Working with Parents:

Guidelines for Early Childhood and Elementary Teachers

Working with Parents:

Guidelines for Early Childhood and Elementary Teachers

SHARI E. NEDLER
UNIVERSITY OF COLORADO, DENVER

ORALIE D. McAFEE
METROPOLITAN STATE COLLEGE

Wadsworth Publishing Company
Belmont, California
A Division of Wadsworth, Inc.

Education and Family Studies Editor: Roger Peterson
Production Editor: Kathie Head
Designer: Cynthia Bassett
Copy Editor: Carol Reitz
Technical Illustrator: Lori Gilbo
Cover and Part Opening Photographs: Elizabeth Crews

Printed in the United States of America

2 3 4 5 6 7 8 9 10—83 82 81 80

Library of Congress Cataloging in Publication Data

Nedler, Shari E
   Working with parents.

   Bibliography: p.
   Includes index.
   1. Parent-teacher relationships.   2. Education, Preschool—Handbooks, manuals, etc.   3. Education, Elementary, Elementary—Handbooks, manuals, etc.
I. McAfee, Oralie, joint author.   II. Title.
LB1033.N4   372.1'1'03   78-10356
ISBN 0-534-00622-1

To our husbands, Sonny and John, our partners in parenthood.
Without their patience and encouragement
this book would never have been written.

Contents

Preface

This book is for classroom teachers who are learning to work with parents. In recent years, research studies and development projects have generated much information on the positive benefits of involving parents in their children's education. Support at both the federal and state levels has encouraged schools to experiment with a variety of ways to involve parents. Citizen–parent groups have been given a greater voice in setting school policy and teachers have turned to parents for assistance, guidance, and support. This is true at both the preschool and the elementary levels. However, many early childhood and elementary teachers are not prepared to work with parents.

There are many approaches to parent involvement, each accomplishing different purposes. A teacher, trying to decide what kind of program would be appropriate, can easily become overwhelmed and confused. We have tried to organize the available information in a systematic and easily accessible way so that teachers can understand these approaches and know how to implement them.

Part One is an introduction to the parent involvement movement in the United States. Readers will develop an understanding of the changing nature of the social, economic, and political forces that affect parent involvement. Landmark events and important research studies are reviewed and related to the identification of program goals.

Part Two presents planning strategies and a process for implementation. These include techniques for identifying needs, selecting goals and objectives, developing activities, motivating parents, and evaluating program impact. We discuss many ideas that have been used successfully by others.

Part Three provides concrete examples of five basic approaches to parent involvement: home-based programs, school- or center-based approaches, home-school partnerships, parent education, and the involvement of parents as policy makers. These chapters describe each approach, discuss advantages and disadvantages, and tell how to implement the programs. Many practical suggestions are included as well as samples of activities. Both prospective and experienced teachers will find the book useful in planning involvement programs that meet the needs of children.

Writing this book has had special meaning for us. As parents, we have watched our own children learn and grow in school. We have fulfilled all the parent roles that we talk about: room mother, pie baker, field trip driver, volunteer aide, PTA member, advisor, and policy maker. As educators developing parent involvement programs, we were alternately despairing and elated. We have tried most of the approaches described in this book and we know that there are no magic answers or cookbook formulas. For those willing to make the commitment, we believe that the rewards of a true home-school partnership are both long-lasting and beneficial to the child and the family.

Acknowledgments

We did not write this book as isolated individuals, but rather as part of a continuity of family, involving both our parents and our children. We thank them for all we have learned. Many others contributed to this effort with encouragement and support. Our colleagues at the University of Colorado and Metropolitan State College shared knowledge and experiences. Appreciation is also extended to Michael Annison, Betty Benjamin, Phil Fox, Jerry Lundquist, George Brooks, and Richard Wylie for their suggestions and interest. Special thanks to Debbie Roberti and Lorrie Spears who helped prepare the manuscript.

We greatly appreciate the suggestions made by our reviewers: Kay Pasley-Tudor of Washington State University, Joyce Huggins of Fresno State University, Betty Garlick of Michigan State University, Merle B. Karnes of the University of Illinois, Chester Youngblood of the College of the Virgin Islands in St. Croix, Marie Van Schuyver of Northeastern Oklahoma State University, Robert Arway of Weber State College, Alvia Bozeman of The Ohio State University, and Phyllis Richards of the University of Texas. Their perceptive comments have been very helpful in revising the manuscript. The assistance provided by the editorial staff at Wadsworth has been invaluable. Thanks to Sheryl Fullerton, Jon Cobb, and Carol Reitz. Most of all, we want to thank Roger Peterson, Wadsworth's education and family studies editor, for his support, patience, and thoughtful guidance.

A school system without parents at its foundation is just like a bucket with a hole in it.

Jesse Jackson

PART ONE
Introduction to Parent Involvement

Educators who effectively involve parents tend to be very enthusiastic about their experiences. They are usually totally committed to the concept of parent involvement and will work actively to convert others to their beliefs. There are, however, many educators who do not want parents involved with either the school or classroom programs. Few people in the education community assume a neutral position on this topic. Very often, both the negative and positive attitudes tend to be based on personal experiences. rather than knowledge of historical events or empirical data.

Chapters 1 and 2 give you a historical perspective of the parent involvement movement in U.S. schools. We review some important research studies that have implications for involvement programs.

Reviewing these historical events should help you understand how attitudes toward working with parents have emerged as well as why certain program strategies have developed. The research studies present strong evidence in support of parent involvement programs, and the expansion of these efforts represents an important movement in education today.

1 *Changing Times*

Historically, each generation of educators has been concerned with the new ideas of the era. For some it has been progressive education, back to basics, open classrooms, or self-contained classrooms. Now parent involvement in the schools is a dominant interest, in part because of the unique problems facing schools and families in today's society.

In the typical kindergarten class of today, you are likely to find a group of children with many of the following types of problems.

Eighteen of thirty children have attended either a preschool or day care program. Going to school is no longer a new experience.

Ten mothers are working full-time. Making arrangements for after-school care is a serious problem.

Eight children come from single-parent homes.

At least four children appear to have special learning problems. They are being referred for further diagnostic testing.

Three children are reading and twenty children can write their names.

One child comes to school with suspicious bruises on her arms and back.

At least five of the mothers stop by once a week to check on their children's progress. They want to know when the reading program will start.

Today's teacher could easily become overwhelmed by the innumerable demands of the classroom. As many teachers cope with these demands, they are rediscovering the advantages of involving parents as partners in the education process.

We will review some key events in the history of early childhood education and parent involvement, two inseparable developments. The term *early childhood education*, as used throughout the text, refers to programs designed for children from infancy through third grade. The growth of nursery schools and kindergartens created an environment that supported parent involvement. By the end of World War II, however, interest in parent involvement began to decline. It was not until the Great Society programs of the 1960s that it was reexamined and massive amounts of federal funds were committed to new and innovative programs.

These cycles of interest and disinterest in working together are tied to larger social and economic changes. Understanding past efforts will help those who must design more effective parent involvement programs for the present and the future.

PARENTS AND SCHOOLS

The answers to the questions of who should educate children and for what purposes have evolved along with our society. Two hundred years ago the answer was simple and uncomplicated. In small, rural, self-contained American communities, the family and church assumed responsibility for socializing and educating children (Lazerson, 1972). As communities grew, more teachers were hired, but the community maintained its control of the schools. Parents were involved in deciding who was to be hired, what was to be taught, and what attitudes and values the school was to stress. The curriculum that grew out of this close relationship between community and school clearly reflected the prevailing culture and beliefs.

During the last half of the nineteenth century, as the United States became an industrialized nation, the population of cities grew, often with large numbers of immigrants. Urban school systems were created to meet these pressures, and the small community school began to disappear (Braun and Edwards, 1972).

In the expanding urban school systems, control of administrative policies, educational programs, and hiring practices moved further away from local community representatives. By the beginning of the twentieth century, superintendents managed school districts and carried out policies set by the school board. Because school board members represented increasingly large numbers of people, they could not maintain close contact with their constituents. Professional educators became the leaders in determining school policy, and the role of parents as decision makers decreased.

Parent Involvement, Social Reform, and the Kindergarten Movement (1870–1910)

The industrialized United States encountered new problems. Many of the recent immigrants were poor and uneducated. They often formed self-contained, cohesive communities where they could maintain their own language, religion, and cultural beliefs.

Immigrants and Kindergarten   Many Americans were concerned about the abominable conditions under which most immigrant children were raised. As part of broad social reform of political corruption, inadequate housing, and unfair labor practices, reformers tried to improve the environment of immigrant children.

Friedrich Froebel had developed a kindergarten program in the 1820s in Germany that recognized the importance of the first seven years of life and emphasized new ways of meeting the special needs of children through a carefully designed educational program. American settlement houses and other philanthropic organizations believed that by offering kindergarten programs for immigrant children they could fight the unsanitary living conditions along with the growth of disease, crime, and delinquency in the slums. During the 1890s, kindergarten classes sponsored by philanthropic groups opened in Boston, New York, San Francisco, Chicago, and other cities (Hill, 1941). Besides play experiences, the programs stressed assimilation into the American culture and taught accepted middle-class values of cleanliness, self-discipline, and cooperation.

These early kindergartens also sought to change family living patterns through parent education programs. Educators visited homes to teach modern American child-rearing techniques. Children went to school in the morning, and teachers visited families in the afternoon. They instructed parents in preparing nutritious meals and the importance of hygiene and cleanliness in the home. The teachers also functioned as social workers, trying to show families how to use community resources. The kindergarten teacher continually emphasized the importance of education as the key to mobility in American society, the vehicle that would ensure future social and financial success for immigrant children.

Public Schools and Kindergarten   Philanthropic agencies, such as the churches, missions, and settlement houses, had limited funds and began to encourage public schools to sponsor the kindergarten programs. By 1911, almost 85 percent of the children enrolled in kindergarten were in publicly sponsored classrooms (Lazerson, 1972). As enrollment increased, the schools began morning and afternoon sessions, and the kindergarten teacher was no longer able to maintain close ties with parents. Publicly supported kindergartens did not have the money to support parent involvement, so the tradition of parent education gradually disappeared.

Parent Groups   Parent involvement was fostered in informally organized groups of middle-class parents. In the latter part of the nineteenth century there were hundreds of mothers' clubs, women's clubs, reading circles, and other self-improvement groups (*Parent Teacher Organization*, 1944). In 1888 the Society for the Study of Child Nature was organized to assist these groups with information and study materials. This group later became the Child Study Association and is the oldest U.S. organization with a continuous parent education program.

In 1897 the National Congress of Mothers was organized. The theme for its first program was "The Need for Child Study" and the discussion included character building, stories and story-telling, physical culture, and dietetics (*Parent Teacher Organization*, 1944).

The Congress of Mothers soon realized that fathers and teachers are also important, and in 1908 the name was changed to the National Congress of

Mothers and Parent-Teacher Associations. Some years later the name was again changed to the National Congress for Parents and Teachers or, as it is more commonly known, the PTA. The activities of the early PTA dealt solely with kindergarten. Efforts to bring together large groups of mothers were made in cooperation with kindergarten leaders, who were among the first to give support to the new movement (*Parent Teacher Organization*, 1944).

The federal government sponsored the first White House Conference on Child Welfare in 1909. This led to the creation of the Children's Bureau in 1912, which is now part of the Department of Health, Education, and Welfare. The bureau has helped bring about reforms in child labor and the treatment of abused and dependent children and has sponsored research in child development. The most widely distributed pamphlet of all times, *Infant Care: Your Child from One to Six*, was first published by the Children's Bureau in 1914. This pamphlet has been published in twelve successive editions, rewritten to reflect changes in child-rearing practices.

The Growth of Nursery Schools (1920–1950)

The first nursery school was started by Rachel and Margaret McMillan in England. Their program was developed to meet the needs of poor children between the ages of one and six (E. P. Dutton, 1919). The McMillans believed that the health problems of poor English children were already too advanced for adequate treatment by school age, so they established a nursery school to offer comprehensive services for younger children. Its goal was to nurture the *whole child* by creating an environment that would serve social, physical, emotional, and intellectual needs. Indoor and outdoor play was encouraged, medical and dental care was provided, teachers were trained in principles of child development, and manipulative educational materials were used in the classroom for stimulating intellectual growth. The McMillans also stressed the importance of working with parents, so teachers visited homes and met with groups of parents to talk about child-rearing techniques.

Settlement Houses and Nursery Schools   Nursery schools in the United States, first organized in the 1920s by settlement houses, were designed to take care of the children of working women and to counteract the ill effects of poverty. Because so many parents worked, several programs began to offer full day care services. Children ranged in age from one to five years and attended for half- or full-day sessions. Program goals were similar to those stressed by the McMillans and included emphasis on physical development, social adjustment, emotional and mental health, and a stimulating environment that would prepare children for *future* educational experiences. Cognitive development goals were considered less important than goals of physical, social, and emotional growth. Parent involvement was not universally included as part of the nursery school program for working parents. When parents were involved, they were usually given advice on how they should raise their children and manage their homes.

The Child Study Movement   Another major event of the 1920s that influenced the growth of nursery schools and parent involvement was the emergence of the child study movement under the leadership of Lawrence Frank (Frank, 1962). Frank was the administrator of the Laura Spelman Rockefeller Fund, and under his direction Institutes of Child Study were established all over the country to increase knowledge of child development and help educators and families improve the quality of child care. Children had become a legitimate subject for scientific study.

The nursery schools that were connected with these institutes or with nearby universities were quite different from those sponsored by settlement houses. The university programs were concerned with teacher training and research in child development. Most of the children came from middle-class homes.

The child study movement stimulated the establishment of a large number of private nursery programs serving middle-class children. Philosophically these programs stressed that children "learn by doing," and social, emotional, and physical development were of primary importance. The teacher guided the children's development, and the nursery school program was seen as preparation for future educational experiences.

Parent education was an important part of most nursery school programs serving middle-class children. The institutes and psychologists wanted to share child-rearing information with mothers. Parents were expected to observe in the classroom, to participate in discussion groups, and to read the latest books on child rearing so that they could raise well-adjusted children.

Parent-Cooperative Nursery Schools   The first parent-cooperative nursery school in the United States was organized by a group of faculty wives at the University of Chicago in 1916 (Lazerson, 1972). By 1929, 500 such schools operated across the country.

Parent-cooperative nursery schools spread rapidly because many middle-class parents wanted programs to promote the growth and development of their young children. Many of these parents could not afford tuition or preferred a program in which they could be part of their children's nursery school experience. These needs were met through a cooperative arrangement that required all parents to work a certain number of hours. Typically, the parents hired one professional staff member to coordinate the program. This staff member had major responsibilities for daily program planning, purchase of food, record keeping, and related program concerns. Each parent volunteered to assist regularly in the classroom.

Almost all the co-op schools had an active parent education program. Mothers usually met in small groups to discuss new information on child rearing, guidance, and human development.

The Great Depression   During the depression (1929–39) the federal Works Progress Administration (WPA) allocated funds for the creation of nursery schools and day care centers as part of a larger effort to generate jobs. Many unemployed teachers, as well as people with no previous experience, were hired and trained as educators. Parents were encouraged to participate in parent education programs, visit classrooms, and meet with teachers to discuss the children's progress.

World War II   When World War II began, millions of women entered the work force, and additional nursery schools and day care centers were opened to care for young children. Federal funds were allocated to support most of these programs. While nursery schools and day care centers continued to stress the importance of the child's total development and the influence of both home and school, active parent involvement began to decline. Many working parents simply did not have the time. Parents were considered essential for providing basic physical care and emotional support, but they were told that their child's development was basically controlled by maturational factors that could not be changed and that skills would emerge when the child was "ready." The nursery school teacher was responsible for the child's preschool education. Parent involvement gradually came to be limited to an annual open house and one parent-teacher conference during the school year.

By the end of the war, nursery school education was widely accepted as a positive experience for young children and their families. Nevertheless, federal funds for nursery schools and day care programs decreased after 1945. While the number of private nursery schools for middle-class children continued to increase, programs for low-income children almost disappeared.

In Retrospect

The spread of kindergarten and nursery school programs, combined with the child study movement, focused attention on the importance of the early years in a child's development. Educators and families accepted many different kinds of involvement for a parent—as an active advisor, a classroom helper, or a participant in educational programs designed to improve child-rearing skills.

Many universities and colleges established professional training programs for early childhood teachers. Professional organizations such as the Association for Childhood Education International (ACEI), the National Association for Nursery Education (NANE), which later became the National Association for the Education of Young Children (NAEYC), and the Society for Research in Child Development (SRCD) were formed to exchange information and research findings. The increased knowledge of how young children develop influenced the kinds of early childhood programs offered as well as the type of advice given to parents on how to raise their children.

Changing Assumptions   By the end of the 1950s, the following assumptions about early childhood education were commonly accepted by parents and educators.

1.   Separation of nursery school, day care, and private kindergarten from the public school program.

2. General lack of concern at the federal, state, and local levels for early childhood programs for low-income children.

3. Confinement of parent involvement to advisory groups, fund raising and room-mother activities, and membership in the PTA. The prevailing attitude in most public schools serving low-income families was that parents were ineffective and uninterested in their children's education.

4. Acceptance of both nursery and public school teachers as the experts working with children. Only the professional educator could determine the goals and philosophy of the program and the kind of instructional techniques used in the classroom.

5. Definition of the parent as reactor to the teacher as initiator. This "teacher teaches, parent cooperates" concept automatically excluded parents from any active decision-making role.

6. Separation of the goals of the nursery school program from those of the primary grades. Nursery school programs emphasized learning through play and concern for the physical, social, and emotional development of the child. Formal cognitive learning began when the child entered first grade. The critical influences of maturation on the child's development continued to be accepted by both educators and parents.

7. Expectations that children and families would accommodate the value system of the schools rather than schools accommodating unique community or population differences.

The last assumption created no problems when the culture of the school and community were the same. However, in many communities, the values, attitudes, and language of the home were different from the mainstream. In south Texas, for example, many children came from homes where Spanish was spoken. However, these children were forbidden by law to use Spanish at school. Materials in textbooks reflected only Caucasian, middle-class, stereotyped models, and the majority of teachers were from the same white culture. The children had no models for their own way of life.

As mentioned, parent involvement in the 1950s was restricted. Professional educators controlled the system and saw parents as unimportant in the process of teaching children. Most poor parents were afraid of both school and teacher and felt excluded from their child's education.

THE GREAT SOCIETY PROGRAM

The War on Poverty

One of the political responses to the civil rights movement of the 1960s was to declare "war on poverty." The condition of this nation's poor children was particularly distressing. Scandalous statistics indicated that these children had been denied access to basic medical care, adequate diet, and decent housing. Many were failing and dropping out of school.

Educational researchers and behavioral scientists presented compelling evidence that the early years were critically important to a child's development and that the quality of the environment influenced later development (Hunt, 1961; Skeels, 1965). If poor children could be given the same kind of advantages available to middle-class children, they might be able to work their way out of the poverty cycle. Some of the advantages thought to be important were nutritious meals, adequate medical and dental care, access to adults who could answer questions and stimulate intellectual growth, opportunities to play with educational toys, and chances to become socially and emotionally adjusted by spending supervised time with peers. Congress allocated federal funds to create new educational programs for disadvantaged (poor) children. Parent involvement was a goal of most programs because parents' interest in their children's education seemed to be one of the advantages enjoyed by middle-class children.

The Elementary and Secondary Educational Act (ESEA) of 1965 doubled federal contributions to education. There were grants to local schools to meet the needs of educationally deprived children (Title I) and to develop supplementary educational centers and services (Title III). These funds were used to develop innovative curricula, purchase audiovisual equipment, train teachers, and hire classroom aides, among other uses. Federal guidelines almost without exception required parent involvement in planning and decision making. After the violence and riots in urban ghettos in the early 1960s, the government saw parent participation as one way to reduce the feelings of powerlessness that were so prevalent among the poor and minority groups. Professional educators could not develop solutions to the problems of compensatory education by working alone—parents had to be involved.

Head Start

The national Head Start program, funded through the Office of Economic Opportunity (OEO), began in 1965 as an eight-week summer experiment designed to serve poor preschool children. Objectives for the program (Grotberg, 1969) included:

1. Improving the child's physical health and abilities.

2. Helping the child's emotional and social development by encouraging self-confidence, spontaneity, curiosity, and self-discipline.

3. Improving the child's mental processes and skills, with particular attention to conceptual and verbal skills.

4. Establishing patterns and expectations of success for the child that will create confidence for future learning.

5. Increasing the child's capacity to relate positively to family members and others, while at the same time strengthening the family's ability to relate positively to the child and his or her problems.

6. Developing in both child and family a responsible attitude toward society.

7. Fostering constructive opportunities for society to work together with the poor to solve their problems.

8. Increasing the sense of dignity and self-worth within the child and his or her family.

Six major components were included in the Head Start program: administration, education, social services, health services, career development, and parent education. The original goals were to be achieved by coordinating these six components to meet specific community needs. The basic plan involved delivering comprehensive services through center-based group programs serving four- and five-year-old children.

Parent Involvement and Head Start   A number of factors influenced the original decision to include parent involvement as a major component of the Head Start program. Educators were beginning to recognize a gap between home and school that often created unnecessary adjustment problems for children, particularly poor children. Parents and teachers working together might be able to reduce some of these discontinuities; parents might be encouraged to reinforce the goals of the program at home. The parents' feelings of self-worth were seen to be closely related to the development of the child's self-concept. If the role of the parent as the child's primary teacher was openly acknowledged by the school as being important, more positive parental feelings about child rearing might develop, and these positive attitudes might create a more supportive and stimulating home environment.

Head Start's Impact   Obviously, these goals were overly optimistic for an eight-week program, so Head Start soon became a year-round experiment. While the program has not accomplished all of its original goals, it has been far more successful than research reports indicate (Cicirelli et al., 1969). One of its greatest accomplishments has been the delivery of comprehensive health services to poor children. Changes in IQ scores, although positive, tended to fade after the children entered the primary grades, except in children from programs in which parent involvement was strongly emphasized. This finding reinforces the idea that a continuity of educational efforts between preschool and elementary programs and parent involvement are necessary to permanently increase the achievement level of children.

Head Start can be considered the first large-scale effort to involve parents in the educational experiences of their children. The Kirschner Report (Kirschner Associates, 1970) discusses four major changes that have occurred in our society as a result of Head Start.

1. *Greater involvement of the poor in making decisions about institutional policies that affect them.* The formation of Parent Advisory Committees (PAC) was required by federal funding guidelines. Parent representatives, working closely with the sponsoring agency, began to make decisions about hiring staff, allocating budget, and deciding the kind of educational program to be offered.

2. *Greater employment opportunities for paraprofessionals in the public schools.* Head Start programs demonstrated that people without formal educational backgrounds could be effective in the classroom. Extensive in-service training programs helped paraprofessionals learn how to work with preschool children and to assist classroom teachers. Many public schools followed the example of Head Start by hiring and training teacher aides.

3. *Increased emphasis on the educational needs of poor and minority groups.* Psychologists, sociologists, linguists, anthropologists, economists, and educators formed multidisciplinary teams to study and develop new educational programs for poor children. Dozens of preschool curriculum models were tested and disseminated nationally.

4. *More adequate health services for the poor.* The health service component of Head Start highlights the need for more efficient delivery of medical care to poor families. Out of these early efforts came neighborhood health clinics, national immunization programs, and early dental care for preschoolers.

Recent reports indicate that low-income children who participated in early education programs were better able to meet the minimal requirements of their school (Lazar et al., 1977). This was reflected by a reduced probability of the children being either assigned to a special education class or held back in a grade. All the programs that reported significant effects had a home visiting component. Parent involvement appeared to have a critical effect on the child's ability to function adequately in school.

Perhaps the major impact of Head Start has been to stimulate other programs that include parent involvement. Home Start, an alternative Head Start model, was the first large-scale effort to demonstrate the potential of working with parents in their homes to enhance their children's learning and development. The Child and Family Resource Program has explored different ways of coordinating the delivery of comprehensive child-centered family services. Parent and Child Care Center programs have been designed to stimulate the development of infants and toddlers along with providing services to parents. Project Follow Through, an extension of Head Start, was developed to help children in kindergarten through third grade maintain the initial gains they had achieved. Federal guidelines for Follow Through require the same kinds of parent involvement mandated for Head Start.

We have learned a great deal from these special programs. Their impact has changed traditional concepts of education in this country. We no longer simply write off large segments of our population as "uneducable." The findings of research and demonstration projects have forced us to acknowledge that every child can benefit in some way when provided with equal educational opportunities. A key part of all these programs has been a serious effort to involve parents and to assess the effect of their involvement on program goals.

NEW ROLES AND SETTINGS

Several politically and educationally significant reports have reaffirmed the importance of the family in determining the level of the child's school achievement. The Coleman Report (1966) concluded that differences in school facilities and curricula are not significantly related to school achievement. The most important single factor in achievement is the home background of the child and fellow students. Important variables are the social status of parents, the number of children in the family, the parents' educational background, and family attitudes toward achievement and schools. Christopher Jencks's research (1972) indicated that schools alone cannot provide equal educational opportunities; the family plays a critical role. In 1973, the International Study of Educational Achievement reported that the home rather than the school is the crucial factor in determining children's overall achievement.

Educational systems are slow to change, but professional educators are beginning to accept the importance of home influences on the child's development. Schools must begin to take the initiative in encouraging active dialogue between teachers and parents to make the child's environment more supportive of development.

Impact of the Great Society Program

Federal funding stimulated an extraordinary amount of development of early childhood programs, child and family research projects, and comprehensive services to the poor. These activities have changed past educational practices and assumptions and have created new questions.

Early childhood education has been redefined to include all children from infancy through age eight. Support for continuity between preschool education and the primary grades can best come about through home-school cooperation.

Expansion of Programs   Programs for children below the age of six now serve a cross section of the population rather than only middle-class children. This has happened because of the increase in federal support for programs serving low-income and other special groups, such as handicapped children; the increase in the number of private nursery schools serving middle- and upper-income families; and the almost universal inclusion of kindergarten as part of public school primary programs.

Parents have assumed a much more active role in working with schools. Federal regulations requiring active parent participation as a condition for funding have undoubtedly stimulated the increase in parent involvement, but the scope of involvement efforts has also expanded. These efforts include not only traditional parent education activities, but also parent participation in program planning, implementation, and evaluation (Stevens and King, 1976).

All Children Can Learn   Early childhood education has moved away from a maturational bias. Educators are accepting the idea that intelligence is not fixed at birth. Although the upper and lower limits of a child's potential are probably set by genetic factors, the extent to which this potential may be realized is probably a function of the child's environment and family interactions. These ideas have dramatically influenced the kinds of programs offered young children. Today's early childhood programs include a strong emphasis on cognitive development as well as social, emotional, and physical growth.

Perhaps the most exciting concept to emerge from the research and demonstration activities of the 1960s is the recognition of the importance of programs that reflect the unique characteristics of a pluralistic society. We have moved away from interpreting differences as weaknesses and instead are accepting them as strengths. Evidence of this is seen in the increased number of bilingual programs funded at both national and state levels, the new and sensitive multicultural curricula, and the growing number of minority group teachers who serve as positive models for young children.

Parents Make a Difference   Strong evidence supporting the effectiveness of parent involvement emerged from the educational experimentation of the 1960s. Research studies reported the powerful influence of home factors, such as parent teaching styles, on the development of children (Hess et al., 1971; Schaefer, 1972). Data from intervention programs indicated that when parent involvement was emphasized, children in the programs scored significantly higher than a comparison group on achievement and IQ measures, and many of the children maintained these gains through the primary grades. Parent involvement is also seen as an appropriate way of responding to pressures for more community control of educational decisions. Parents want to have a voice in the policy-making process. Evans (1975) cites still more benefits.

Most obviously, even a minimal effort to involve parents in their children's education can bridge the continuity gap which often exists between home and school . . . properly informed and equipped parents can provide home practice opportunities for their children in many school related activities. This can be extremely important for children whose educational progress is problematical . . . by contributing in meaningful ways to their child's development and education, many parents may achieve an improved sense of self-worth and respect. If so, the general affectional relationships among parents and children may also improve.

Emerging Roles for Teachers

Our society has become so complex that no one institution can meet the needs of all our children. Groups that have traditionally worked in isolation, separate from each other, must now learn to work together.

Today's classroom teachers must be flexible, open, and willing to involve parents. They should be aware that many schools receive special funds from the federal or state government that require involvement of parents. Teachers must consider all these special regulations in planning programs and be certain that guidelines are followed.

Relating to Parents   Working with parents calls for all sorts of professional skills. Very often, these skills are not emphasized or included in traditional teacher education programs. Trying to educate another adult can create a lot of anxiety. How do you get parents to come to your first meeting? How do you develop a program that will hold their interest? Where do you find the time for the planning and preparation necessary for a successful program? There are no easy answers, and teachers must commit themselves to evaluate every phase of their program. Without evaluation there can be no improvement.

Interpersonal skills are critical for working effectively with parents. Inexperienced and experienced teachers alike often have conflicting feelings regarding their relationships with parents. They might be overwhelmed at the idea of having to plan a program that goes beyond working directly with the children in the classroom. Other teachers might be used to self-contained classrooms and react negatively to having more than one adult in the classroom.

The other side of the coin must also be considered. Parents have their own feelings about school involvement. Very often they will be intimidated by the classroom teacher and will hesitate to expose themselves to any judgments by a professional educator. Parents who believe that schools have the major responsibility for educating children will be angry that schools are asking them to devote their time to parent involvement. Teachers must learn to be sensitive to what they see and hear in others, as well as to their own feelings, attitudes, and beliefs. Only by knowing yourself can you relate effectively to others.

Planning for Others   Parent involvement often means new classroom organizational patterns. Instead of one adult or a team of educators in a classroom, the program must accommodate the nonprofessional parent volunteer. Each extra person in that classroom means increased planning time, more materials, and on-the-job training and supervision. Only time and practice simplify the complexity of this process.

Teachers must do more than simply commute from home to school if they want to improve their classroom effectiveness. Each school serves a unique community, and classroom programs should reflect the culture of that community. Teachers must become sensitive to the special characteristics of both the families and children by becoming familiar with the culture, attitudes, and values stressed in the home. This can be considered part of a larger effort to provide continuity for children.

Teaching Adults   Involvement programs often focus on giving child-rearing information to parents. Teachers must make every effort to be well-informed in this area. This implies continuous development through formal course work or extensive self-directed reading. Many teachers, particularly those who are young and inexperienced or have no children of their own, will feel very uncomfortable in this role. It is important to remember that even though a teacher may be inexperienced as a parent, his or her professional preparation has provided special insight and information that can be extremely helpful to parents.

Parent involvement often means that the setting for education will change. At times teachers may find that to reach their goal, the home or the community is the most effective classroom.

Emerging Roles for Parents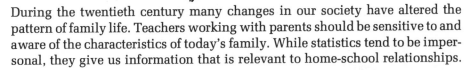

During the twentieth century many changes in our society have altered the pattern of family life. Teachers working with parents should be sensitive to and aware of the characteristics of today's family. While statistics tend to be impersonal, they give us information that is relevant to home-school relationships.

- Over 50 percent of all women are in the labor force; over 30 percent of all women with children under age six work outside the home.

- The U.S. divorce rate is now the highest in the world. Out of every two marriages, approximately one will end in divorce.

- About 10 million children under the age of eighteen come from homes with divorced parents.

- The number of single-parent families is increasing, both because of divorce and because the parent never remarries.

- The number of women without husbands heading their families has increased to more than 7.2 million.

- Stable, multi-age communities and the extended family have been replaced by communities linked by interests, age, and income level.

- Childbearing among young adolescents is increasing. In our society these young people have had little or no exposure to young children and even less exposure to rearing a child.

McAfee and Nedler (1976) have identified changes and breakdowns in the fulfillment of two basic functions of our society: (1) the way children are reared and (2) the way parents and future parents learn about child rearing. Traditionally, the family has raised and cared for the child, but many children are now cared for away from the home for part of the day. Some are simply left alone. The baby-sitter and day care center are as much a part of many American families as grandmother and aunt used to be. Because divorce is usually a transition period between marriages, many children relate to two or more sets of parents. Unfortunately, child-rearing help and support from a spouse or other family members are not always available to parents. Isolation and frustration may result when no one can take over and provide some relief. Often physical punishment and control of behavior are sanctioned (Gil, 1970). The constraints that keep this violent tendency within the bounds of physical safety seem to be less rigid, perhaps reflecting the increase in violence in our total society.

The ways in which parents learn to care for their children have also changed. Smaller families and a mobile society result in fewer younger siblings or nearby cousins on whom to practice; and grandparents, aunts, and experienced neighbors are often unavailable for advice. Too often, the information and advice given to parents does not take into account the high emotional content and stress associated with child rearing.

Parents as people are being subjected to all the strains of a changing technological society. These factors must be considered by schools as they attempt to establish meaningful links between the home and classroom.

Home-School Goals

Roles for Parents   Variations of parent involvement are endless and the extent of involvement should ultimately be determined cooperatively by parents and teachers. Certainly no parent should be made to feel guilty for choosing a minimal level of involvement. Teachers must be sensitive to the many other demands on a parent's time and plan an involvement program that considers and responds to individual needs. No cookbook formula will be appropriate. Goals and activities should match the particular group with which the teacher is working and should start where the parent is, not where the school *expects* the parent to be.

Goodson and Hess (1975) have described four very different ways of involving parents: (1) as policy makers, (2) as more effective teachers of their own children, (3) as supporting resources for the school, and (4) as better-informed persons.

Roles for Teachers   The teacher's role is to work with parents as they jointly identify goals that are particularly relevant to their needs. Reasonable goals might include:

- Creating an environment in which parents and teachers work together to bring about a partnership between home and school.

- Providing a setting where parents are free to choose the level of their involvement and the kind of involvement desired.

- Developing a program that recognizes the parent as essential to an educational process stressing continuity between home and school.

- Providing an environment in which different cultural backgrounds, value systems, attitudes, and goals for children are shared and respected by school and home.

- Creating a setting where conflicts in goals and ways to reach these goals can be resolved honestly and openly so as to serve best the needs of the child.

SUMMARY

Parent involvement has always been part of our educational tradition, yet historical events have shaped the degree of involvement as well as the kinds of roles assigned to parents and teachers. For the first time in our history, however, the effectiveness of involvement has now been studied in a fairly systematic manner. Data supporting the importance of the parental role in educational settings can be cited.

The overriding goal of any parent involvement effort must be to assist the family and school to meet the emerging developmental needs of all young children through quality education programs. In order to achieve this goal, both parents and teachers must be willing to look at their roles in new ways and develop those skills needed for effective home-school cooperation.

FOR DISCUSSION AND FURTHER STUDY

1. Survey three or four different primary grade or early childhood programs in your community and describe their programs for involving parents. How do these programs relate to historical attitudes about parent involvement?

2. Interview three parents of young children and describe their attitudes toward taking part in parent involvement activities. What kinds of things would they like to do?

3. Describe the reasons nursery schools generally serve children from middle-class homes.

4. Visit and observe a parent-cooperative nursery school. Interview the director and some parent volunteers and describe the roles and responsibilities of parents in this type of program.

5. Discuss the reasons that parent involvement was emphasized so strongly as part of the Great Society programs of the 1960s.

6. Describe three ways in which the Great Society programs have influenced current involvement programs.

7. Identify one program in a school or center in your community that is funded through a special federal or state grant. Describe any special guidelines that teachers in these programs must consider or follow in working with parents.

8. Discuss how family life patterns in the United States are changing. What are the implications for the classroom teacher?

9. What kinds of goals would you consider most important for a parent involvement program?

10. Survey three schools in your community. Discuss and compare the roles of parents and educators in setting policies and determining goals of the education program.

BIBLIOGRAPHY

Braun, Samuel. "Nursery Education for Disadvantaged Children: A Historical Review." In *Montessori in Perspective*, ed. Lucile Perryman. Washington, D.C.: National Association for the Education of Young Children, 1966.

Braun, Samuel, and Esther Edwards. *History and Theory of Early Childhood Education.* Worthington, Ohio: Charles A. Jones, 1972.

Cicirelli, V., et al. The impact of Head Start. An evaluation of the effects of Head Start on children's cognitive and affective development. *Report to the U.S. Office of Economic Opportunity by Westinghouse Learning Corporation and Ohio University.* Washington, D.C.: Government Printing Office, 1969.

Coleman, James, et al., *Equality of Educational Opportunity.* Washington, D.C.: U.S. Government Printing Office, 1966.

Evans, Ellis. *Contemporary Influences in Early Childhood Education.* New York: Holt, Rinehart and Winston, 1975.

Frank, Lawrence. "The Beginnings of Child Development and Family Life Education in the Twentieth Century." *Merrill-Palmer Quarterly* 8, no. 4 (1962): 207–27.

Gesell, Arnold, and Frances Ilg. *Infant and Child in the Culture of Today.* New York: Harper & Row, 1943.

Gil, David. *Violence against Children: Physical Child Abuse in the United States.* Cambridge, Mass.: Harvard University Press, 1970.

Glick, Paul. *Some Recent Changes in American Families, Current Population Reports.* U.S. Department of Commerce, Social and Economic Statistics Administration, Bureau of the Census, 1974.

Goodson, Barbara, and Robert Hess. *Parents as Teachers of Young Children: An Evaluation Review of Some Contemporary Concepts and Programs.* Stanford, Calif.: Stanford University Press, 1975.

Gordon, Ira. *Parent Involvement in Compensatory Education.* Urbana, Ill.: ERIC Clearinghouse on Early Childhood Education, 1970.

Grotberg, Edith. *Review of Research: 1965–1969.* Washington, D.C.: Project Head Start, U.S. Office of Economic Opportunity, 1969.

Hess, Robert, Marianne Block, Joan Costello, Ruby Knowles, and Dorothy Largay. "Parent Involvement in Early Education." In *Day Care: Resources for Decisions,* ed. Edith Grotberg. Washington, D.C.: OEO Pamphlet 6106–1, 1971.

Hill, Patty. "Kindergarten." *American Educator's Encyclopedia.* Lake Bluff, Ill.: United Educators, 1941.

Hunt, J. McVicker. *Intelligence and Experience.* New York: Ronald Press, 1961.

Jencks, Christopher, et al. *Inequality: A Reassessment of the Effect of Family and Schooling in America.* New York: Basic Books, 1972.

Karnes, Merle, et al. "Educational Intervention at Home by Mothers of Disadvantaged Infants." *Child Development,* 41 (1970): 925–35.

Kirschner Associates, Inc. *A National Survey of the Impacts of Head Start Centers on Community Institutions: Summary Report.* Report. Report No. 889–4638. Washington, D.C.: U.S. Government Printing Office, 1970.

Klaus, Rupert, and Susan Gray. "The Early Training Project for Disadvantaged Children: A Report After Five Years." *Monographs of the Society for Research in Child Development* 53, no. 120 (1968).

Lazar, Irving, Virginia Hubbell, Harry Murray, Marilyn Rosche, and Jacqueline Roche. *The Persistence of Preschool Effects: A Long Term Followup of Fourteen Infant and Preschool Experiments.* Ithaca, N.Y.: Community Service Laboratory, New York State College of Human Ecology, Cornell University, September 1977.

Lazerson, Marvin. "The Historical Antecedents of Early Childhood Education." In *Early Childhood Education: The Seventy-first Yearbook of the National Society for the Study of Education,* ed. Ira Gordon. Chicago: University of Chicago Press, 1972.

Levenstein, Phyllis. "Cognitive Growth in Preschoolers through Verbal Interaction with Mothers." *American Journal of Orthopsychiatry* 40 (1970): 426–32.

Marital Status and Living Arrangements: March 1975. Current Population Reports. Population Characteristics. U.S. Department of Commerce, Bureau of the Census, 1975.

McAfee, Oralie, and Shari Nedler. *Education for Parenthood: A Primary Prevention Strategy for Child Abuse and Neglect.* Denver: Education Commission of the States, no. 93, 1976.

McMillan, Margaret. *The Nursery School.* New York: E. P. Dutton, 1919.

The Parent Teacher Organization: Its Origins and Development, Chicago: National Congress of Parents and Teachers, 1944.

Schaefer, Earl. "Parents as Educators: Evidence from Cross-Sectional Longitudinal and Intervention Research." In *The Young Child: Reviews of Research,* vol. II. Washington, D.C.: National Association for the Education of Young Children, 1972.

Skeels, Harold. "Effects of Adoption on Children from Institutions." *Children,* 12 (1965):33–34.

Stevens, Joe, and Edith King. *Administering Early Childhood Education Programs.* Boston: Little, Brown, 1976.

Weikart, David, and Delores Lambie. "Early Enrichment in Infants." In *Education of the Infant and Young Child,* ed. V. Dennenberg. New York: Academic, 1970.

2 Parents, Teachers, and Children

If you ask parents whether they are important in influencing the growth and development of their children, their answer almost always will be yes. If you ask the same parents how or why their behavior makes a difference, they will probably have difficulty giving specific examples. What happens if you ask teachers the same questions? Most will agree with the parents, but again will be uncertain as to how or why this is so. The research literature clearly supports the importance of home environments and parent-child interactions to human development. The attitudes, values, and behaviors of parents influence and affect the child's physical, social, emotional, and intellectual behavior in school and in later life. Experimental data confirm what most people would accept as common sense; parents do make a difference.

Many questions, however, remain unanswered. Are there certain behaviors that parents should use? Is there a common set of values that should be adopted by all? Are some parent attitudes more supportive of healthy growth and development than others? Are there, instead, a broad range of behaviors, values, and attitudes that are acceptable for effective parent-child interactions? How does one make sense of all the available information?

Answers to some of these questions will emerge as we review the child-rearing research. We will discuss some of the desirable parenting behaviors that have been identified by various researchers and the implications of these findings for the design of parent involvement programs.

RESEARCH ON CHILD REARING

Although child rearing is a significant task for adults in any society, few parents in this country have ever received any systematic instruction to prepare them for this job or help them carry it out effectively. Until relatively recently, social science research in the United States did not include studies of applied problems in raising children.

Recent Influences

Before the 1950s, very little information on effective child rearing was available. The few child-rearing books that had been written were read by a very small portion of parents. The information in these books was based primarily on theoretical notions about child development rather than on actual research data. The theories that were used to develop ideas about child rearing, particularly those in the psychoanalytic tradition, were typically developed by studying neurotic and psychotic adults and extrapolating these findings to young children.

The work of Arnold Gesell and colleagues (1943) focused on development in physical and psychomotor areas that are largely under the control of physical maturation. These investigators gave little attention to child development in the cognitive and social-personal areas. Their heavy maturational bias led them to suggest that children go through a series of innately programmed stages regardless of parental behavior or environmental events. Parents were told by doctors and teachers that when their child was "ready," he or she would learn to read and write. Readiness was tied to a specific chronological age and parents were actively discouraged from tampering with the child's natural sequence of development. The role of the parent should be confined to knowing about and passively watching and reacting to the child's behavior during these stages. The same maturational bias pervaded the books of Benjamin Spock (1945). Although he gave a great deal of direct advice on the health and physical care of children, he had practically no suggestions for parents regarding the child's cognitive development.

Over time, the American behaviorist tradition helped break down this maturational bias in child rearing. The early behaviorists saw the child as much more responsive to environmental differences and therefore more open to the molding influences of child-rearing practices. Skinner's research (1953) provided additional support for the effects of environmental factors on the child's growth and development. Reinforcement was seen as critical in molding the child's behavior and influencing learning. Bandura (1969) and other social psychologists explored the phenomenon of learning by example or through exposure to social models. These studies revealed that much of what a child learns is determined by what he or she observes in the environment.

Other researchers had looked at the effects of environmental experiences on growth and development. Skeels and Dye (1939) studied twenty-five retarded infants who lived in an orphanage. Half of these children were transferred to an institution for the mentally retarded, where they were placed in an adult ward and cared for by the female patients and staff. These children were given a great deal of individual attention and affection by their caretakers. The other children stayed in the orphanage and received relatively little individual attention or stimulation.

Both groups of children were tested over thirty months and the differences between them were startling. Those children who remained in the orphanage showed an average IQ loss of 20 points, while the children placed in the institutional ward gained an average of 32 IQ points. A follow-up study more than twenty years later revealed significant and dramatic findings (Skeels, 1966).

Most of the children who had been in the institution had been adopted, their median education level was twelfth grade, and as adults they were self-supporting. The orphanage children had either remained in this setting or been transferred to state schools or institutions for the retarded. Their median education level was less than third grade and those who were employed held only menial jobs.

This study provided strong evidence that the quality of a child's environment can be crucial in determining the eventual level of intellectual and social functioning. Other researchers in the 1950s and early 1960s began to investigate the relationship of parent behaviors and other environmental influences on such traits as intelligence, school achievement, aggression and hostility, achievement motivation, affiliation and sociability, sex typing and sex-role learning, and self-esteem.

Findings must be interpreted cautiously because of methodological problems such as small sample sizes, the use of interviews rather than direct observation, differing criteria for measuring achievement or self-esteem, and the impossibility of randomly assigning children to parents and controlling home treatment. Nevertheless, the findings indicate that cognitive and affective child traits are predominantly shaped by the people, objects, and events in a child's environment rather than by genetically determined innate factors. While the newborn infant is not totally a "blank slate" as early behaviorists advocated, there is evidence that his or her cognitive development (to some degree) and social-emotional development (almost completely) are heavily dependent on the child's formative experiences, especially the attitudes and behavior of parents.

The Developing Child

School was over for the day, and Mrs. R. was sitting at her desk thinking about the children in her first grade class. Some of them were easy to work with and teach. They seemed to love school, were interested in the work, and were able to carry out assignments independently. At the other extreme were youngsters who seemed to require her constant attention. Somehow they never heard the directions she gave, they needed regular supervision, and were much more interested in playing outside during recess than in coming to reading groups. As in every class she had worked with, there were a few children who caused her great concern. Johnny always came to school tired. He was very quiet and rarely became involved in the classroom activities. Mary, on the other hand, was so active that it was almost impossible to get her to settle down and finish a task. Mrs. R. sighed and wondered if she was actually meeting the needs of the youngsters in her class. The district superintendent talked about how each teacher individualized her program to match the curriculum to the developmental level of each child. She really wondered if it was humanly possible for any one teacher to truly individualize a program in that way.

Anyone who has spent time in a classroom will immediately recognize the problems Mrs. R. faces. Each human being has a unique genetic endowment and an equally unique environment in which to grow and develop. A child entering school has already been exposed to all sorts of educational experiences that begin at birth, or before. These early learning experiences are crucial in determining the child's total development. Parents, as the key adults in the home, are the first and probably most important teachers that the child will ever have.

Schaefer (1972) has identified several important factors that characterize the parent's interaction with the child. The duration of the relationship usually extends from birth to maturity. Other significant adults such as teachers and baby-sitters move in and out of the child's life, but the parent remains as a continuing influence. The intensity of this relationship lays the groundwork for language and cognitive development, interests, and all kinds of personality characteristics. All parents have their own sets of consistent behavioral patterns. They reward certain responses, have basic expectations for their children, and model important behaviors. Our society acknowledges that parents have primary responsibility for raising children. Most handle this task well and are able to accept the child, interact effectively, and meet basic needs. A smaller number are incapable of fulfilling this role, and abuse and neglect often occur. Great variability exists among parents, creating optimal environments for some children and deprived environments for others.

Studies of Parents and Children

Several studies have examined the relationship of the parent's behavior to the child's affective and cognitive development. By the time children enter school, there are already clear differences in their levels of functioning. The studies we will describe looked at various aspects of mother-child interactions in an effort to identify the parental behaviors that might account for these differences.

Infant Studies   Yarrow et al. (1972) examined the impact of the inanimate and social environment on the child's development. Their subjects were five- to six-month-old infants, and their mothers were from both low- and middle-income black families. The inanimate environment was rated in terms of the number of toys and other kinds of objects available to the child. Variety, responsiveness, and complexity of inanimate objects were analyzed. The social behavior of the mother was also examined for variety and level, responsiveness to the child, and positive effect as reflected in her behavior.

The variety of objects available to the child appeared to be the most significant factor in predicting gross motor development and general mental and psychomotor development. The responsiveness of these objects to the child's developmental level also appeared to affect development. As one might suspect, the mother's socially responsive behavior was a significant factor correlating positively with the child's development. The findings of this study appear to support the importance of providing a physical environment for the child that reflects variety and responsiveness as well as a social environment in which the mother responds contingently to the child's behavior.

Clarke-Stewart (1973) studied thirty-six nine-month-old, first-born infants and their mothers from low-income families. The children were observed seven times during a nine-month period, and assessments were made of language, cognitive, social, and emotional development. The quality of maternal care appeared to be a significant factor in determining the competency of the infant. Some of these quality attributes included the warmth of the mother in responding to the child, the mother's ability to involve the child with objects in the environment, the mother talking to the child about what he or she was doing, and a general positive attitude toward the child's behavior. The more competent mothers were usually attentive to their infants during the early months of development and responded consistently to the child's behaviors and demands. The behavior of the mother and the child appeared to influence each other. The responsiveness of the mother, for example, could very well communicate to the child that he or she had some measure of control over what happened, which could then motivate mastery learning. Mothers of the more competent infants (as measured by their behavior at eighteen months of age) all consistently went beyond providing basic physical care to the child.

The studies of mother-infant interactions indicate that more competent parents have a large number of short interactions with their children. As the child grows older, frequency appears to be less important and the quality of the interactions becomes more critical. White et al. (1973) studied the development of competence in young children. Although there were some methodological problems with this study (the number of children studied was particularly small), the researchers did identify some differences in the behaviors of the more competent mothers. These mothers were much less restrictive in allowing the child to move around the house freely and explore the objects in the environment. The more competent children engaged in a larger number of language interactions with their mothers and had mothers who responded to the things the child was interested in and wanted to talk about. In other words, the child initiated the contact and the mother responded. A key difference between the competent and less competent mothers was that the more competent mothers were significantly less controlling and restrictive in their interactions with the children.

Preschoolers and Mother-Child Interactions   Hess et al. (1968) studied many different aspects of mother-child interactions. Their sample included 163 black families representing four groups. The mothers in the first group had completed at least four years of college. They were not working and the fathers were employed in either professional or managerial jobs. The second group included mothers who had completed high school. Again, these mothers were not working and the fathers were employed in either skilled blue-collar or white-collar jobs. Mothers in the third group had attained no more than a tenth-grade education and did not work; the fathers were employed in unskilled or semiskilled jobs. The fourth group of mothers had no more than a tenth-grade education. There were no fathers in the home and the mothers received welfare aid. All of the children in the sample were within three months of their fourth birthday; half the sample were boys and half girls.

The findings of this study reflected significant social class differences. Mothers were questioned about their perceptions of whether or not they had the ability to control their environment through their own efforts as opposed to feeling a sense of powerlessness. The less educated mothers felt that they could not control or predict what happened to them. In contrast, the more highly educated mothers felt that they were very much in control of their lives and could bring about change through their own efforts and attitudes. While both groups described the same kind of goals and hopes for their children, they had very different perceptions of their abilities to influence attainment of these goals. The more educated mothers saw themselves as taking a very active role in assisting their children to reach particular goals, whereas the less educated mothers felt they played a more passive role. These mothers had a tendency to see the future as totally unpredictable and controlled by external events.

When questioned about how they handled discipline problems at home, social class differences again emerged. The less educated mothers mentioned the use of punitive techniques much more often than the more highly educated mothers. The latter group gave answers that reflected a desire to give the children information and explanations about why they expected certain kinds of behavior. It appeared that explanations would be stressed rather than simply telling the child or punishing inappropriate behaviors.

Each of the mothers was observed in videotaped teaching situations. Again, significant group differences were noted. During the introduction to the tasks, the more highly educated mothers repeatedly gave their children a lot of specific information. They consistently told the children what the task would be like and what they should do. When a child made a mistake, these mothers provided feedback and attempted to assist the child in correcting the error. The less educated mothers tended to respond only to the child's behavior. They were not as likely to go beyond the particular response of the child or to give additional instructions.

It seems reasonable to assume that the same kinds of behaviors would be found in the homes of these children. Most probably, the better educated parents frequently interact with their children and provide a higher level of cognitive stimulation. The child raised in a home where the mother does not offer this type of interaction is forced to try to figure out the meaning of the world alone. Since the child's knowledge base is tentative and shaky, informative feedback is of critical importance. Without input from caring adults, young children are likely to acquire knowledge filled with errors and inconsistencies. They are less likely to develop the ability to focus on the critical factors in the environment and attend to those features that might help them make basic discriminating judgments. When these children begin school, the teacher is likely to find that they are less prepared for the demands of formal learning.

Affective Influences   Hess et al. (1971) reviewed studies that examined affective influences on the child's cognitive and emotional development. They identified several clusters of parental behavior that influence the child's social and affective growth.

1. Maternal warmth, high emotional involvement and interaction, and the parents' general interest in the child appear to be positively correlated with the child's achievement.

2. The development of independent behavior on the part of a child seems to be related to parental behavior that focuses on training the child from an early age to be independent in both actions and thinking.

3. While encouragement of early independence appears to prepare the child for success in school, as the child grows older the more effective parent establishes well-defined limits for behavior. The establishment of these limits also seems to be related to higher school achievement.

4. The most positive pattern of parental control is that in which parents explain their requests, consult with the child, and give reasons for the discipline techniques used.

5. The attitudes, values, and expectations of the parent seem to significantly influence the child's behavior and aspirations. The competent parent communicates a sense of control over the achievement level to be reached by the child as well as a high level of expectation for the child's abilities.

6. The child's self-concept and sense of control over the environment seem to be related to the parents' acceptance of the child, the degree of clear rules established in the home for the child's behavior, and the respect the parent has for the individuality of the child.

Intervention Studies

Goodson and Hess (1975) reviewed twenty-nine programs designed to serve low-income preschool children and their parents. A major goal of each of these programs was to train parents as teachers of their own children. Many different approaches were used, including home-based intervention, school and home settings combined, group sessions for parents, and individual tutors. All of the programs in the review were developed and implemented in the middle and late 1960s; three basic assumptions regarding parent involvement guided the design of the programs. First, the home environment of the children was considered to be inadequate for preparing them for future school experiences. The research of Deutsch (1964), Bereiter and Engelmann (1966), and others identified what were thought to be significant differences in the home environments of middle- and lower-class families. These differences included the amount and kind of stimulation available to the child, the language modeled, motivational strategies, and the interaction between parent and child. The second assumption was based upon the work of Bloom (1964) and other researchers on the concept of critical periods in development. Bloom's longitudinal study of growth indicated that the early years of a child's life were critically important. He argued that by age four one could predict with reasonable accuracy a child's potential for future intellectual growth. Since the early years were times of great intellectual and cognitive development, we could assume that intervention during this period would have maximal impact on the child. The third assumption was related to the influence of the family on later school achievement. The Coleman Report (1966) indicated that the family was a significant factor in the child's educational experience and was a major determinant of educational outcome. Building upon these assumptions, each program designed a particular intervention strategy for parent involvement.

Goodson and Hess identified a number of problems related to cross-program comparisons (1975, pp. 13–14).

Program effectiveness is primarily judged in terms of the criterion of cognitive gains for children, but many programs were designed to achieve other important goals. . . . There are methodological problems. Comparable tests are not used in all program evaluations. . . . There is variation among the programs on factors that are not examined, such as age of children and number of hours of intervention. . . . It is likely that programs which fail to produce results are not reported, leaving a reviewer with a biased sample of programs showing varying degrees of success. . . . Some of the most important questions about the effects of parent participation require follow-up data, and such data are often not available.

The findings of this review should be interpreted cautiously. There were great variations among the programs in sample selection, instrumentation, program specificity, implementation strategies, and data analysis techniques. The conclusions are tentative but promising.

Intelligence Test Data Twenty-six programs reported intelligence test data on the children at the end of the intervention period. The majority (23 programs) indicated that children in the program had significantly higher IQ scores than control groups. Nine programs tested the children in follow-up studies that ranged from three months to five years. Data from the child-centered group programs (where parents were part of a center-based program) indicated that the children maintained consistently higher scores than the control groups. Both groups, however, showed a decline in scores after about two years. Two home-based programs reported much more positive results (Gordon, 1973; Madden et al., 1974). Program children consistently scored higher than control groups and maintained these gains after two and three years of follow-up.

Achievement Test Data Only three programs collected achievement test data using standardized achievement instruments. Again, there were significant differences in favor of program children through the third grade. More of the program children scored at or above the 50th percentile, received passing grades, and were less likely to require remedial classes. Teachers who were asked to rate the classroom behavior of both program and control children gave significantly higher ratings to the program children on factors such as achievement motivation, appropriateness of self-concept, and other psychosocial behaviors.

Parent Emphasis   Each of the twenty-nine programs placed different emphasis on working with parents. Some focused totally on the parent as the prime subject of intervention and shared information through home visits, group meetings, or a combination. Other programs worked directly with parents and children. A center-based program was offered to all children, and related activities were available to the parent through both home visits and group meetings. Analysis showed that those children making the greatest IQ gains had parents who received home visits either alone or as part of the preschool program. Follow-up data revealed that more of the program children maintained their IQ gains when the program emphasis had been on working directly with the parent.

Program Content   Different kinds of content goals were emphasized by the programs, including attention to language stimulation, sensorimotor stimulation, cognitive development, and knowledge of child development principles. The specific content of programs did not appear to influence gains in the children's intellectual scores. A key factor, however, was the degree of active involvement of the parents in the program activities. Content designed to ensure active parental responsibility for the child's development seemed to be most effective.

Changes in Parents   Significant attitudinal changes in parents of program children were reported. Parents who were most heavily involved in program activities appeared to feel much more in control of the events in their lives. The attitudes of program parents reflected realistic expectations about their child's development, less authoritarianism, and increased flexibility in behavior.

A number of changes occurred in the quality and dynamics of parent-child interactions. Parents were more likely to use language in reinforcing their child and gave more positive feedback. The language patterns of the parents became more complex and elaborate. They tended to listen to the child and expand on what he or she said. Most parents appeared to be warm, sensitive, and relaxed with their children. They were more likely to be actively involved in teaching their children and responding to their needs.

Most of the programs reported that, as positive changes appeared in the parents' behavior, program children significantly outperformed control children. These findings support the strategy of direct intervention in training low-income parents to become more effective teachers of their own children. Additional research is needed before recommendations can be made for large-scale program implementation, but the feasibility of the approach has been demonstrated and provides encouraging support for parent involvement programs.

Effective Parent-Child Behavior

Investigators have studied the relationship of home variables and school achievement. Gordon (1976) classified these home variables into four categories: family structure, family attitudes toward achievement and school, family process variables, and home-school interactions.

Family Structure   These variables include the number of children in the home, the occupation of the father and mother, the educational background of the parents, family income, religion, and language of the home. While social class has consistently been reported as an important factor related to school performance, the structure of the home does not appear to be as important as the attitudes and practices within the home (Keeves, 1975).

Family Attitudes   This category includes the attitudes of the parents toward their child's educational level, their ambitions for the child, and the child's own aspirations. Parent interest in the child is correlated with higher school achievement (Keeves, 1975).

Family Process   A large number of family process variables have been identified (Bloom, 1964; Dave, 1963; Wolf, 1964). These include press for achievement, language models, academic guidance, family activities, dominance patterns, independence training, work habits and order, and stimulation and reinforcement practices. Important factors within the home related to school achievement include the use made of books and library facilities, the kind of arrangements made for homework, the encouragement of independence and curiosity, and reinforcement strategies.

Home-School Interactions   Coleman (1975) reported that in the United States, for ten-year-old children home factors were twice as important as school factors in accounting for reading achievement. He further stated that for reading, science, and literature, the total effect of home background is considerably greater than the direct effect of school variables (p. 381). According to Jencks (1972), the home and social system have a much greater influence than schools on achievement.

Cognitive Factors   Evidence strongly indicates that the behavior and attitudes of parents influence the achievement of the child in school. Some investigators have identified what they believe to be desirable parent behaviors, both cognitive and affective (Dave, 1963; Hess, 1969; Wolf, 1964). Some of the factors that have been reported in the cognitive domain include:

1.   Parents who see themselves as teachers of their child.

2.   Parents who talk *with* their child rather than *at* him or her.

3.   Parents who consistently provide some sort of academic guidance for their child.

4.   Parental behavior that consistently reflects praise and reinforcement.

5. A high level of verbal interaction within the home.

6. Homes that have a variety of books and materials for the child.

7. Parents who provide information and feedback to the child about the environment.

8. Parents who listen to, share, and plan with the child.

Affective Factors   Affective factors have been identified that also appear to be correlated with the child's development.

1. The parents' sense of self-esteem and confidence.

2. Consistency in managing the child.

3. Discipline that reflects rationality and explanations.

4. A willingness to spend time with the child and devote efforts to child rearing.

5. Parental feelings of control over the events in their lives.

6. Parental ability to work within the social and economic system and operate within the framework of established institutions.

Taken together, these variables probably represent the ideal situation for child rearing. We cannot at this time identify any one of these factors as being the most crucial for the child's development. Most probably, no one pattern or set of factors will ever be identified as representing the ideal parent. Just as we know there are many examples of effective teaching behavior, so also there appear to be many examples and varieties of effective parenting behavior.

PROGRAM IMPLICATIONS

What conclusions can be drawn from our knowledge of how children develop and the research findings on parent-child interactions? What implications might these data have for the design of parent involvement programs? While there are still many unknowns, we can begin to make the leap from research to practice by analyzing the major findings and developing strategies for putting these techniques into practice through parent-school cooperative efforts.

The suggestions that follow should be considered reasonable in view of our current state of knowledge. Remember that new information will be reported constantly. Teachers must make every effort to stay informed and to revise programs accordingly. There are many ways to stay abreast of new findings: by attending conferences, in-service programs, and lectures, and by reading new books, journals, and magazine articles dealing with parent involvement. Current beliefs will become outmoded as new information emerges.

Meet Physical Needs

The child's physical development, while largely controlled by genetic factors, still requires basic support that can be provided only by adults. Both parents and teachers should be aware of their responsibility to meet the child's physical needs. This means a proper diet, medical checkups, and opportunities to rest, exercise, and explore. A basic assumption must be that children's physical needs must be met before they are ready for the more complex tasks of childhood.

Share Control and Power

Research clearly shows that the parents' feeling about themselves, their sense of worth, esteem, and control, must be positive if they are to meet the needs of their children. While schools cannot intervene by providing good jobs and an adequate income for all families, they must do everything possible to build up the parents' self-concept. This means that an involvement program must be carried out not simply because it is required, but because the teacher really believes that what parents do makes a difference in the child's life. Teachers can communicate positive expectations regarding the parents' role and be willing to share some of the decision-making functions that determine the direction of the school program. Parents should have some feeling of control and power over their child's educational experiences. If they believe that what they do is important, they will be more likely to communicate to the child the importance of education.

Exchange Child-Rearing Information

The research literature has emphasized the importance of the quality of parent-child interactions. Teachers can share this information in parent involvement programs. The information should include the importance of parents being responsive to children and their interests. Long-term goals can be discussed to assist the child in becoming independent and responsible. This process is a gradual one and parents must be aware of the kinds of rules they set up and whether or not these rules facilitate the development of independence. The foundations for effective coping are established early in life and grow out of the cumulative effects of numerous parent-child interactions.

The parent is one of the most consistent role models for the child. The behaviors modeled by the parent will be observed and imitated by the child. Imitation learning has implications for all aspects of the child's development, including language, social behaviors, and many individual personality traits. Aggressive behavior, coping styles, problem-solving techniques, and a multitude of other traits are first acquired as children observe their parents' behavior. Often parents are not aware of the effects of incidental learning episodes, so parents and teachers should explore these aspects of behavior and begin to acquire those skills necessary to monitor their own behavioral patterns and how these influence children.

Create Supportive Environments

The environments of the home and school provide the child with many opportunities to interact with objects, people, and events. Young children should be given access to their environment (within the limits of safety and sanity) and be encouraged to explore and discover on their own. The adult's role is to provide children with corrective feedback as needed and information that will permit them to internalize the meaning of environmental events. The process of constructing a knowledge base is slow and continuous. Parents and teachers must explore realistic ways of providing the child with the kinds of opportunities needed to interact meaningfully with the environment.

Share Expectations

Another area that needs to be explored by parents and teachers is the use of reinforcement techniques. Do the home and school reinforce and praise the same kinds of behaviors? Are they instead confusing the child by reinforcing and attending to very different kinds of behaviors? The child will most likely repeat those behaviors that are reinforced consistently. Typically, the young child wants to please adults but this becomes difficult when important adults reinforce different kinds of behavior. For example, suppose parents reinforce the child to speak only when spoken to. On the other hand, the teacher in the classroom encourages the children to develop oral language skills. A different behavior is reinforced in the classroom, and the young child is uncertain as to what is expected of him. Parents and teachers working together can discuss the kinds of expectations they have for the child and provide continuity between home and school.

Ideally, the most significant outcome of any parent involvement effort would be the development of continuous goals for home and school. This has rarely occurred in American education and is certainly a very difficult goal. The advantages of providing continuity for children are obvious. Instead of inconsistencies of goals between settings, children will have the opportunity to encounter the same kinds of expectations, values, and attitudes regarding their behavior, and the adults in their environment will be consistently responsive.

SUMMARY

A tremendous amount of information is available for those who wish to design parent involvement programs, and the fund of information increases at a rapid pace. While the implications of some studies or reports remain unclear, we can identify findings that guide program planning.

1. The quality of a child's environment is a crucial factor in determining the level of intellectual and social functioning eventually achieved by the child.

2. The behavior of parents (particularly the mother or primary caretaker) as they interact with their child can significantly affect intellectual and social-emotional development.

3. The ways that parents interact with their children appear to be related to factors such as socioeconomic status, educational background, and the general social responsiveness of the parents.

4. The family appears to significantly influence the child's educational experiences and has a major effect in determining educational outcomes for the child.

5. Preschool programs that involve parents report significant differences betweeen program and comparison children on intelligence and achievement test scores.

6. Program designers should be sensitive to factors such as meeting the child's physical needs, sharing control with parents, exchanging child-rearing information, creating supportive environments, and sharing information about child expectations.

Working with children can and should be a joyous experience. Too often we allow problems to overwhelm us and forget the very deep rewards that come from involvement with children. Programs that enable parents and teachers to work together and share this task are much more likely to succeed in creating an environment for the child that is responsive to unique developmental needs.

FOR DISCUSSION AND FURTHER STUDY

1. Explain the kind of child-rearing advice a maturational advocate would give to parents of young children.

2. Give five examples of parent behaviors that can affect the child's intellectual development.

3. Give five examples of parent behavior that can affect the child's social or emotional development.

4. Arrange to visit the home of a preschool child. Observe the child and note how he or she interacts with objects and people in that environment. What suggestions would you have for the parents?

5. Prepare a five-minute speech for parents of young children, focusing on creating an ideally supportive home environment.

6. Select three goals for a parent involvement program and show how these goals are supported by research findings.

7. List ten things parents could do (supported by research findings) to stimulate the intellectual and emotional development of a young child.

8. Explain why educational programs that involve parents appear to be more effective than those working only with children.

9. List five conclusions about child rearing that can be drawn from some of the research studies cited in this chapter. Discuss how this information could be used in setting up a parent involvement program.

10. Develop a checklist of important things to look for when visiting homes of infants, preschool children, and children in primary grades. Explain how you selected the items on your list.

BIBLIOGRAPHY

Bandura, Albert. *Principles of Behavior Modification.* New York: Holt, Rinehart and Winston, 1969.

Bereiter, Carl, and Siegfried Engelmann. *Teaching Disadvantaged Children in the Preschool.* Englewood Cliffs, N.J.: Prentice-Hall, 1966.

Bloom, Benjamin. *Stability and Change in Human Characteristics.* New York: Wiley, 1964.

Brophy, Jere. *Child Development and Socialization.* Chicago: Science Research Associates, 1977.

Clarke-Stewart, Alison. "Interactions between Mothers and Their Young Children: Characteristics and Consequences." *Monographs of the Society for Research in Child Development.* Chicago: University of Chicago Press, 1973.

Coleman, James. *Equality of Educational Opportunity.* Washington, D.C.: U.S. Office of Education, 1966.

Coleman, James. "Methods and Results in the IEA Studies of Effects of School on Learning." *Review of Educational Research* 4, no. 3 (1975): 335–86.

Dave, R. "The Identification and Measurement of Environmental Process Variables that are Related to Educational Achievement." Unpublished Ph.D. dissertation, University of Chicago, 1963.

Deutsch, Martin. "Facilitating Development in the Pre-School Child: Social and Psychological Perspectives." *Merrill-Palmer Quarterly* 10 (1964): 249–63.

Gesell, Arnold, and Frances Ilg. *Infant and Child in the Culture of Today.* New York: Harper, 1943.

Goodson, Barbara, and Robert Hess. *Parents as Teachers of Young Children: An Evaluative Review of Some Contemporary Concepts and Programs.* Stanford, Calif.: Stanford University Press, 1975.

Gordon, Ira. *The Florida Parent Education Early Intervention Projects: A Longitudinal Look.* Institute for Development of Human Resources, College of Education. Gainesville, Florida: University of Florida, 1973.

Gordon, Ira. *What Are Effective Learning Environments for School Age Children?* IDHR Conference, Gainesville, Florida, 1976.

Hess, Robert. "Parental Behavior and Children's School Achievement: Implications for Head Start." In *Critical Issues in Research Related to Disadvantaged Children*, Seminar #5. Princeton, N.J.: Educational Testing Service, 1969.

Hess, Robert, Marianne Block, Joan Costillo, Ruby Knowles, and Dorothy Largay. "Parent Involvement in Early Education." In *Day Care: Resources for Decisions*, ed. Edith Grotberg. Washington, D.C.: OEO Pamphlet 6106–1, 1971.

Hess, Robert, Virginia Shipman, Jere Brophy, and Roberta Bear. *Cognitive Environments of Urban Preschool Negro Children*. Report to the Children's Bureau, Social Security Administration, Department of HEW, 1968.

Hunt, J. McVicker. *Intelligence and Experience*. New York: Ronald Press, 1961.

Jencks, Christopher. *Inequality: A Reassessment of the Effect of Family and Schooling in America*. New York: Harper & Row, 1972.

Keeves, John. "The Home, the School, and Achievement in Mathematics and Science." *Science Education* 59, no. 4 (1975): 439–60.

Madden, J., Phyllis Levenstein, and Sidney Levenstein. *Longitudinal IQ Outcomes of the Mother-Child Home Program, 1967–1973*. Verbal Interaction Project, Family Service Association of Nassau County, Inc., and State University of New York at Stony Brook, Freeport, N.Y., 1974.

Schaefer, Earl. "Parents as Educators: Evidence from Cross-Sectional Longitudinal and Intervention Research." In *The Young Child: Reviews of Research*, vol. II. Washington, D.C.: National Association for the Education of Young Children, 1972.

Skeels, Harold. "Adult Status of Children with Contrastive Early Life Experience: A Follow-up Study." *Monographs of the Society for Research in Child Development*, serial no. 105, vol. 31, 1966.

Skeels, Harold, and H. Dye. "A Study of the Effects of Differential Stimulation in Mentally Retarded Children." *Proceedings of the American Association on Mental Deficiency* 44 (1939): 114–36.

Skinner, B. F. *Science and Human Behavior*. New York: Macmillan, 1953.

Skodak, Marie, and Harold Skeels. "A Final Follow-up of One Hundred Adopted Children." *Journal of Genetic Psychology* 72 (1948): 85–125.

Spitz, Rene. "Hospitalism: A Follow-up Report." *The Psychoanalytic Study of the Child* 2 (1946): 53–74.

Spock, Benjamin. *The Common Sense Book of Baby and Child Care*. New York: Duell, Sloan, and Pearce, 1945.

White, Burton, et al. *Experience and Environment: Major Influences on the Development of the Young Child*, vol. I. Englewood Cliffs, N.J.: Prentice-Hall, 1973.

Wolf, Richard. "The Identification and Measurement of Environmental Process Variables Related to Intelligence." Unpublished Ph.D. dissertation, University of Chicago, 1964.

Yarrow, Leon, J. Rubenstein, F. Pedersen, and J. Jankowski. "Dimensions of Early Stimulation: Differential Effects on Infant Development." *Merrill-Palmer Quarterly* 18 (1972): 205–18.

PART TWO

Basic Considerations in Planning for Parent Involvement

Parent involvement programs come in all shapes and sizes. Teachers can ask parents to supervise playground activities, make instructional materials, demonstrate a special skill, read stories to children, or serve as room mothers. Federal or special program guidelines might require involving parents in an advisory or decision-making role.

How can a teacher develop an involvement program to meet the needs of parents in the community or school? One way is to use a "shotgun" approach and try four or five ideas that have been successful for others. One or two of these ideas might work, but the others will probably be dismal failures.

Another option, and one that we advocate, is to follow a systematic planning process designed to identify goals and objectives for each group of parents. Committing time to planning will delay the start of parent group activities, but when activities do begin, they will be based on the actual needs and interests of parents. By building a firm foundation for a relevant program, teachers will be able to offer an effective approach to parent involvement.

3 Relating to Others

OVERVIEW

Mary has been in first grade for three months and her mother, who is a member of the school board, is very pleased with the progress she has made. Being particularly sensitive to the complexity of teachers' roles and knowing how rarely anyone praises their efforts, Mary's mother has requested a conference.

Karen Brown was worried. Mary's mother is an outspoken member of the school board and has requested a conference. Karen knows that the conference means trouble. What is she doing wrong?

Johnny's mother received a note from Lila Maple asking her to come to school for a conference. Johnny's parents are divorced and his mother works nights, so she has not attended any of the parent meetings held that year. She knows from her own school experience that the note means there are problems. What had Johnny done?

Miss Maple had noted that Johnny's parents are divorced and that Johnny's mother seems to be doing her best to take care of her family. Johnny is doing well in the first grade, and Miss Maple thought that it would be nice to share this information with his mother.

These are two examples of how past experiences create barriers to communication. In the first case Karen Brown assumed that the only time parents ask for a conference is when they have a complaint. In the second case, the parent believed that conferences are scheduled only when the child has a problem. She did not even consider the possibility that meetings could be held to share positive information.

Barriers such as these can be broken down easily if teachers are sensitive to potential misunderstandings and anticipate problems. In this chapter we will explore some basic assumptions about human relations and communicating with others. Teachers often have mixed feelings about working with parents, and parents have the same kinds of feelings about working with teachers. We will identify some of the emotions involved and discuss how they can get in the way of effective communication.

We will give some ideas on how schools can create an atmosphere that helps parents and children feel comfortable and welcome even before school starts. The last section of this chapter deals with parent-teacher conferences as a strategy for improving communication between home and school.

UNDERSTANDING PEOPLE

All people function in three ways at the same time: we think, we feel, and we behave. While we are often told (and would like to believe) that we are rational human beings, we do not always behave in rational ways.

The Parent-Child Relationship

As decisions take on more personal meanings, our behaviors become more and more influenced by emotions. The parent-child relationship, in particular, is loaded with emotional factors. While most parents can discuss other children's behaviors rationally, their perceptions of their own child are significantly altered by strong emotional relationships, regardless of how educated, experienced, or intelligent they might be.

Faust (1967) has identified what he calls *cripplers* to effective functioning and learning. These cripplers are excessive fear, excessive guilt, and excessive anxiety. Each of these can cause large amounts of adrenaline to be released into the body. When this happens, the ability to think logically may be greatly diminished. Parents, children, and teachers who are experiencing these emotions will not behave as they would in more normal situations. They cannot analyze their concerns, explore alternatives, or make rational decisions.

How can teachers reduce this stress? Joseph Breuer, a physician in Vienna more than 100 years ago, discovered a very important principle about human functioning. He found that "talking helps people." The principle has implications for the classroom. All of us have had the experience of being extremely upset and going to a friend with whom we were able to talk about our feelings. While the friend may or may not have helped us reach a solution, at the end of the discussion we felt better and were able to think more logically. Very often, parents who are terribly upset come to school ready to complain to the teacher about some supposed injustice that has been done to their child. Rather than responding in anger, the teacher should help the parent express the feelings and allow time for rational thinking to replace the emotional reaction.

Arthur Combs compares some of our actions to those of a turtle. When a turtle is safe and free from attack, it sticks its head out, eats, and explores the environment. If, however, a turtle is in an unsafe, hostile environment, it withdraws into its shell, is not open to growth, and eventually dies. The same is true for people. In home-school relationships, open communication can occur only when the environment for both teacher and parent is supportive, nurturing, and safe.

The Parent's Self-Concept

Almost without exception teachers want to help children develop positive self-concepts, but often they forget that parents need the same care. Parents differ from each other in the feelings they have about themselves. If they see themselves as able and adequate parents, they will behave with their children in ways that are consistent with this belief. If, however, they see themselves as inadequate, their behavior will tend to be consistent with this perception. For example, parents who believe that they are doing a good job raising their children will usually volunteer to help the teacher in the classroom in any number of ways. They are comfortable about their own parental abilities, and the expectations they hold for their children are generally positive. Other parents might be very hesitant to volunteer for classroom activity. They are unsure of their own skills and are unwilling to risk being judged inadequate. Teachers should remember that the behavior they see is often a reflection of the parents' perception of themselves. Keeping this in mind should help teachers in learning to deal with parents who appear to be angry, hostile, or uncooperative.

Teachers can try to change the self-concept of parents through hearing, believing, and becoming. Parents need to hear from others frequently that they are indeed able, competent, and loving. This can help them begin to believe these new perceptions of themselves. After hearing and then believing that they are worthwhile persons, their behavior can begin to change consistent with this new belief.

At this point you are probably saying to yourself, "That's great, but who has time to do that with the parent of every child in the classroom?" We agree that this would be an impossible task. Remember, however, that not all parents need intensive encouragement and support. Most feel good about who they are and what they are trying to do. There will be times when some parents need extra support in handling their child-rearing role, however, and teachers should try to respond appropriately.

TEACHERS HAVE FEELINGS

Parents and teachers often find it difficult to work together cooperatively. Many teachers may have really tried to start a parent involvement program but have not been successful. Others do not want to be bothered and can give many reasons why working with parents is unimportant. They might give lip service to the concept but communicate in subtle and not so subtle ways that they do not expect the program to work. Talking to teachers reveals many reasons for these attitudes.

My job is complicated enough just working with these children in the classroom and teaching them basic skills.

Those that do come to the classroom don't seem to know what to do. By the time I explain everything, it would have been easier to do it myself.

I don't want parents telling me what the school program ought to be. They're not trained, they don't understand what we're trying to do, and they shouldn't be allowed to make decisions about the educational program.

An annual conference and an open house once a year are enough. Let me do my job and they can do theirs.

If you talk to enough teachers you will hear all of these comments and more. Let's explore some of the reasons (both real and imagined) behind these attitudes.

Experience Makes a Difference

Beginning teachers are under tremendous pressure to demonstrate that they are competent in the classroom. Suddenly they are responsible for teaching thirty children, maintaining order in the classroom, and meeting all the other requirements of the school's program. The tasks are complicated, and it is a rare beginning teacher who is not anxious, afraid, and feeling very inadequate. Starting out in a new professional role means that everything takes longer than it should. Teachers work nights and weekends, and barely stay ahead of the children. All teachers go through a stage of feeling unable to cope, and some become so discouraged that they drop out of the profession. For these teachers, working with parents is just one more task that they feel they cannot handle. The best solution is for teachers to start slowly, set limited, short-range goals, and plan to expand the parent involvement program as they become more comfortable in their teaching role.

Many teachers do not have children of their own, so they often feel very uncomfortable when parents ask them for advice. How can they tell a parent what to do if they have never been through the experience of raising children themselves? Certainly all teachers are not experts on child rearing in the home, but they have been trained professionally to work with children and deal with developmental issues. Teachers also have the advantage of being able to look at the children in the classroom fairly objectively, so they are not as emotionally involved as their parents. There is no reason that teachers cannot discuss problems of concern with parents if they keep their role in perspective. Teachers can be of real assistance by answering questions and resolving problems and issues of child rearing, by giving reassurance, or sometimes just by listening. At other times, teachers might have to refer the problem to another agency.

The feelings of the experienced teacher have been influenced by a whole series of positive and negative encounters with parents. These probably include the friendly parent, the aggressive parent, the helpful parent, the parent expert who tries to tell the teacher what to do, and the parent who just does not seem to care. Each of these encounters leaves a mark and affects the teacher's perceptions of parent involvement.

All teachers need advice on working with parents, and there are a number of ways to get it. One is to have a parent involvement resource person who can work with classroom teachers and help them develop effective techniques for communication. Teachers also might consider taking special courses in interpersonal techniques or parent involvement. Finally, resources often unrecognized by teachers are their own professional colleagues. If the faculty can agree that parent involvement is an important goal, teachers can plan meetings to exchange information. Teachers can also get many good ideas through informal contacts with each other.

Demands on Time

Where do teachers find the time to work with parents? Their day is already filled to overflowing. Bringing parents into the classroom to work as volunteers might sound helpful, but it means extra planning and effort for the teacher. Is it really necessary? Our answer is yes, absolutely and positively. In the long run nothing will pay off more for both teachers and children than getting parents involved. The classroom will gain at least one extra pair of hands to help manage daily classroom routines. Many parents can be extremely effective as instructional aides and can help teachers individualize programs. Another benefit that is often overlooked is that parent volunteers usually become strong advocates for school programs. These are the citizens who are willing to fight and work for passage of bond issues, development of innovative programs, and support for classroom teachers.

There are no simple techniques for using time wisely, or any magic solutions for engaging those parents who do not want to be involved. Achieving effective parent involvement will often depend on the effort the teacher is willing to make. We all set priorities on how we use our time, and if parent involvement is important, it will be near the top of a priority list. You might try a simple time study for a week. At the end of every day, keep track of what you actually did and ask yourself if this is the best use of your time. Perhaps you have fallen into a comfortable routine in which you do things because you have always done them that way. A teacher aide might be able to assume responsibility for some of the things you do. Could parent volunteers take over a few of the time-consuming tasks?

Remember that you as a professional must learn to use your time in such a way that you get the most payoff for your effort. You have certain special skills that no one else can bring to the classroom. Develop a plan for yourself that will allow you to find the time to work with parents. If the priority of parent involvement is important, you will manage to find a way to fit it in.

Demands on the Teacher

A sad fact of life is that the reward system of many schools does not recognize the efforts of teachers who work effectively with parents. Accountability has become the byword, and every teacher is expected to produce gains in achievement test scores. In addition, most principals and preschool directors expect the teacher to maintain an orderly classroom with well-behaved children. Evaluations are often based on whether or not the teacher has managed to achieve these goals. These pressures are very real and crucial to a teacher's future employment.

Once we acknowledge that accountability is a fact of life, it might make sense to say that a teacher's responsibility is to work only with children in the classroom. Teachers really have not been trained to work with adults, no one expects them to be experts in this area, and besides parent needs usually fall outside of traditional school concerns. The question a teacher must ask is, "Can I educate this child by myself?" Can the child's school performance be separated from his or her life at home? Can the goal of schooling be achieved without the cooperative efforts of parents and teachers? The research literature clearly supports increased continuity and communication between home and school. Academic goals will be more difficult to achieve if teachers work in isolation from families. Remember, a teacher has the child for one year, whereas the parent stays with the child as a continuous influence.

Doors Have to Open Many teachers believe that the classroom is their private domain and that teaching children is their responsibility alone. They are protective and possessive of the time they have with youngsters in their class, and they really think that they will be less effective if other adults are in the classroom. Implied in these findings is that other adults will be judging or evaluating the teacher. Teachers can accept evaluation from a supervisor, but critical comments from parents fall into another category. Most often, teachers resent these comments and believe that parents are unqualified to make such judgments. One way to resolve this issue is to simply keep parents out of the classroom.

A widely used excuse for closing the classroom door is to say that when a parent is in the room, his or her child is likely to misbehave. The parent volunteer creates additional management problems for the teacher, and many believe that other adults in the classroom interfere with children's progress. This is true only if the teacher refuses to deal with and confront the issues. Children are reasonable beings who enjoy and take pride in having their parents volunteer in the classroom. The teacher needs to explain to both the children and parents what the role of the parent volunteer will be, the rules of acceptable behaviors, and how they are all to work together. After the first week or so, most children accept the arrangement naturally, allowing the parent volunteer to function effectively. Parents also have to be assured that they will be able to handle their new responsibilities as they gain more experience. They must be prepared for the possibilities of having to cope with children who show off, cling, or even have tantrums. Teachers should convince parents that the children will settle down in time if all the adults in the classroom are firm and consistent in their behavior.

Settings Must Change When home visiting is part of a parent involvement program, teachers often feel uncomfortable about moving out of the classroom to a new setting. While it is natural to feel uneasy, there is no reason to be unduly apprehensive. Common sense and everyday rules of courtesy should help overcome any initial barriers. Parents are trying to cope with their role from day to day just as teachers try to cope with their teaching responsibilities. Active listening, serious efforts to communicate, and allowing time for the relationship to develop should establish the foundation for a comfortable relationship.

Implications for Teachers

You bring your feelings about working with parents into the classroom. These feelings are part of who you are, where you come from, your past experiences, your attitudes, and your value system. Having these feelings is fine if you are aware of the emotions that will affect your relationship with parents. It will take some of you longer than others to reach a point when you are really comfortable in these relationships. Set reasonable expectations for yourself and know that you will change slowly and gradually.

Teachers who work effectively with parents really believe in the concept of involvement. They are comfortable with themselves and know their strengths as well as their weaknesses. They are willing to take risks and open the classroom door to both praise and criticism. Their expectations for parents are positive and they communicate a willingness to share, discuss, and explore issues. Because these teachers know that they cannot educate children alone, they are eager to have parents as partners in the educational process.

PARENTS HAVE FEELINGS

Almost without exception, parents want their children to do well in school. Most parents believe that if children do well in school they will also be prepared to do well in life. This also implies that parents have done their job well. The intense emotional factors associated with a child's performance in school can set up an adversary relationship between parents and the teacher. Parents (often unconsciously) believe that the teacher, whom they perceive as an expert, will make judgments about how effective they have been in their role. This often triggers strong feelings of guilt, anxiety, and inadequacy.

While teachers know that children develop at different rates and that individual variations in abilities are to be expected, parents are disappointed and concerned when their child is not rated as outstanding in every area. Discussing performance in terms of *average* achievement can set off emotional reactions rather than rational dialogue focused on what the child can or cannot do. Unrealistic expectations often get in the way of accepting where the child is and feeling good about his future.

The Parents' Perception of the School

The school as an institution is often perceived as intimidating by both well-educated and less-educated parents. Each parent brings his or her own unique experiences to the parent-teacher relationship. Memories of school and the feelings they evoke include failures, successes, clashes with authority figures, and all the fears and anxieties associated with peer relationships, as well as enjoyable moments. Add to these memories all the rules for parents regarding visiting classrooms, calling for appointments, checking in at the office, and talking to the professional educator and you can begin to see why parents often feel overwhelmed. Many of the rules have been set up for administrative convenience rather than for community needs.

Schools are often seen by parents as distant and unsympathetic to the many pressures of their everyday lives. Notes are sent home regularly telling them to put their children to bed early, to provide a quiet place to study, and to be sure that the children eat a balanced diet. Imagine the frustration faced by parents when they live in homes that are small and crowded, or when the parent is unemployed. When real home-school communication exists, teachers will be aware of individual situations that create strain and hardship for families. Unfortunately, this kind of communication is rare, and schools continue to send the same note home to all parents without considering unique problems and the feasibility of doing what is asked. Feelings of inadequacy, guilt, and alienation inevitably increase as parents find themselves unable to meet the requirements imposed by the system.

Many parents react by putting distance between themselves and the school. They stay away because they know they will be judged as not fulfilling their responsibilities. Very often, if their children begin to have problems in school, they will receive a note from the teacher asking them to come in for a conference. Since communication has clearly been one-way, initiated only by the school, parents know that the conference means new problems. Again, they will probably be told what they should be doing, which will reinforce their belief that they are not coping adequately.

The Parents' Perception of Their Role

Our society has never acknowledged and recognized the importance of the parenting role. We give lip service to the concept, but rate parenting as an unskilled job. Schools have reinforced this attitude by assuming the major responsibility for the child's formal education.

For many years, only the professional was permitted to work in the classroom. Recently there has been a movement toward accepting paraprofessionals and volunteers as active members of the instruction team. But many teachers continue to believe that the paraprofessional or volunteer should not have instructional responsibilities, and they are not willing to let them work directly with the children.

The belief that only the professional can teach is often accepted without question by parents. Mothers, in particular, tend to believe that anyone can do their job. Because they often lack formal training, they think they cannot contribute much to their child's educational experiences. This attitude, reinforced by home, school, and the media, increases the barriers to sharing and communicating.

New problems are emerging as our society changes. More mothers are working and there has been a tremendous increase in the number of single-parent families. Our idealized television families always have a mother who stays at home and cares for her children. Complementing the idealized mother is a father sharing the responsibilities. Working parents and single parents are constantly bombarded with signals that create feelings of guilt. They often have to miss special classroom programs or activities and can see their child's disappointment. Their nagging fear is that their children are being cheated. These guilt feelings are compounded when their children have problems in school. Busy teachers can be insensitive to these emotional factors and unwittingly reinforce the parents' sense of inadequacy. The judgments implied in their comments and requests make it even more difficult for parents to feel good about what they are able to do.

Talking to the Teacher

What happens when parents and teachers meet? The traditional setting for these meetings is the classroom, the teachers' home territory and perhaps unfamiliar to parents. Without realizing what is happening, teachers communicate that they are in charge and that important things happen in school, not at home. The parent walks into the classroom and usually finds the teacher seated at the desk. The desk between the two can create additional barriers. Sometimes the teacher is busy working and doesn't immediately get up to greet the parent. The message is, "When I am ready, we will begin."

Jargon Creates Barriers   Educators tend to forget that not everyone is familiar with the jargon of their profession. They throw out such terms as "percentile ranks," "quartiles," "mastery learning," and "over- and under-achieving." Many parents are reluctant to ask for a definition of these terms. They listen patiently as the teacher talks and neither understand the point that is being made nor expect to understand.

Some teachers really believe that parents are incapable of comprehending new instructional techniques and innovative curricula; they expect the parent to accept what they are doing on faith. The message is clear: parents are not trained, they do not understand educational change, and they are not supposed to question decisions.

Parents soon learn that even when they have reasonable complaints, the system regroups to protect its own. Most principals or directors will support the teachers in their program, at least on the surface. Parents are often caught in the dilemma of trying to decide if they should go to the school when they have real concerns, or whether it might not be better to ignore the problem and hope that it will pass. They think that their complaints might create new problems for their child. These feelings of uncertainty and helplessness reinforce the idea that power is based in the school rather than in the community.

Teacher Knows Best   Teachers have all kinds of advantages in their relationship with parents. Their role and their responsibilities have been clearly described. Parents, on the other hand, are uncertain as to their actual rights. Are their expectations reasonable? Are they asking too much of the classroom teacher? Are they asking too little? What is their role in relationship to the school as an institution? Many parents believe that they are the only ones having problems raising their children. These hidden fears concerning their roles and responsibilities create even more barriers between home and school.

The teacher's responsibility is to create a setting of trust where open dialogue can help the home and school better meet the needs of children.

Implications for Teachers

If we are serious about the importance of parent involvement, schools will need to change their traditional mode of operation to encourage and permit parents to assume more active roles. What can facilitate these changes?

1. Awareness of differences in parents must be reflected in any programs developed. You can learn to use these differences to strengthen parent involvement. This means that you must make individual contacts with parents, get to know them, and base plans on this individualized knowledge.

2. Forget the idealized, romanticized picture of the American family and learn to accept parents as they are. Most parents are truly concerned about their children. Acknowledge the incredible difficulty of the child-rearing task and be openly supportive of the many ways parents can reach important goals.

3. If we are to interact effectively with parents, we must respect that they are the true experts when it comes to knowing their own children. Listen to what they have to tell you and share what you have seen in the classroom. As partners you each have a contribution to make.

4. Give parents genuine opportunities to participate in school decisions. Be prepared for some ideas with which you disagree, but consider what can be learned through these experiences. Just as you want to help each parent build a positive self-concept, you also want them to develop realistic expectations about themselves and others.

5. Involvement implies action and doing. If you expect that you will talk and parents will listen, then you can predict a large number of drop-outs. Involve parents in planning and selecting goals for themselves and have them suggest ideas for group activities or resource people to conduct sessions.

6. We all need feedback and reinforcement if we are to maintain our interest. Praise the efforts that are being made and the changes you see in both the parent and the child.

7. No one has unlimited time for involvement and not all parents can be involved. Parents are busy people and have many other important commitments. Be practical in your planning and do not expect more than a parent can reasonably do.

8. Learn all you can about the community in which you work. There will be a mixture of many different cultures, value systems, attitudes, and traditions. You will be much more effective in your teaching role if you understand and accept these different belief systems.

9. Improvement grows out of self-criticism. Don't get too comfortable or complacent. Parent involvement programs should change from year to year because of your experiences. The goal of perfecting your program will never be totally reached because each year the cast of characters will change and your parent involvement efforts will accommodate these new needs.

INVOLVEMENT STARTS EARLY

Parent involvement should begin long before the child starts school. If we expect parents to assume an active participatory role, schools and programs must take the initiative and communicate their interest in working with families. The activities we will discuss are not necessarily expensive or time-consuming. They do, however, require a serious commitment to communicating with families and a willingness to plan ahead. The major responsibility for these early outreach efforts must be assumed by the school administrator, who has the authority to plan and coordinate the efforts of both the school faculty and parent volunteers. Plans will vary according to local situations, but efforts should focus on the development of regular outreach activities. All of the following suggestions could be adapted to elementary or preschool settings.

Information Packets

Giving parents materials that describe the school program and its expectations for children and parents will help remove the mystique that surrounds the changing educational system. The anxiety that so many parents feel regarding the judgments of teachers about their children can be reduced through the exchange of concrete information. After reading these materials, parents who have questions should be encouraged to contact someone at the school who can give them more information.

Information pamphlets should include descriptions of the school curriculum and the goals of the program. They can discuss the kinds of experiences children will have when they start school and the sorts of things parents can do to prepare children for an easy adjustment, for example, going to the library together, reading books, telling stories, playing games outdoors, and cooking simple foods. The suggested activities can be easy and part of everyday routine. The importance of the child's social and emotional development can be stressed and reinforced with specific ideas. Other suggestions might include places to visit in the community, special events of interest to young children and their families, and community resources that meet special needs.

The children should also be included. They could receive a note or a simple picture story about school or other topics, such as learning self-help skills or playing with a friend. These early messages can communicate a sense of recognition and welcome to children.

Invitations to Visit

Every school has its own policy regarding visits to classrooms. Very often these policies have grown out of traditions that no longer make sense. If school administrators and teachers want to establish communication between home and school, then they must be willing to take the first step by opening their doors. This does not necessarily mean that every day is visitor's day. Some schools, because of their schedules, would prefer to designate one or two days per week or month as visiting days. The decision will very likely depend upon the resources available to handle the mechanics of school visits.

Staff or volunteers set the tone of these visits by welcoming people as they come into the school. Information should have been sent out ahead of time telling them where to go to check in, the kinds of things they will be able to see, and some simple courtesy rules for classroom observation. Someone should be available to take them around the building, answer questions, and visit with them informally. The ideal arrangement is to have a special room designated for parents or a corner set up in the office for parents. Parents will not feel welcome if they do not have a place to sit, talk, or observe. The entire staff, from secretaries to the principal or director, must reinforce the attitudes of cooperation, acceptance, and sharing.

Registration

By the time school registration arrives, parents, children, and teachers should be ready for school to begin. The schedule for registration should be planned in such a way that there is a chance for personal contact between the parent, child, and school staff. Very often this means staggering the schedules so that only a limited number come at one time. Again, materials should be prepared and mailed ahead of time to answer many of the questions parents are likely to have about starting school.

The setting for registration should be conducive to the comfort of both children and adults. Perhaps a portion of the room can be set up with low chairs, tables, and some interesting toys and books for the children. While they play in one part of the room, parents can meet with the school staff to discuss procedures and answer questions. It is always helpful to have other parents, perhaps PTA representatives, take part in the registration activities. Parents who are already involved with the school can serve as powerful models for new parents. Special resource people such as the speech therapist, school psychologist, school nurse, and even the cook might talk about their roles and the special services they provide. If children are to be screened then or at a later time, the process can be explained to parents.

Parents and children should always be given an opportunity to visit the classrooms the children will enter when school begins. As they meet the teachers and see the classrooms and the children working in them, they will begin to feel comfortable about the future.

Starting School

There are many ways to handle the start of school. Some teachers prefer to divide their class into smaller groups and ask each group to attend for one hour for the first two or three days. Others might want to stagger the days of attendance during the first week of school and have each group attend on two assigned days. Another variation is to have half the group attend one day, half the next, and by the third day bring the entire group together. School policy, teacher preference, and whether or not parents work will determine the arrangements made for the first week of school.

Regardless of the schedule, parents should be encouraged to come with their child and to stay if they wish. Working parents often make special arrangements to be with their child on the first day of school. This day is often as traumatic for the parent as it is for the child; it is a milestone in the parent-child relationship and emotions are close to the surface. Teachers should be sensitive to the anxiety associated with this separation and help the parents and children make this transition. Parents should be reassured that many children find this initial separation difficult but that in time they will be able to adjust to school.

Involvement that begins long before the child formally starts school can pay off in many ways. The child and parent have been prepared gradually, are familiar with the school setting, and are much less likely to be apprehensive or anxious about the new experience. Parents who have received clear messages of welcome are more likely to be comfortable and excited about the new roles they might assume. The school staff has also had the advantage of early contacts and the chance to meet informally with the parent and child. These techniques can reduce the confusion that usually accompanies the first weeks of school and can facilitate an easier transition for everyone.

PARENT-TEACHER CONFERENCES

Conferences between parents and teachers are usually scheduled in both preschool and primary grade programs, and the conference is often the major vehicle for discussing the child's progress. Children in primary grades receive report cards periodically and the conferences are used to supplement information given to the parent through the written report. Many teachers feel very uncomfortable conducting conferences with parents. Often they feel uncertain about the best way to begin, worry about discussing problems, and generally dislike the whole conference procedure.

Some General Considerations

Parent conferences should be looked upon as an invaluable source of information. No one knows the child better than his or her own parent. Behaviors or attitudes that the teacher has seen in the classroom can often be explained by the parent. This information can be very helpful to the teacher in working with the child at school. Parent conferences can develop support for what the school is trying to do by encouraging parents to reinforce certain behaviors at home. For example, parents can provide extra help, encouragement, or enrichment experiences that make it easier for the child to learn.

Many teachers feel very uncomfortable conducting conferences with parents. One of the reasons for this is that they are not always sure what to expect.

The teacher can never be totally in control of the situation when dealing with other adults who have their own ideas as to what their role ought to be. Their perception can be quite different from that of the teacher. For example, some parents might see the conference as a time to check out the credentials of the teacher. How much experience does the teacher have? What kinds of skills are stressed in the program? This parent feels like an expert monitoring the teacher's qualifications.

Teachers must acknowledge before they even begin planning for their conferences that parents will behave in ways that reflect differences between them. Some parents will be very knowledgeable about schools, others will not. Some will be comfortable in their parenting roles, others will be uncertain or apprehensive. A few parents will need special help, support, and patience. Their unique backgrounds will require personalized responses and behaviors. The message for the classroom teacher is to be realistic, to expect these differences, and to accept each parent as an individual.

The majority of parents are really concerned about their children but will respond in different ways to this concern. All will be interested and at the same time worried about what the teacher will report to them. Some parents have unrealistic expectations for their children and will demand too much. Others will be overanxious. Teachers must learn to listen to what parents say and be sensitive to the feelings they are communicating.

Planning the Conference

The first step in preparing for a conference is to be absolutely clear about its purpose. The specific purposes should relate to the needs of the child. You might want to discuss the progress the child has been making or the developmental abilities you have observed in the classroom. Out of this discussion could come a plan for home-school cooperation.

Another purpose might be to find out what kinds of goals, feelings, or expectations the parent has for the child. How has the parent assessed the child's performance and progress?

An important purpose might be to talk about differences in beliefs or ways the parent and teacher interact with the child. What kinds of behaviors and attitudes do the parents reinforce? What discipline techniques are used at home? Are the school and home in agreement or do they need to accommodate to each other? Once you have identified the purpose for the conference and the tentative outcomes, further planning can proceed.

Set up the time and place for the meeting in person, if possible. A telephone call will give you an opportunity to talk with the parent about the reason for the conference. Be prepared to offer two or three alternative dates and times. Also be prepared to meet either at school or in the parent's home. Once the initial arrangements are made, be sure that you have allowed enough time to discuss items of interest to both you and the parents.

Identify materials related to the things you are going to talk about. Samples of the child's work will provide examples of the points you wish to make.

Collect anecdotal records or observations that have been made on the child's classroom behavior, such as finishing tasks on her own or learning writing skills. Be prepared to relate the child's behavior and progress to the goals of the school program. Use many concrete examples and clear language, and avoid technical terms.

Next, take a look at the setting for your meeting and be certain that it ensures privacy. If the conference is to take place in the classroom, try to avoid sitting behind your desk and having the parent sit across from you. The desk often represents a symbol of authority. If a table is available, arrange the chairs so that you can sit side by side where each of you can see the materials in the child's folder. If you must use your desk, arrange the chairs so that they are adjacent to each other.

Conducting the Conference

When the parent enters the room, extend a warm greeting that communicates respect and appreciation for the effort that has been made to keep the appointment. Always remember the demands, pressures, and realities of family life. You are not there to sit as a judge of the parent but rather as a partner sharing mutual concerns.

A good technique to use in beginning the conference is to start with a positive statement about the child and try to get the parent to tell you how he feels about his child and the school experience. As the parent talks, he will begin to feel more comfortable in this new and strange setting and some of his anxiety should be reduced. If you find yourself talking to a parent who is very shy, defensive, or hesitant to say too much, be prepared to begin talking about the child's work, progress, and some of the goals of the program. Try to clarify the points you are making by summarizing information and giving the parent time to ask questions. Encourage comments from the parent that indicate what his feelings or reactions might be. As you discuss the child, be honest, direct, and specific in your suggestions.

If there are specific problems to be reviewed, present them in such a way that the issues are in perspective. Parents tend to overreact to any problems, and often they are not sure how important or critical the problems really are. You as a teacher are in the best position to help the parent see a problem as something that can be worked through in time with some special effort. Very often parents will tell you that they see the same kind of behavior at home. Once the teacher brings this out into the open, parents are usually relieved to have someone with whom to share their concern. Be certain that you have at least tentative suggestions in mind for any problem that is discussed. Before you make any suggestions, however, get ideas from the parent as to what you both might do.

Every conference should end on a positive note. You might talk about some specific things the parents can do at home with the child. If there are no special problems, these plans can revolve around goals for the rest of the school year and some reinforcement or enrichment activities that would be interesting and fun for the parent and the child to do together. In cases with special problems, you may want to encourage the parent to return in a month or so for another conference. In other cases you can agree to stay in touch by telephone. For many others, the contact between school and home will be maintained through ongoing parent involvement activities.

Follow-up Activities

The conference is not over when the parent leaves. You should keep careful records of the parent conference discussion, suggestions that have been made, and notes of follow-up activities that have been agreed upon.

Sometimes you will need to investigate the possibility of special referrals for particular kinds of needs, such as suspected physical, emotional, or learning disabilities. Notes from the conference file can be shared with resource personnel and can often help in making decisions for future referrals.

You should develop a personal file of special community services available to families. This information file should include the kinds of services, who the people are, what they can do, their professional qualifications, procedures for contacts, and any costs connected with the service. When a parent has a special problem, you should not have to fumble around and make inquiries as to how to meet the need. A professional responsibility is to have this information at your fingertips, accessible, and ready to be shared.

Parent-teacher conferences can provide invaluable opportunities to share and exchange information. Both the home and the school have their own special responsibilities in meeting the needs of the child. Open and honest dialogue should enable each to be more effective. You must feel comfortable enough with your own abilities to set realistic goals for yourself and for the parent. Expect imperfect solutions, some progress, and always new needs that will emerge as you learn to communicate and relate to each other.

SUMMARY

Relating to parents in a positive way can be both demanding and rewarding. While we are all supposed to be rational human beings, none of us ever behaves in completely rational ways at all times. Teachers should remember this as they attempt to respond sensitively to parents by listening carefully and allowing sufficient time for learning to communicate with each other.

The way we behave is almost always consistent with the perception we have of ourselves. Teachers should learn to recognize parents with low self-concepts and give them the encouragement they need to believe that they are competent and worthwhile people.

We have seen that teachers have both positive and negative attitudes toward parent involvement. These feelings can be influenced by the teacher's experience in the classroom, ability to use time efficiently, and existing demands within the system. Since feelings can influence the effectiveness of any involvement program, teachers must be aware of their beliefs and select realistic program goals.

Parents also have mixed feelings about becoming involved, and at times these feelings can interfere with effective relationships. Schools must try to be more sensitive to the pressures and demands of being a parent in today's world. As dialogue opens up between home and school, new and more relevant ways to involve parents should emerge.

Ideally, involvement begins before the child starts school. Some ways to bring this about include sending information packets to homes, inviting parents and children to visit schools, sharing information at registration, and planning the first days of school in a way that helps parents and children adjust easily. Once the child is enrolled in the school program, parent-teacher conferences can be used as a vehicle for facilitating meaningful communication between home and school.

FOR DISCUSSION AND FURTHER STUDY

1. List five things a teacher might do to enhance a parent's self-concept.

2. Interview three teachers and ask them to share their feelings about working with parents.

3. Study your interviews with teachers and list their negative and positive comments about working with parents. How could these negative attitudes be reduced?

4. Interview three parents and question them about their attitudes toward parent involvement. How do they perceive their role in this type of program? What feelings do they have about working with the school?

5. Develop an information packet that could be given to parents of children registering in school for the first time.

6. Role-play a parent-teacher conference in which you meet with:
   a. The parent of a child who is doing well in kindergarten.
   b. The parent of a first-grade child who is having difficulty learning to read.
   c. A parent who appears to be disinterested or hostile.

7. Develop a list of supportive resources available to a preschool or elementary school program in your community. How could these resources meet the special needs of children and families?

8. Role-play an attempt to involve a parent who never attends group meetings or activities. What information would you need before contacting the parent?

9. Describe five factors that a teacher should consider in planning an involvement program responsive to the feelings of parents.

10. Discuss four reasons for negative teacher attitudes toward parent involvement. What could be done to change these attitudes?

SUGGESTED READINGS

Barker, Larry. *Listening Behavior.* Englewood Cliffs, N.J.: Prentice-Hall, 1971.

Egan, Gerard. *You and Me: The Skills of Communicating and Relating to Others.* Monterey, Calif.: Brooks/Cole, 1977.

Johnson, David. *Reaching Out: Interpersonal Effectiveness and Self Actualization.* Englewood Cliffs, N.J.: Prentice-Hall, 1972.

Lair, Jess. *I Ain't Much Baby — but I'm All I've Got.* New York: Doubleday, 1972.

Mehrabian, Albert. *Silent Messages.* Belmont, Calif.: Wadsworth, 1971.

Purkey, William. *Inviting School Success: A Self-Concept Approach to Teaching and Learning.* Belmont, Calif.: Wadsworth, 1978.

Ross, Raymond. *Persuasion: Communication and Interpersonal Relations.* Englewood Cliffs, N.J.: Prentice-Hall, 1974.

Verderber, Kathleen, and Rudolf Verderber. *Interact: Using Interpersonal Communication Skills.* Belmont, Calif.: Wadsworth, 1977.

BIBLIOGRAPHY

Breuer, Joseph, and Sigmund Freud. "Studies on Hysteria." In *Standard Edition.* Vol. II. London: Hogarth Press, 1955.

Brim, Orville. *Education for Child Rearing.* New York: Free Press, 1965.

Carkhuff, R. R. *The Development of Human Resources: Education, Psychology, and Social Change.* New York: Holt, Rinehart and Winston, 1971.

Combs, Arthur, and Donald Snygg. *Individual Behavior: A Perceptual Approach to Behavior.* New York: Harper & Row, 1959.

Faust, Verne. *The Counselor-Consultant in the Elementary School.* Boston: Houghton Mifflin, 1967.

Heffernan, Helen, and Vivian Todd. *Elementary Teacher's Guide to Working with Parents.* West Nyack, N.Y.: Parker, 1968.

Hymes, James. *Effective Home-School Relations.* Sierra Madre: The Southern California Association for the Education of Young Children, 1974.

McCormick, Mary. "The Role of Values in the Helping Process." *Social Casework* 42, no. 1 (January 1969): 15–19.

Parents-Children-Teachers: Communication. Association for Childhood Education International, Bulletin no. 28-A. Washington, D.C., 1969.

Raths, Louis, Merrill Harmin, and Sidney Simon. *Values and Teaching.* Columbus, Ohio: Merrill, 1966.

4 Setting Goals: Options and Decisions

Parent involvement can take many forms, each with unique goals, staffing patterns, and objectives. Consider the following situations. You are a teacher in a center-based preschool program. The director calls a staff meeting and announces that the center has received a special grant to develop a home-visiting program. You will be expected to spend half your time in the classroom and half your time working with parents in their homes.

The personnel manager at the Blue Sky School District calls to say that a job has finally opened up and the district wants you. She adds that you will be working as a first-grade teacher in a Title I school. Title I guidelines require teachers to develop and carry out extensive parent involvement activities.

At a district-wide in-service training workshop, the elementary curriculum coordinator presented the fourth curriculum package you will be expected to teach in your second-grade classroom. You can hardly believe it! If you could barely get three packages into an instructional day last year, how are you going to manage this year? You don't see how you can handle all the teaching on your own. What you need is at least one extra pair of hands in the classroom. Maybe part of the answer would be to ask parents to work as volunteer aides.

Although the educational settings are quite different, the problems faced by these teachers are similar. Each one is being asked to develop a parent involvement program. The teacher in the Title I school will probably have access to a parent involvement coordinator who will be able to assist in planning and designing program activities. Teachers in the other settings will most likely be expected to plan and carry out their own programs. One way to avoid being overwhelmed with this responsibility is to approach the planning of a program as systematically as possible.

In this chapter we will look at a planning process that teachers can adapt and use in developing parent involvement programs. We will review some of the key questions that can be answered through this process. This process provides a framework for finding out what parents are interested in doing as well as ways to set priorities so that goals can be reached and effective programs developed. We will also discuss techniques for forming and working with parent advisory groups.

SOME KEY QUESTIONS

Regardless of the setting, the ages of the children, or the availability of special resource staff, the same kind of information is needed by anyone who is trying to make intelligent decisions about program planning. This information will influence the goals that are eventually selected as well as the strategies for reaching those goals. A preliminary step for the teacher is to spend some time reviewing the following questions and considering possible answers.

What Parent Involvement Goals Will Best Serve the Needs of Children?

Society has placed great pressure upon schools to solve problems that are often caused by external factors such as economic, political, and social conditions. There are times when schools simply are not the appropriate action agency; for example, if the unemployment level is high in the community, schools cannot respond directly to the economic problems that are created. However, if children are not getting nutritious meals at home, schools can offer balanced meals through special food programs, develop a series of basic nutrition programs for parents, or send home copies of recipes for inexpensive nutritious meals. Whatever can be done to improve the quality of family life is always an important consideration for teachers and schools, but their primary responsibility must be active support for activities that will benefit children. The major purpose of any parent involvement effort must be to strengthen classroom programs so that children's needs are met more effectively than would otherwise be the case. The following are illustrations.

Instructional Materials   As the planning process begins, the teacher or parent involvement coordinator should review the many different ways parents can strengthen the school program. Perhaps there is a need for more instructional materials for children to use in classroom learning centers. Some teachers might want to focus early involvement efforts on encouraging parents to make these materials for the classroom.

Volunteers   Other teachers might feel that there is not enough individualization built into the daily instructional schedule. One answer could be to bring more adults into the classroom as volunteer teacher aides. This decision would mean looking at the feasibility of setting up a parent volunteer program.

Parent Education   Suppose a teacher was concerned about the general low level of the children's physical health. This teacher might want to explore the possibility of developing a family life education program to give parents information about meeting their children's basic physical needs.

Policy Making   Another area from which goals could emerge is school policy making. What if the school district was facing a severe budget crisis? The

school board, in responding to the crisis, could consider eliminating 50 percent
of the teacher aides. Teachers, knowing how effective instructional aides are in
the classroom, believe that eliminating them would seriously jeopardize the
quality of the educational program. In this case a major goal for parent involvement would be to encourage parents to work actively with the school board to
influence budget decisions.

What Parent Involvement Goals Will Best Serve the Needs of Parents?

Parents are not likely to support active home-school involvement unless the
needs that they think of as important are considered. Teachers, therefore, must
identify parent needs and plan involvement strategies that include goals for
both parents and children. The following examples show how involvement
programs might be designed to meet the needs of both groups.

Need to Be Needed   Suppose one of the broad goals identified as important
for children is to help them develop independent classroom work habits.
Teachers believe that children can learn to accept responsibility for their own
classroom behavior. One of the ways this can happen is through the use of
age-appropriate, individualized instructional materials in classroom learning
centers. Let's assume that an assessment of parents' needs indicated that a large
number of mothers feel isolated at home and excluded from their children's
school experiences. Many of these parents have younger children and are not
able to work regularly as classroom volunteers. One way to coordinate these
two sets of needs (children working independently in the classroom and parents feeling they are part of their children's educational experiences) might be
to set up half-day workshops for small groups of parents. Working together
under the direction of the teacher or another parent volunteer, they can create
individualized instructional materials for the children to use in the classroom.
If necessary, child care services can be provided for younger children.

Acceptance of Individual Differences   Another need of children is an
educational program planned in such a way that each child can learn at his or
her own rate. The teacher believes that individual differences among children
are to be expected and learning goals should be based upon individual rather
than group norms. A need for parents is to help them understand and accept
these individual differences as positive. The goal for parents might be to
encourage the development of realistic expectations for their own child's performance or behavior. One way to achieve these two sets of goals would be to
have parent volunteers work with small groups of children in individually
planned learning experiences. This kind of program strategy allows each child
to individually master curriculum objectives while parent volunteers can observe the learning and social behavior of many different children. The sensitive
teacher will recognize and capitalize on many informal opportunities to discuss
with parents realistic expectations for children in this age group.

What Parent Involvement Goals Will Best Serve the Needs of Teachers?

The classroom teacher is really the key ingredient in any parent involvement effort. Unfortunately, the expectations and responsibilities placed on classroom teachers today border on being unrealistic. Teachers are expected to educate the child, meet any special needs that might exist, relate positively to the community, and be accountable for all educational activities. No wonder many teachers feel frustrated, overwhelmed, and even confused about their professional role. Teachers have a responsibility and a right to examine their own needs when selecting and considering parent involvement goals. Unless teacher needs are considered in an early stage of planning, the teacher implementing the program may not be effective and enthusiastic about carrying out the parent involvement effort.

Katz (1972) has discussed the needs of teachers in four developmental stages: survival, consolidation, renewal, and maturity. Although the length of time spent in any one stage can vary, most teachers seem to move through the stages sequentially and experience the concerns and behaviors typical of each stage of development.

Survival   What are the needs of a teacher who is just beginning a professional career? The big issue at this stage is what Katz refers to as *survival*. Anxiety runs high as the teacher attempts to cope with instructional responsibilities, classroom management, paper work, children, parents, and colleagues. Surviving the day, the week, and finally the academic year is a key concern, and anything beyond survival often overwhelms the teacher.

Suppose the principal or program director tells this teacher that she expects parent involvement to be part of the classroom program. How can the inexperienced teacher identify parent involvement goals and at the same time respond to the need to survive? Some ideas might be to invite parents to assist on field trips, participate in planning special parent programs such as an open house, or serve as resource people for selected curriculum units. These kinds of activities minimize direct involvement of adults in the classroom, which an inexperienced teacher might find very threatening. There is nothing unusual about feeling threatened, but teachers should know why they are uncomfortable at the thought of more extensive parent inolvement. New teachers should set goals for themselves that will gradually help them become comfortable with the idea of working closely with parents.

Consolidation   After the first year or so of teaching, most teachers move into the next developmental stage of *consolidation*. By this time, teachers have seen that they can make it through the day, the week, and a full academic year. They are beginning to feel comfortable about themselves in the classroom and are much more at ease with the principal and fellow teachers. Finally, they are ready to stand back and look at the needs of individual children. Parent involvement goals at this point can often include moving out of the classroom and into the community. Teachers might begin to initiate closer contacts with families through home visits. Each of these visits gives them an opportunity to get to know the parents and to feel more comfortable talking to them. Gradually, as teachers begin to develop more confidence in their own abilities to relate effectively to parents, they might invite parents to observe in the classroom or to serve as volunteers for selected classroom events.

Renewal   After two or three years of teaching, most teachers are ready for new challenges and are looking for ways to improve their classroom program. Katz calls this stage *renewal*. Teachers who have reached this stage should be ready to bring parents into the classroom as volunteers. They are comfortable with their own abilities, realize that no one is ever perfect as an instructor, and are actively looking for new ways to meet the needs of children. It does not always take two or three years before teachers are ready to bring parents into the classroom as volunteers, but learning to juggle all the pieces of a teacher's role takes time, experience, and practice. Goals for parent involvement that include an extensive volunteer program will most often be selected by those teachers who have learned to handle comfortably their instructional and classroom management role.

Maturity   Katz describes the fourth stage of development as a period of *maturity*. Such teachers are comfortable with themselves and have reached a point in their professional careers where they actively seek new information at both an applied and a theoretical level. These teachers are able to work with and accept parents as full partners in the process of educating children. Their teaching experience has helped them develop the stable sense of self needed to work with other adults without feeling threatened or intimidated. The parent involvement programs they develop are most likely to have goals that are comprehensive and creative, reflecting a willingness to collaborate with the home in educating the child.

PLANNING THE PROGRAM

The process we describe in this section can be used in planning either an extensive parent involvement program or one designed to serve a single classroom. This process can be carried on within a school district, preschool center, or elementary school building. In order to make intelligent decisions about the kind of parent involvement program to offer, teachers need to gather basic information that forms the *data base* for planning. This data base is not a mysterious computer printout with meaningless numbers and figures, but rather a collection of relevant information that gives answers to important questions.

Ideally, the goal is to develop a plan (see Figure 4.1) that will include the following.

Figure 4.1
Planning a Parent Program

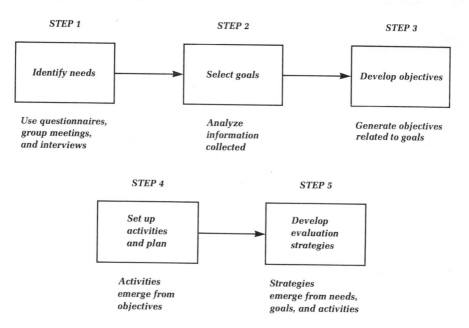

1. A description of any unique needs in the classroom or school.

2. The identification of goals that are logically related to these needs.

3. A statement of realistic objectives that can be achieved.

4. A description of program activities appropriate for reaching the objectives and goals.

5. A description of ways to evaluate the effectiveness of program activities.

Some teachers reject the idea of committing time to an organized planning effort. They believe that if a parent involvement program has to be developed, teachers should simply invite parents to observe or volunteer in the classroom. These teachers forget that parent involvement can take many different forms, so it takes time to consider what is most relevant for a particular school or classroom. Think of the plan as a road map that will guide you to your destination. Imagine trying to visit a friend who lives in a city 100 miles south of your home. Even though you know the general direction in which to drive, without a map you are likely to miss the most direct route. You might get there in a reasonable length of time, but chances are that it will take you much longer than necessary. You will probably get lost or discouraged and end up turning back toward home. If you approach the development of a parent involvement program without a plan, you are like the driver without a map. Many haphazardly planned activities will not be successful, parents will not seem excited about becoming involved, and you will probably get discouraged.

Within a short time you may be heading back toward a more traditional teacher role that minimizes the involvement of parents.

Forming an Advisory Group

An essential element in the planning process is an active parent advisory group. Very often, educators take it upon themselves to design a parent involvement program without talking to parents. This approach will jeopardize any program from the start. The message that will be communicated is that the "expert" knows what is best for the "naive" parent. Designing effective parent involvement programs is not an exact science. Both the parent and the educator have a contribution to make, and the planning process represents the first step in establishing a collaborative home-school relationship. If school programs are to have any credibility, parents must have a role in exploring the options for involvement.

There are other ways in which a parent advisory group strengthens the planning process. Parents are able to examine goals and strategies in terms of how relevant they might be for other parents. An educator's opinion of relevance will not necessarily be the same as that of parents. Teachers tend to be so involved with classroom learning objectives, such as reading and math skills, that they forget the importance of the affective or humanistic aspect of the relationship between adults and children.

"Educating from the heart," a phrase coined by a group of parents in Denver, was the theme of a successful involvement workshop. All program sessions focused on activities designed to capitalize on the joy of adults and children sharing creative experiences such as dance, music, puppetry, and cooking. These kinds of ideas are much more likely to come from parents who tend to be sensitive to the needs and feelings of other parents.

The long-range benefits of working with an advisory group are that the program goals selected are likely to be credible and relevant. Furthermore, parents who participate in planning will already have a deep commitment to make the program work by getting other parents actively involved.

Selecting the Group   The actual formation of the advisory group can be handled in a number of ways. Meetings can be held before or after the school year begins to elect representatives, or parents can be asked to volunteer to serve on the advisory committee. Another option is to work with the Parent-Teacher Association executive committee or center board members and have them select the group. Whatever process is used, once the committee is formed the immediate task is to gather all of the information needed to design a parent involvement program. The process described in this section provides only general guidelines, not specific prescriptive advice. Every situation differs and individual modifications should always be made. Some people, for example, might work in a program funded through a special federal grant, so the goals of the program are probably specified by the funding agency. The advisory group in this case would begin by reviewing the specified goals and then plan ways to identify program objectives and activities to achieve the goals. Another example might involve a center director who has decided to have each classroom teacher develop an individual parent involvement program. Teachers are told to form advisory groups to identify relevant goals for children and parents. Regardless of the specific situation, following a systematic planning process is the most efficient way to gather useful information for designing a successful program.

Sharing Information   At the first meeting of the advisory group, the members should review some of the reasons for having parent involvement. The research findings (see Chapter 2) regarding the effects of the family on a child's school performance should be emphasized. The evidence supporting the importance of the parental role in a child's success can be a powerful motivator for involvement. The importance of parent involvement to help teachers individualize programs for children is another point to make. All parents may not clearly understand why involvement is important or how it can strengthen the school programs. This information should be shared and parents encouraged to generate more ideas about the benefits to be gained from active involvement.

Identifying Relevant Questions   The group should next consider the kind of information that is needed for program planning. At this point, the teacher, who has already been thinking about tentative goals, can present examples of questions, such as the following.

1. What are the unique needs of children, parents, and teacher?
2. What kinds of goals might be appropriate for meeting these needs?
3. Who will actually participate in this program?
4. What will the program setting be—home, school, or both?
5. Who will be responsible for designing and carrying out the program?

Teachers who have already identified unique classroom problems or needs can share this information with parents. Suppose that all funds to pay bus drivers for field trips have been eliminated from the school budget. There is a need for parent volunteers to provide transportation for a certain number of field trips. This information could be discussed with the advisory group, and if they agree that drivers for field trips are important, ways of recruiting parents and organizing such a program could be explored. Again, parents should be encouraged to ask any other questions they feel are important.

Planning with the Advisory Group

As we discuss how this process can work, we will assume that the advisory group has already had its initial meeting, discussed why parent involvement is important, and reviewed the kinds of general questions that should be considered in the process of identifying needs. We will also assume that the group has talked about the importance of first identifying needs and then developing program goals and objectives.

Identifying Needs   Before decisions can be made regarding goals, objectives, and activities, the advisory group should identify special needs or topics of interest that most parents consider important. This can be done by preparing questionnaires that can be sent home with a letter of explanation or through group meetings or interviews held at home or school. The questions can range from general to specific, depending upon the amount of structure the advisory group wishes to impose. Some examples of rather general questions would be the following.

1. Would you like to learn more about how children grow and develop?

2. Would you like to know more about different ways of keeping your family safe and well at home?

3. Do you feel that working as a volunteer in your child's classroom would be an interesting and worthwhile experience for you?

Below are some examples of more specific questions dealing with these same general content areas.

1. Would you like to know more about how your child's self-concept develops during the first five years of life?

2. Would you be interested in taking a first-aid course?

3. Would you like to sign up for an orientation program that would prepare you to work as a volunteer in the classroom?

The information collected from parents should be studied carefully. The group can tally the responses and determine how many parents agree about particular areas of interest. This frequency information (the number of parents agreeing with particular statements) can then be reviewed as the advisory group moves into the second step: goal selection.

Selecting Goals   Once the major areas of parent interest are determined, the advisory group can begin to function as a decision-making body. Major program goals can be discussed. Ideally, goals emerge from the questions asked of parents in the first step of the process.

Suppose that the three general questions given above (each reflecting different needs) had been selected by a majority of the parents as most important. How can goals be generated from the questions? The first question identified as important was: Would you like to know more about how children grow and develop? This general question can be stated as a goal in the following way:

Parents will be involved in a series of meetings in which child growth and development specialists will lead group discussions on selected topics of interest.

The second question identified as important was: Would you like to know more about different ways of keeping your family safe and well at home? A related goal would be:

Parents will become familiar with and understand techniques that can be used in the home to create a healthy and safe environment.

The third question was: Do you feel that working as a volunteer in your child's classroom would be an interesting and worthwhile experience for you? An appropriate goal related to this question would be:

Parents will participate in different types of classroom volunteer activities throughout the school year.

Each of these goals is a broad statement reflecting a general way of meeting the need identified in the planning process.

Developing Program Objectives   Once goals have been selected the group should be ready to move to the next step of specifying program objectives. These objectives should be clear statements of what is going to happen as the program attempts to achieve particular goals. Many people are intimidated by the term *objective* and seem to believe that objectives are a very mysterious kind of statement that only experts can make. Nothing could be further from the truth. An objective is simply a precisely phrased statement that makes it possible to determine whether or not you have accomplished what you set out to do. Mager (1962) lists three characteristics of instructional objectives.

1. The statement identifies and names the overall behavioral act.
2. The statement defines the important conditions under which the behavior is to occur.
3. The statement defines the criterion of acceptable performance.

An example of an objective in the area of growth and development related to the goals already described could be:

By the end of the school year, 75 percent of the parents who have attended the discussion groups will be able to identify correctly five behavioral characteristics of the preschool child.

Another example related to the goals of safety and health might be:

By the end of the school year, 75 percent of the parents will be able to correctly demonstrate artificial respiration techniques.

In Chapters 5 and 6, we will discuss how objectives can be used to develop a detailed program plan designed to achieve specific goals. The important point to remember during the planning period is that objectives should be described and agreed upon by the teacher, administrative staff, members of the advisory group, and any other parents who participate in the involvement program.

Developing an Activity Plan   This step involves the selection and design of activities to help achieve goals and meet needs. Very often, people plan their program simply by designing activities. They operate under the mistaken assumption that if they can describe what will happen on a day-by-day basis, that is enough planning for the program. Unfortunately, planning activities without first determining needs, goals, and objectives often results in a program filled with ineffective or irrelevant activities.

The most effective way to achieve the objectives is to consider the collection of information about possible activities as an ongoing process that begins with the first step of planning. Information about the kinds of instructional techniques and activities that parents find most appealing can be noted continuously through formal and informal contacts. When the activity plan is actually worked out, it will usually be necessary to collect more information about content or instructional methods, such as the use of lectures, discussion groups, role-playing, videotapes, or printed materials. Guidelines for designing program activities will be presented in more detail in Chapters 5 and 6. The major point here is that the activities that are selected should be based on information collected through the identification of goals and objectives.

Developing Evaluation Strategies   The final step in planning involves finding ways to determine whether or not program goals have actually been accomplished. The term *evaluation* often arouses feelings of anxiety, negativism, and inadequacy. There is really no reason to fear assessment. One cannot improve any kind of program unless information is collected to determine what has worked.

Evaluation is a process of systematically examining what was done and what happened as a result of a particular activity. The information collected can then be used to revise or change the program goal, objective, or activity. Most people involved in the design of a new program should not be surprised to find that at least 50 percent of what is tried does not work. There is no reason to become discouraged because some ideas are not as effective as they appeared to be during planning. This information is invaluable for developing new program activities that eventually will achieve the objectives. The evaluation plan is a key element in collecting information needed to make intelligent program decisions.

Matching Goals to Resources

Throughout each step of the planning process the advisory group must continually ask whether resources are available to implement the program plan. Resources include not only available dollars but also the kinds of people needed to carry out the recommended program activities. Are people with special expertise available through the community or school faculty? If there is a need for special school resource people, such as a psychologist, speech therapist, or home economics teacher, do they have the time to commit to program activities? If paraprofessionals are to be used in home visiting, who will be responsible for training? Who will train teachers to work effectively with parents?

Another task is to review the total plan and clarify roles and responsibilities for coordinating the program. Will the teacher take this on as part of the usual professional responsibilities? Does the teacher have enough time to do this? Will parents be asked to volunteer and assist the teacher in running the program? If it becomes clear that there are not enough people resources available for achieving objectives, then the plan must be revised. Unrealistic goals can do more to discourage people in a program than any other factor. The advisory group must work until it develops a plan that includes both short- and long-range goals, and then it must identify key check points that can be used to review progress toward achieving these goals. The group should not try to implement an overly ambitious plan with inadequate resources.

Legislative Mandates   Another area to study before making the final selection of goals is the legislative mandates at both the federal and state levels. In programs such as Title VII (bilingual), Title I, Head Start, and Follow Through, the mandates for parent involvement are clearly stated. These program guidelines are determined at the federal level and grantees are expected to follow the regulations. For example, Title I requires that school districts establish active parent advisory groups to work with the administrative staff as it implements the educational program. The advisory group is to assume an active role in specific areas of decision making.

Feasibility   Other questions to be studied as final program decisions are made involve feasibility, practicality, usefulness, and relevance. How feasible is the plan in terms of the characteristics of the parent group? If an extensive classroom volunteer program has been designed, will most parents be able to participate? If not, are other kinds of activities suited to the needs of those who cannot volunteer during school hours?

Practicality   How practical is the plan in view of the resources (people, time, money) available? Suppose a program goal is to offer parents a course in child growth and development. If most of the parents did not complete high school and the literacy level of the group is quite low, special reading materials will have to be developed, relevant films should be identified, and anyone presenting sessions will have to be trained to use a variety of multimedia techniques that will hold the interest of this group of adults. Since locating and developing these materials will be complex, time-consuming tasks, it might be more practical to reconsider the child development course as a long-range goal and allow enough time to put together a strong instructional package. An interim or short-range goal for which activities could be designed immediately might be to organize discussion groups focusing on a topic of special interest to parents, such as discipline.

Usefulness   How useful is the plan to both children and parents? An elaborate or lengthy group meeting on the importance of taking young children to places of interest in the community would not be particularly useful to a group of well-educated middle-class parents. Printed materials describing places of interest could be prepared and either mailed home or handed out at the parent meeting.

Relevance   How relevant is the plan to the particular community? Are the activities consistent with the culture or life-style of the families? Has consideration been given to incorporating unique cultural factors such as foods, holidays, music, art, dance, artifacts, language, and other customs and traditions?

Careful Review   Be prepared to seriously examine these questions before final program decisions are made. Review the plan with administrative staff and colleagues. Get as much input as possible before the action plan is finalized. Different people will often bring valuable insight and perspective to difficult issues or questions.

If the plan is reviewed by others, they may identify ideas that simply won't work. An example of this might be planning a series of home activities in which parents are encouraged to use mealtime as a learning experience for their children. For low-income families who live under severely crowded conditions, there may be no area in the home large enough to accommodate everyone. In middle-class families the mother and father might both work and the whole family never sits down to meals at the same time. Developing home learning activities for mealtimes without getting further input from parents will definitely ensure failure. Some simple checking around or discussion with members of the advisory group would uncover the information needed to develop other kinds of activities for achieving the same kinds of objectives.

Figure 4.2 gives examples of a plan that might emerge from a process such as the one described in this chapter. These are samples of final decisions made by both the teacher and members of the advisory group. They are a road map to guide the development of the program. A planning process can never provide all the answers or anticipate all the problems that will arise, so the group must be prepared to revise and change the plan as additional information is collected.

The major advantage in using a planning process to develop a written description of activities is that the teacher, administrative staff, advisory group, and other parents are more likely to have a clear idea of what will happen during a period of time. Everyone will know what must be done and who will be

Figure 4.2
Sample Program Plan

Need	Goal	Objective	Activity	Evaluation
Children: Need a more individualized classroom program. Parents: Need to be more closely involved with their child's educational experiences. Teacher: Needs assistance from other adults in order to individualize the classroom program.	Parents will be involved in working cooperatively with the classroom teacher to explore and implement ways of assisting the teacher in the classroom.	At the end of a four-hour in-service training session, 80 percent of the parent participants will be able to correctly demonstrate techniques for presenting a language arts experience to first-grade children. Ninety percent of the parents who volunteer to serve as classroom aides will actively participate in the program for the entire school year.	Planning and presentation of two two-hour in-service training sessions for parents. Appropriate instructional techniques for working with small groups of children will be demonstrated, discussed, and role-played (classroom teacher, teacher aide, parent volunteer). Teacher will keep daily attendance records of parent volunteers (classroom teacher).	Observation of parents role-playing instructional activities. Analysis of attendance records.
Children: Need adults who understand and will respond appropriately to their behavior. Parents: Need to know how to respond to their child's behavior and developmental needs. Teachers: Need parents to consistently reinforce the child's efforts to master developmentally appropriate tasks.	Parents will be involved in a series of meetings in which child growth and development specialists will lead group discussions on selected topics of interest.	By the end of the school year, 75 percent of the parents who have attended the discussion group will be able to correctly identify five behavioral characteristics of the preschool child.	Planning and presentation of two two-hour group meetings focusing on multimedia examples of the characteristics of the developing preoperational child (classroom teacher, school psychologist, pediatrician, speech therapist). Planning, observation, and discussion of videotaped segments of the classroom program (classroom teacher, library media coordinator, school psychologist).	Each parent will discuss what he has observed on the videotapes, and will correctly identify specific behavioral characteristics of the preschool child.

responsible for carrying out the task. The result should be a design for an involvement program based on real rather than perceived needs.

WORKING WITH THE PARENT ADVISORY GROUP

One very important reason for forming an advisory group is to provide a setting where parents and educators can cooperatively explore alternative directions for the parent involvement program. There are many parent roles, goals, objectives, and types of activities to be considered. While teachers could simply make their own preferences known and then see how many parents would be willing to participate, this approach rarely generates much active support. The best way to motivate parents (or other adults) is for teachers to provide early opportunities for their involvement in program planning and the selection of relevant goals.

The role of the advisory group leader is complex and demanding. There are, however, a number of important attitudes and behaviors that can be useful in helping teachers become more effective in this role.

Define Roles

One of the first tasks for the group in order to function effectively is to cooperatively define the role and responsibilities of the parents, teacher, and administrative staff. They should agree on who will be responsible for key tasks and on how each group member contributes to the planning process.

Model Respect

The teacher's behavior should consistently reflect respect and appreciation for the efforts made by members of the advisory group. For example, the teacher actively listens to what is said, encourages every member to talk, and avoids overly emotional reactions to suggestions. It is the teacher's responsibility to create an atmosphere in which everyone is given the opportunity to contribute ideas and suggestions. Parents, particularly in the early stages of working in an advisory group, will tend to defer to the "education expert." The goal is to help parents feel comfortable working with the school as full partners, and to achieve that goal the group behavior must reflect a desire to openly share information and jointly make decisions.

Confront Frustrations and Conflict

The process of leading a group can at times seem personally threatening and cause feelings of inadequacy. These feelings are not unique and are most often caused by inexperience in a new role. People are inevitably going to disagree, spend time in tangential discussions, interrupt each other, or even become angry over what is said or recommended. There will almost certainly be moments of frustration or anger over the behavior of at least one member of the advisory group. The test for any group comes when disagreements arise, not when all members agree. It is at this point that leadership skills become critical. Someone has to remind the group that its major purpose is to work together in order to select goals that will meet the needs of children.

Suppose, for example, that a parent is strongly opposed to a suggestion that an extensive volunteer program be developed. This particular parent has been one of the few who has worked regularly in the classroom since school began. The teacher suspects that the parent feels threatened at the possibility of losing or having to share a role of importance. A sensitive leader could respond by acknowledging the quality of the volunteer's work and suggesting that this parent might coordinate the more extensive program or assist in training new parent volunteers.

Use the Expertise of Others

Once the group moves into the stages of planning and collecting information, leadership skills become especially important. If the advisory group asks a question that the teacher cannot answer, the teacher as a leader has a responsibility to acknowledge that no one can be an expert in every area and that they must seek help and get information from others who have special expertise.

Develop Clear Agendas

The leader should prepare an agenda for meetings, giving everyone an opportunity to speak to the agenda items. The group should stay with issues until decisions are reached. When time is limited, they can allocate a certain amount of time to each agenda item or speaker.

Monitor Your Own Behavior

A useful technique for checking your effectiveness as a leader is to tape an early advisory group meeting. After the meeting, play the tape back and listen to the kind of language used in talking with parents. Do you hear a lot of technical terms? How much "teacher talk" do you hear compared to the amount of "parent talk"? Do you accept criticism and avoid making excuses for any mistakes that have occurred? Have you consistently acknowledged efforts that others have made? Are you reinforcing these efforts with a word of thanks or encouragement? These are all critical interpersonal skills that should be used in interacting with others. Learn to monitor your own behavior and become sensitive to all the incidental learning that takes place. As a model for others in the group, be aware of the kind of behavior and attitudes you are projecting. Parents will receive both hidden and overt messages, so try to refine those skills that facilitate effective communication. Your responsibilities as a leader are to listen to what the parents are saying, synthesize their ideas when necessary, and share information that will help the group function effectively. Remember these key points:

1. Believe in the parents who serve on the advisory group and communicate this belief.

2. Define roles for all members of the group.

3. Define responsibilities for all members of the group.

4. Always show respect and appreciation for the efforts made by the group members.

5. Be prepared for disagreements and monitor your own behavior as conflicts are resolved.

6. Be honest and direct as you work with others.

7. Be sensitive to the needs of others and try to respond appropriately.

SUMMARY

The success of a planning effort depends to a large extent upon the interpersonal skills of teachers. A very basic decision for teachers is whether or not they believe that schools alone can cope with the task of educating children. When they honestly believe that parents have a critical role to play in the educational process, they will be more likely to commit the time and effort necessary for effectively planning cooperative home-school programs.

One step of the planning process leads to the next. The most important points to remember are listed here.

1. Think about any special needs for children, parents, or the teacher.

2. Review in your own mind the kinds of goals to be considered.

3. Form the advisory group.

4. Schedule an orientation session that focuses on:
    a. The reasons for parent involvement activities.
    b. Clarification of the roles and responsibilities of all members of the group.
    c. Description of the planning process.

5. Identify goals, that is, make use of interviews, group meetings, questionnaires, or other survey methods.

6. Develop objectives and review them in terms of cultural relevance, practicality, feasibility, and availability of resources.

7. Describe the activities.

8. Identify assessment techniques.

The outcome of this process, a written program plan, will not be perfect but will be an invaluable aid to all who participate in the parent involvement activities.

FOR DISCUSSION AND FURTHER STUDY

1. Why is it important to first consider the needs of children and then those of parents and teachers in planning a parent involvement program?

2. Interview and observe two teachers. Can you determine their developmental stage of teaching? Discuss the evidence you have for placing a teacher in a particular stage.

3. Describe how the concept of a teacher's developmental stage relates to the kind of involvement program planned by the teacher.

4. Identify your own developmental teaching stage. List and discuss five goals and objectives for a parent involvement program that would be consistent with your developmental concerns.

5. What are the advantages and disadvantages of working with a parent advisory group?

6. Role-play what you might say to an advisory group about the importance of having a parent involvement program.

7. Develop a questionnaire that could be used with parents to identify program needs.

8. List the essential parts of an instructional objective. Write an objective dealing with the development by parents of home teaching experiences for their children.

9. Develop a checklist that you could use in program planning to match goals with available resources. Why is this coordination important?

10. Describe some of the skills necessary for working effectively with an advisory group. Role-play a situation in which conflict has arisen. How would you handle this conflict?

BIBLIOGRAPHY

Bridge, Gary. "Parent Participation in School Innovation." *Teachers College Record* 77, no. 3 (1976): 368–89.

Brim, Orville. *Education for Child Rearing.* New York: Free Press, 1959.

Davies, Don. "Perspectives and Future Directions." In *Schools Where Parents Make a Difference*, ed. Don Davies. Boston: Institute for Responsive Education, 1976.

Gallagher, James, Richard Surles, and Andrew Hayes. *Program Planning and Evaluation.* Chapel Hill, N.C.: TADS, 1973.

Grotberg, Edith. *Day Care: Resources for Decisions.* Washington, D.C.: Day Care and Child Development Council of America, 1971.

Jelinek, Janis, and Andrea Kasper. "Exchanging Information." In *Teaching Parents to Teach,* ed. David Lillie, Pascal Trohanis, and Kenneth Gain. New York: Walker and Co. 1976.

Katz, Lillian. "Developmental Stages of Pre-School Teachers." *Elementary School Journal* 73, no. 1 (1972): 50–54.

Lillie, David "An Overview to Parent Programs." In *Teaching Parents to Teach,* ed. David Lillie, Pascal Trohanis, and Kenneth Gain. New York: Walker and Co., 1976.

Mager, Robert. *Preparing Instructional Objectives.* Palo Alto, Calif.: Fearon Publishers, 1962.

Northcott, Winifred, and Shirley Fowler. "Developing Parent Participation." In *Teaching Parents to Teach,* ed. David Lillie, Pascal Trohanis, and Kenneth Gain. New York: Walker and Co., 1976.

Pickarts, Evelyn, and Jean Fargo. *Parent Education.* New York: Appleton-Century-Crofts, 1971.

Rich, Dorothy, and Cynthia Jones. *A Family Affair: Education.* Washington, D.C.: Home and School Institute, 1977.

Sayler, Mary Lou. *Parents: Active Partners in Education.* Washington, D.C.: American Association of Elementary-Kindergarten-Nursery Educators, 1971.

Swick, Kevin, and Eleanor Duff. *Parent Involvement in Early Childhood Education: A Process Approach.* Columbia: University of South Carolina, 1977.

Wilson, G. and G. Panloff. *Adult Involvement in Child Development for Staff and Parents.* Atlanta: Humanics Press, 1972.

5 Strategies for Involvement

If you look behind the scenes of successful parent involvement programs, you will find some common elements. Teachers who are effective in recruiting and working with parents use strategies that include getting administrative support, making sure that they have allowed enough time for careful program planning, and developing realistic program goals that reflect the needs of children, parents, and teachers.

In addition, the effective resource person or teacher must know how to capture the interest of parents and maintain their involvement. This chapter will present ideas that can be used for encouraging and maintaining the involvement of parents. Many of these strategies are closely tied to program management techniques. Because these plans have been tried in a variety of settings, some will be more appropriate for you than others. The purpose of this chapter is to share as much information related to motivational and involvement techniques as might be needed to plan and implement different approaches to working with parents.

DEVELOPING AN EFFECTIVE INVOLVEMENT PROGRAM

There are both advantages and disadvantages associated with parent involvement programs. Having a teacher aide can be extremely helpful, but every teacher who has worked with an aide knows that extra time must be given to planning for and training that second person in the classroom. Certain issues and problems are common to all parent involvement approaches regardless of the goals, settings, or roles filled by parents. Teachers who work with parents should be aware of these issues and should clarify their own feelings. They cannot hope to be successful in their efforts to involve parents unless they are honestly committed to this concept. Problems must therefore be examined and resolved before the program plan is implemented.

Working with Parents Can Be Difficult

Training   One of the most common criticisms from teachers is that parents are not trained to work effectively with children in classrooms and cannot understand how to help children achieve school-related goals. Too many teachers and administrators believe that it is not worthwhile to take the time needed to educate or train "naive" parents. The historical roots of the "expert" educator ignoring the "naive" parent are strong and in many cases very difficult to overcome.

The solution to this problem is not difficult or complicated. Orientation meeetings, discussion groups, or carefully planned workshops can do wonders in helping the so-called naive parents to develop the skills and confidence needed to be more effective as resource people, policy makers, and teachers of their own children.

Getting Parents to School   Another complaint is that it is difficult to get parents to school for meetings. This issue is even more complicated in urban and rural communities where children are bused to school. Very often parents who live far away from the schools find it difficult to make transportation arrangements to attend meetings.

A transportation committee can be very helpful in coordinating arrangements for different parents. Car pools can be organized and parents without cars can ride with neighbors or with their children on the school bus.

It's Not Important   Parents might not attend meetings because they really do not understand the reasons for parent involvement. Many parents do not see themselves as teachers of their own children, as resources for the school, or as influential in political decisions.

These kinds of attitudes and perceptions will not change overnight and require more effort than simply a letter inviting parents to a meeting. When parents are reluctant to become involved, time must be devoted to home visits, small neighborhood group meetings, or any other form of personal contact where dialogue can be developed between home and school.

Disruptions in the Classroom   Another common complaint is that when parents come into a classroom they tend to cause more commotion than the teacher can handle. Very often the parent's own child is the behavior problem and many teachers would rather not try to cope with these kinds of disruptions.

Teachers who have learned to handle this situation have usually developed classroom management strategies that anticipate the probability of disruptions. These teachers work with the children and set up clear rules of acceptable behavior. They communicate the expectation that each child will work cooperatively with the parent volunteer and not misbehave. Children are amazing in their ability to accept rules that have been explained, discussed, and enforced consistently.

Parents Are Not Dependable   It is often said that parents are not very dependable. They promise to work in the classroom every other Thursday morning but tend to call at the last minute with an excuse for not coming. They promise to be at home to meet with the teacher to review home learning activities, but they are not there when the teacher arrives. They say they will attend a school board meeting at which important policy decisions will be made, but they never show up.

No one will deny that these things happen, but often the parent has a legitimate reason for not being able to meet a commitment. One effective technique for avoiding these kinds of problems is to anticipate and face them early in the parent involvement program. The advisory group might discuss the consequences of absenteeism and work out ways of handling last-minute emergencies. Perhaps the parents will decide to develop their own substitute list. They might, instead, have a volunteer coordinator responsible for getting other parents to the classroom or to a school board meeting. A baby-sitting pool might be part of the answer. Whatever the solution, the parents should be responsible for their own commitment to the program.

Working Parents   The working parent who is unable to participate in many daytime activities creates special problems for program planning. Teachers often assume that these parents cannot make arrangements to be part of a daytime involvement activity that is particularly important to their child.

When the parent knows that a meeting or event is important, he will usually make an effort to attend. Working parents do, however, have special needs that can be met through parent involvement programs. Very often, these are the parents who feel guilty because they cannot spend time with their children during the day. A parent involvement program that is sensitive to these special needs can plan evening or weekend meetings that permit working parents to attend activities or simply stay informed about the school program.

Extra Work for Staff   Some teachers say that a parent involvement program really means a great deal of extra work for staff. Different aspects of the involvement program will be easier to deal with than others. For example, if parents who are working in the classroom forget to put materials away after an activity, a simple solution is to post a checklist for cleanup. Many parents are unaware that the supervising adult and children are responsible for maintaining an orderly classroom environment. On the other hand, developing home activities for parents to present to children is much more complex. This is really a long-term project that can extend over two or three years, so teachers should be realistic about what can be accomplished within any one academic year.

Tension between Home and School   The economic conditions in education today, along with the issues of race, culture, and goals, have created tension between the community and schools. Teachers are well aware that bond issues are being turned down by voters in all parts of the country as citizens indicate that they are unwilling to allocate more funds to the operation of public schools. Questions are raised about how money is being spent, and accountability is demanded over and over again.

Many teachers react to the tension in their community by avoiding the parent voter. A much more effective solution is to open the doors of schools and classrooms. Teachers should invite parents to see what the educational system is trying to do, acknowledge problems and concerns, and encourage parents to work with educators to develop innovative solutions.

Working with Adults   Many teachers are concerned about whether or not they can work effectively with adults. The teachers who feel threatened or intimidated by this challenge will often reject the concept of parent involvement because they are unsure of their ability to handle such a program.

Developing the skills to work with adults requires time and training. Teachers can take courses at a local college or university or ask for special in-service training courses. If nothing else is available in the community, several teachers can organize a study group and acquire these skills together.

There will always be issues or problems unique to a particular community. Each problem, however, has some kind of solution. Whether or not the solution will be found depends upon the attitudes of the teacher, parent resource person, and administrative staff. If the goal is to develop a program that really works, solutions to problems will be found. If, on the other hand, the goal is to show why parent involvement cannot work, the problems will probably remain unsolved.

Parent Involvement Pays Off

Home-School Continuity   An important benefit from every parent involvement program is the establishment of a link between home and school. Continuity goals could involve parents and teachers working together to help a child learn to read, to put a puzzle together, or to develop a positive self-concept. Communication between home and school is necessary for creating environments where the needs of children are consistently met. These needs should go beyond intellectual goals and should include responsiveness to social, emotional, and physical concerns.

Individualizing Instruction   There are many direct benefits for the classroom program when parents become involved. For example, the teacher who has parent volunteers working in the classroom can plan a program based on reduced group size. One teacher working with thirty or thirty-five children cannot meet the needs of each child. Using parents as instructional aides is an effective way of implementing the concept of individualization.

Volunteers can often be extremely helpful by preparing instructional materials for the home or classroom. Developing games, lotto cards, manipulative activities, and personalized books are very time-consuming tasks. Parents who volunteer to prepare these materials have the advantage of being able to see the product of their efforts in the classroom and at home. This is a direct form of reinforcement that can be extremely satisfying to the volunteer.

Children Relating to Different Adults   When parents work in the classroom, children learn how to relate to many different adults. These kinds of experiences can be important in preparing children for interpersonal relationships in future adult roles.

Special Help   In any classroom there are children who need special help. These could be handicapped children who have been placed (mainstreamed) in a regular classroom (Cohen, 1974), or children who simply have difficulty in a particular content area. Often teachers are aware of these special needs, but they have no time to work individually with the children. Parents as volunteers can help the teacher meet these needs. Daily schedules can be arranged in such a way that either the teacher or the volunteer works with a particular child on a one-to-one basis. Perhaps a small number of children who share a common need can be grouped together.

Parents as Resources   Every group of parents represents an untapped pool of talent. There are musicians, artists, master carpenters, electricians, plumbers, nurses, and attorneys, each with special knowledge that can be shared. Multicultural education begins in the community (King, 1977); it is not necessary to purchase elaborate curriculum materials, film strips, or films to promote the diversity of cultures. Parents should be encouraged to share in planning multicultural aspects in the classroom curriculum and capitalize on activities to enhance the self-concepts of both children and parents.

Look at the Parent's Side

There will be times when the teacher or advisory group plans activities and finds that parents do not come. While this can be very discouraging, it would be unrealistic to expect every parent to participate. There are some very legitimate reasons that would prevent parents from becoming actively involved in all kinds of programs. Teachers should be aware of what these reasons are and should try to modify their programs to be more responsive to special needs.

Make Arrangements for Child Care   Many parents have younger children at home who require a great deal of attention, tend to be ill, or cause unexpected family emergencies. Parents with younger children are often unable to become involved in many program activities. Schools can try to respond by offering child care services or scheduling meetings at times when one parent is at home and the other can attend. Special activities can also be planned to include children of all age groups.

Alternate Meeting Times   The times at which meetings or special activities are scheduled can also create problems. Because one time will never be convenient for every family in the group, teachers should try to alternate the days and times for program events in order to give as many options as possible.

Plan More Than One Type of Involvement   A different kind of problem is created when only one kind of involvement is planned. The particular type of activity might not be appealing to some of the parents; if they had other choices, more of them might participate. However, such diversity is not always possible. Resources could be unavailable, time might be extremely limited, or teachers might not be ready to handle more than one type of activity. The goal should be to gradually offer more program options to parents.

Be Sensitive to Needs of Parents   Some parents are reluctant to become involved with schools because their culture, value system, or attitudes are quite different from those of the larger community. Perhaps they do not speak English and cannot communicate easily with the classroom teacher. What if their own school experiences have been negative and they hesitate to expose themselves to what might be a recurrence of unpleasant relationships? When parents are uncomfortable in an educational setting, they will avoid planned encounters. One way for the teacher to respond is to be sensitive to signs of avoidance and make every effort to reach out and encourage parents to participate in the program. This might mean making home visits, asking other parents to bring friends to meetings, communicating via letters or telephone calls, or planning a very special program to appeal to particular parents. Attitudes do not change overnight and teachers must often be satisfied with a gradual increase in interest.

Keep the Program Interesting   We often overlook the most obvious reason for avoiding involvement activities: parents may find them uninteresting and do not want to participate. One way to prevent this problem is to encourage as many parents as possible to assist in program planning. Another strategy is to systematically evaluate activities. The information from evaluation forms should tell teachers how the parents are reacting and should provide ideas about ways to improve the program.

Reach the Shy Parent   Just as we sometimes fail to notice the quiet child in the classroom, we also tend to overlook the quiet parent who is often uncomfortable in the group. This parent might attend one or two meetings but then avoid any other contact. The sensitive teacher, aware that some people need more support than others, will try to demonstrate warmth and acceptance. A friendly greeting, calling the parent by name, and encouraging questions or comments are all very effective techniques for pulling the parent into the group.

Group Parents   Thought must also be given to the size of groups for different program activities. Sometimes an activity will lend itself to a large number of people, whereas at other times the group size should be limited. When an outstanding guest speaker is scheduled, as many parents as possible should be encouraged to attend. Sometimes, however, the effectiveness of the planned activity depends upon giving everyone a chance to actively participate. Suppose there are five or six parents whose children have special learning needs.

These parents might want to meet together in order to discuss unique concerns about their children's progress. In another instance, a small group of parents might be interested in developing strategies for combating child abuse. Perhaps they feel that with training they can provide needed support to the abusive parent. This group might also want to develop and disseminate educational materials about child abuse to other parents in the school. These special groups will usually form when opportunities are provided for discussion and exploration of topics of interest.

Listen to Reactions   All parents should be encouraged to react to selected program goals. This kind of feedback can be obtained by talking to parents at school. Teachers should get early reactions to the instructional strategies planned for group activities. How do the parents feel about games as a way to learn? What about role-playing? Discussion groups? Films? A speaker from the community? Involvement programs will be strengthened by suggestions that can come only from the parents who will be participants.

THE ADMINISTRATOR'S ROLE

An essential element for the success of any involvement program is support from the school administration. The administration can include the preschool center director, school principal, school district central staff personnel, or funding agency representatives. The key person for the classroom teacher is the building principal or center director, because this person makes the policy decisions that will facilitate or hinder the planned involvement activities.

Open-Door Policy   There are all kinds of program needs that can best be met by a supportive administrator. An open-door policy is absolutely essential to the development of school-home partnerships. The principal or center director who wants to encourage parent involvement communicates and extends this welcome to the parents from every staff member in the building.

All-School Newsletter   An all-school newsletter is another tool that can be used by the administrator to communicate support of a parent involvement program (Andrews, 1976). These can be sent out regularly and can include information on school menus, transportation schedules, and dates of upcoming holidays. The administrator can write a column for parents that discusses planned program events, special family activities, a review of new books of interest to parents, and other items about the community.

Parent Place   The administrator can arrange to designate one room for use as a "parent place" (Gilmar and Nelson, 1975). The furnishings might include a washer, dryer, stove, sewing machine, sink, refrigerator, typewriter, duplicating equipment, comfortable chairs, books, and games of special interest. Parents can use this room when they want to visit with teachers or other parents, work at school, or attend a meeting. The room can also be used for parent education programs, policy committee meetings, and workshops. Setting up the parent place can be a school project organized by parent volunteers. Often community groups will donate items to furnish the room.

Family Information Center   If an unused room is unavailable for parents, some space should be found for a family information center. Again, the person who can allocate this space is the school administrator. An information center can be in the corner of a classroom, in the school office, or on a hallway bulletin board. All kinds of information can be collected and shared with parents to publicize special events in the community and highlight upcoming parent involvement activities (Marion, 1973). A family information center indicates that the administrator and faculty are willing to commit time and effort to maintaining communications with parents.

Design of Materials   The administrator can organize and encourage an all-staff project to develop materials for parents to use at home with their children. A total school effort would ensure that sequential materials are designed for every grade level. The administrator must be certain that teachers or parent volunteers are given the time and any other support they need to design materials and test them on small groups in order to be sure that they are clearly written and easy to use. The administrator then follows through by having the materials duplicated, publicized in the school newsletter and the family information center, and sent home where they can be used.

In-Service Training   Finally, and perhaps most important, the administrator provides leadership for training the staff in the school or center building. Supporting the concept of parent involvement makes no sense unless staff training programs are developed. In-service development sessions should be planned and scheduled, resource people contacted, and sufficient time allowed for staff participation. Some administrators might encourage teachers to take a special course at a local college or university, attend a particular workshop, or read a new and relevant book. Whatever strategies are used, the goal is to increase the skills of staff members so that they can work effectively with parents.

RECRUITING PARENTS

The strategies for recruiting parents should be related to program goals, the community setting, and the parents involved.

Strategies Unlimited

Spring Registration   Spring is an ideal time to hold meetings to introduce the involvement program to parents of children beginning school. There should be printed materials to reinforce and summarize the information covered at the meeting. The principal or center director, teacher, and parent volunteers can discuss goals of the involvement program and the kinds of activities tentatively planned for the school year. If the program is just getting started, the planning process can be reviewed and volunteers can sign up for the advisory group.

PTA Meetings   Back-to-school nights offer another opportunity to share information about parent involvement. Printed materials, sign-up forms, and questionnaires can be distributed to parents. Those who are interested in becoming involved can indicate this and tentative plans for beginning the program can be discussed.

Posters and Announcements   Posters can be prepared before school begins and displayed prominently throughout the building. They might announce an orientation meeting, special speaker, or just the news that a parent involvement program is being organized. Printed brochures or flyers can be sent home in conjunction with the posters. These materials can include information about upcoming meetings as well as other news of special interest to parents.

Home Visits   When time permits, a personal home visit from the classroom teacher can pay off. The teacher moves out into the community, sees the child in the home environment, and meets the family in a setting familiar to them. All sorts of information can be shared about the child, and the teacher will have a perfect opportunity to encourage parents to become involved. The potential benefits to both school and home can be discussed and parents will have an opportunity to voice any special concerns.

Newspaper and Radio   Very often a local newspaper or radio station will cooperate in disseminating information about a parent involvement program. A newspaper article with a human interest emphasis can be extremely effective in catching the attention of readers. Whoever makes the contact with the media must communicate the sense of excitement generated by the parent involvement program.

Classroom Newsletters   Another way to recruit parents is through a classroom newsletter. This newsletter is different from the all-school publication. The content is totally related to the children and parents in the class, tells what parents are planning for the involvement program, and acknowledges their contributions. The teacher shares information of special interest to parents and invites them to attend an organizational meeting.

Social Occasions   Social events such as potluck suppers, family picnics, and coffees are good ways to meet parents and discuss the program. Several kinds and combinations of different events may be necessary to recruit enough parents to begin the program. The exact formula will depend upon the local situation.

Other Motivators Some other traditional techniques to involve parents are based on the concept of mild coercion. These include door and room prizes offered by the PTA for high parent attendance at meetings. The basic motivational strategy here is to set up competition between classrooms, teachers, or children. Very often the children are encouraged to pressure their parents to attend a meeting or PTA function. While there might be times when these strategies can be used effectively, some less coercive methods for motivation may be preferred.

Many teachers use the motivational technique of communicating positive messages. They tell parents that the involvement program will be fun for them. Parents will have the opportunity to get out of the house to do something that they will enjoy and that will benefit their children. The teacher stresses that participation will give parents an opportunity to help children make a contribution to the community and help them develop new skills and friendships.

If all else fails, there is one strategy that almost always guarantees high parent attendance. A program presented by the children is an event few parents can resist. Some teachers prefer not to use children in this way, while others are comfortable accepting the technique as a means to reach more important goals.

Each of these ideas can be used at different points in the program. The motivational techniques used will most probably be consistent with the school's style of relating to others.

From Recruitment to Involvement: One Approach

Marcia teaches kindergarten at the Blue Sky Elementary School. This is the second year of her parent involvement program. During the first year she worked closely with an advisory group, exploring needs and developing a program plan for the parents of her kindergarten students. As a result of that activity, Marcia developed a program that concentrated on using parents as resources in the classroom. While she intends to form a new advisory group representing parents of children currently enrolled in kindergarten, she also wants to continue the program developed the previous year.

Three weeks before school begins, Marcia sends a letter inviting the parents to an orientation meeting. The letter includes a tentative agenda of the topics to be covered, such as bus schedules, the school calendar, car pool arrangements, special instructions for field trips, clothing, lunch money, absences due to illness, safety rules, procedures for parent-teacher conferences, and an introduction to the parent involvement program. Marcia has developed a printed handbook that reinforces and extends the material covered at the meeting. Marcia is counting on parents making a special effort to attend because of the important information that will be shared. In her letter she stresses that there will be time for questions, a tour of the school building and classroom, and a review of the educational program as well as time to get acquainted.

Marcia has also prepared a short questionnaire and checklist for the parents to identify their special talents and skills that could be used effectively in the classroom, and to find out how many would volunteer to work in the classroom. These forms are duplicated in Figures 5.1 and 5.2. She intends to distribute the questionnaire and checklist after she has discussed the goals of the volunteer program and the different kinds of roles available to parents. Those interested in classroom responsibilities could provide clerical support such as grading papers, keeping attendance records, or collecting lunch money. Others might want to serve as instructional aides and work directly with small groups of children. Parents could also make materials for use in classroom learning centers.

If Marcia wanted to implement a program focused on the parent as a better teacher of his own child or a better informed parent, she would ask other kinds of questions and describe different sorts of parent activities. For example, she might want to identify important discussion group topics or find out what types of instructional materials parents want for use in their homes. The content of the questionnaire will always be related to the goals and objectives that have been identified by the advisory group. Marcia's meeting is planned to help her collect information that will be used to implement a parent classroom volunteer program.

After the group orientation meeting, Marcia follows up with home visits or telephone calls to those parents who were unable to attend the group meeting. Marcia discusses the material covered in the handbook and asks parents to return the questionnaire by the end of the first week of school.

By the beginning of the second week of school, Marcia is ready to analyze the information and organize the parents into groups according to common interests. She puts the names of those who will be unable to volunteer for any classroom time in a separate folder. Some of these parents have special talents or interests and have indicated a willingness to come to school for special events or curriculum units. Other parents have volunteered for clerical work, supervision of children, preparation of learning materials, and instructional aide work.

Marcia knows that each of these roles will require some training and she has already developed some techniques for orienting each group. She had worked with her advisory group the year before and had presented some short in-service training programs for parents that had been fairly effective. The topic names were catchy and seemed to appeal to the parents.

- Keeping the wheels turning: Clerical support

- Getting into the curriculum: Instructional aides

- Media monsters: Developing and duplicating materials

- Keeping the house in order: Housekeeping chores

- Four eyes are better than two: Supervising children

Figure 5.1

PARENT QUESTIONNAIRE

Date_____

Name_____   Telephone_____

    I am taking a survey of parents of children in my class to find out what activities or roles they have taken part in at school and in the classroom, and what activities they would like to take part in now.

1. What activities have you performed in the classroom or at school?

2. What activities would you like to take part in?

3. Which of these activities do you feel would most benefit your child through your participation?

4. Do you have any other concerns or questions about parent involvement in the classroom?

Figure 5.2

CHECKLIST FOR PARENTS

Name_____

Would you like to:

Mother   Father

1. _____   _____   Read a story to some of the children?

2. _____   _____   Teach a song or some other musical activity?

3. _____   _____   Do something in art?

4. _____   _____   Work puzzles or play games?

5. _____   _____   Share your hobby with the class? (If your child
                        is interested, the class will be, too.) If so,
                        what is your hobby?_____

6. _____   _____   Show some children how to use simple carpenter
                        tools?

7. _____   _____   Bring a guitar (or other instrument) and show
                        how it works?

8. _____   _____   Tell the children something about your occupation;
                        for example, a doctor could give a peek inside
                        his or her bag, a police officer could describe
                        helping people and show a uniform?

9. _____   _____   Show us your butterflies, mice, rabbits, insects,
                        etc.?

10. _____   _____   Wear a costume from another country and tell us
                        about it?

11. _____   _____   Lead the group in a large motor activity (balls,
                        ropes, etc.)?

12. _____   _____   Churn butter?

13. _____   _____   Make cookies?

If none of these appeals to you, what would you like to do?

1. _____

2. _____

Remember: You are welcome to visit the classroom at any time.

This year Marcia wants to ask her new parent advisory group to work with her in developing a written handbook for parent volunteers. She wants the handbook to include much of the same information covered in the training sessions, such as how to work with small groups of children, use duplicating equipment, supervise field trips, watch the playground, and tell stories. Marcia believes it will be helpful for the parents to first attend the training sessions and then have a written handbook that reviews all of the information.

After Marcia has analyzed the information collected through the questionnaires, she prepares a note to send home with each child. This note announces another group meeting for organizing the parent involvement program. Since the parents will be asked to elect an advisory group, Marcia stresses the importance of attending this meeting. The meeting is scheduled for the evening and arrangements are made for child care services. Marcia asks each child to remind his or her parents to return the reply form indicating whether or not they will attend.

The agenda for the group meeting focuses heavily on organizing the parent involvement program. Marcia has prepared name tags for everyone and after a brief period for informal visiting, they move to introductions and selection of the advisory group. Marcia reviews the function and responsibilities of the advisory group and asks those who are interested to volunteer. Each volunteer talks briefly about why he or she wants to serve on the advisory group; after all have spoken, a closed ballot election is held. Five parents are elected and Marcia asks each member to stay and meet with her briefly after the general meeting. Next, Marcia reviews the information gathered through the questionnaires and organizes the parents according to areas of interest. Marcia tells each of the groups that she will present a short training program for them to define their roles and responsibilities. They select a convenient date, time, and place for their groups to meet.

After the large group meeting, Marcia meets briefly with the advisory group and discusses some of the tasks that remain to be done. They pick a meeting time to organize their own roles and responsibilities. Some of the tasks they see as important include another needs assessment that could identify new areas of interest, development of a written handbook for parent volunteers, and plans for program activities during the school year. Their program calendar will include a schedule of planned events such as discussion groups, training sessions, guest speakers, and advisory board meetings, and will be planned in a way that allows for some flexibility in responding to special needs or interests.

By the end of the fourth week of school Marcia is ready to begin her first parent in-service meeting. The year before she had not been able to hold this meeting until the third month of school. The experience and practice of the previous year made it much easier for Marcia to get her program organized. She wonders what she will learn this year and how this will change what she does the following year. Marcia also reviews in her own mind some of the questions that are always of concern to teachers. Is the plan reasonable? Does she have enough help to carry out the program? Will more volunteers be needed? Should she cut back on some of the planned activities that seem to be overly ambitious? Marcia knows that she will have to try the plan as it has been developed and make changes during the year. She has been able to recruit parents, organize the advisory groups, and get the initial involvement activities under way. Her next concern is that the parents' involvement and interest are maintained.

 ## MAINTAINING INVOLVEMENT

Recruiting parents and gaining initial commitment are only the beginning. Many programs start out with great enthusiasm but after three or four months interest begins to fade. Just as there are many techniques for recruiting parents, there are also many strategies that can be used to maintain initial parent interest.

The Teacher's Attitudes

The teacher's attitude toward working with parents is critical to the program's success. The classroom teacher or parent resource person sets the emotional climate for the entire program. While every teacher is different, certain inter-personal qualities are particularly important in relating effectively to others. The teacher who is concerned about maintaining the involvement of parents will go out of his way to be friendly and warm whenever they meet. The sensitive teacher initiates the greeting and offers a personal comment about the parent's child or an involvement experience shared by the teacher and parent.

No matter how many crises or unexpected interruptions might occur, the teacher tries to model both a sense of humor and the ability to cope with events. Teachers often forget that they are powerful models for parents as well as children. Parents face the same kinds of stress in their daily home life as teachers face in the classroom. Unfortunately, there are not too many effective role models available to them in most communities. Teachers can meet a very important need of parents by developing the interpersonal skills that will encourage parents to continue their involvement in school programs.

Communication Techniques: Staying in Touch

Parents must know that the program is alive and well. There should be no extended periods of time without some contact between home and school. There are all sorts of ways to maintain communication and all of these techniques can be tried at different times of the year.

A monthly calendar of events should be sent home on the first day of every month (Rich and Jones, 1977). It can include a description of special program activities that have been scheduled and list the names and dates when volunteers will be working in the classrooms. It can also mention special observation sessions for instructional aides; the dates for parent advisory board, PTA, and school board meetings; any field trips that have been scheduled; the regular substitute list; and some drop-off child care services available in the community.

Teachers can also make use of the newsletter, the classroom bulletin board, and announcements to maintain communication. A telephone call to parents sharing positive information about their children is always welcome.

When possible, instructors should try to continue home visits throughout the school year. Each home could be visited once during the year. These visits mean a great deal to the children and their families. Another advantage of the home visit is that when conference time arrives, the parent and teacher have already met and know something about each other. At the conference, they are more likely to be able to concentrate on the child, his progress, and areas of concern for both school and home. These conferences will be much more productive when the initial period of unfamiliarity has passed.

Another way to encourage communication is to put a suggestion box in a place convenient for parents. They should be encouraged to make comments and suggestions on ways to strengthen the involvement program.

Special Events

We all enjoy an unexpected event that represents a change from our regular routine. We tend to remember the details of these happenings because they are unusual, involve new people, and often include different kinds of information on ways of dealing with issues. Parents will also react positively to special events planned as part of the involvement program. Teachers need to capitalize on this interest by scheduling new and different kinds of events throughout the school year.

About twice a year the school could plan a clothing, toy, and book exchange for the families of children (Rich and Jones, 1977). Another idea that is particularly appealing to children is to feature a "family of the week" as part of the classroom curriculum. Select a different family each week and ask parents to send baby and family pictures along with special objects from home. Invite the parents and child to come to school and help arrange the classroom display. Perhaps the parent can visit for an hour during the week and share information about the family, its cultural background, and customs.

Teachers might want to prepare and send home tips for home activities related to the classroom program (Wheeler and Henderson, 1976). Another idea would be a book list of titles selected by a librarian or other expert in children's literature (Lincoln, 1974). Very often, a parent volunteer can take the responsibility for putting the tip sheet together, including suggestions for rainy days, things to do when children are sick, some thoughts about "tender topics," or recommendations for television viewing.

Another very exciting idea is videotaping the classroom program. While some teachers will hesitate to do this, others will be ready to experiment. They can videotape children in classroom learning centers, working with the teacher in reading groups, involved in a social studies unit, playing in the housekeeping or block areas, or participating in music, art, or whatever may interest the parent. These tapes can be shown to individual parents or at a group meeting with a follow-up discussion of what was seen.

Workshops can be scheduled at special times of the year. A parent committee can develop ideas for gifts that can be made during the workshops. A small fee can be charged for materials and soon a busy parent group is involved, sharing information about themselves, and really getting to know each other.

Special programs could deal with the needs of handicapped children, the topic of child abuse, organizing a community-wide immunization program staffed by volunteers, or a new program that will train parents to tutor children having reading difficulties (Pickarts, 1973). If the topic is of concern to parents, they will come and participate.

It is important to include events that are purely social in nature. During a coffee or tea at the end of the year the teacher can thank volunteers for their contributions. This is also a good time to review progress made, mention ideas and events that were tried, and share once again the successes and failures. If an important goal of parent involvement programs is to break down barriers between home and school by really getting to know each other, there must be enough time for this to happen throughout the year.

Demonstrating Concern

Little things can make a difference. A pleasant setting for a meeting with comfortable chairs and a place for everyone who attends can create an environment that helps people get to know each other. If, on the other hand, the room has poor ventilation and is crowded, the participants will drift away or not return for the next meeting.

There should be name tags and time for parents to visit and get to know each other before starting the formal agenda for the meeting. A volunteer committee can plan and serve simple nutritious refreshments.

When parents have taken the time to volunteer in the classroom, provide transportation for a field trip, supervise children on the playground, go to a school board meeting, or make instructional materials, the effort should be acknowledged. The teacher and the children must always thank parents. They like to feel that what they do has been noticed and appreciated.

SUMMARY

As you gain more experience in working with parents, you should find that the activities you plan are increasingly successful. Just as you stand back and monitor the progress made in the classroom program for children, you should stand back and monitor your parent involvement program. Are those parents who were enthusiastic at the beginning of the year still volunteering? What about other parents? Are they beginning to volunteer and participate in program activities? Do parents feel comfortable about dropping in after school and asking questions? Is the parent advisory group generating new ideas for programs? Are you able to delegate more responsibility for coordinating the program to parent volunteers? Do the parents seem to be enjoying the experience and learning from what they are doing?

These are all important questions that should be asked, both formally and informally. Periodically distribute a parent questionnaire about program effectiveness. Get the information needed to improve the program so that it is truly responsive to children, parents, and teachers.

Remember some of the options available as meetings and activities are planned. Make arrangements for child care, alternate meeting times, be sensitive to the needs of different parents, and try to plan interesting program activities.

Work at encouraging the support of your principal or director. As leaders and decision makers they can provide needed resources for achieving goals.

Learn to use many different strategies for recruiting parents and maintaining involvement. Ideas include registration programs, PTA meetings, posters, school and class newsletters, home visits, special programs, and special appreciation events. If you alternate these strategies, you will be able to maintain the interest and involvement of parents.

FOR DISCUSSION AND FURTHER STUDY

1. Develop a set of rules for children that a teacher can use when bringing parents into the classroom as volunteers.

2. Develop a set of rules for parent volunteers that a teacher can use when parents work in the classroom.

3. Interview parents and teachers in your community. Identify and discuss particular issues or problems that are unique to your local community and are related to implementing a parent involvement program.

4. Generate a list of fifteen tasks for a parent volunteer. What would the benefits be to the children, teacher, and parent?

5. Pretend you are a school administrator and write a column to be published in the school newsletter for parents. The purpose of the column is to encourage parents to participate in the school's programs.

6. Design a brochure or poster that a teacher could use to announce the first parent involvement meeting of the year.

7. Select a grade level and design a program orientation handbook that could be given to parents at the beginning of the school year.

8. Develop a resource file of places in the community that would be of special interest to parents and their children. Include ideas of how parents can use these visits to stimulate their child's intellectual, physical, social, and emotional development.

BIBLIOGRAPHY

Andrews, Palmyra. "What Every Parent Wants to Know." *Childhood Education* 52, no. 6 (April 1976): 304–305.

Cohen, Shirley. *Parent Involvement in the Education of Young Handicapped Children.* New York: City University of New York, Center for Advanced Study in Education, 1974.

Gilmar, Sybil, and John Nelson. "Centering Resources for Learning: Parents Get into the Act." *Childhood Education* 51, no. 4 (February 1975): 208–10.

Gordon, Ira, and William Breinogel. *Building Effective Home-School Relationships.* Boston: Allyn and Bacon, 1976.

Higginson, George, Carl Swanson, and Reeve Love. *Calipers: Planning the Systems Approach to Field Testing Educational Products.* Austin, Texas: Southwest Educational Development Laboratory, 1969.

King, Edith. *Working with Culturally Different Parents.* A paper prepared for the conference "Toward the Competent Parent," Georgia State University, Atlanta, Georgia, February 22, 1977.

Lincoln, Robert. "Reading to Young Children." *Children Today* 3 (May–June 1974): 28–30.

Marion, Marian. "Create a Parent-Space: A Place to Stop, Look and Read." *Young Children* 28, no. 4 (April 1973): 221–24.

Pickarts, Evelyn. "Learning to Read—With a Parental Assist." *Today's Education* 62, no. 2 (February 1973): 31–37.

Pickarts, Evelyn, and Jean Fargo. *Parent Education.* New York: Appleton-Century-Crofts, 1971.

Randall, Robert. "An Operational Application of the CIPP Model for Evaluation." *Educational Technology* 9, no. 7 (July 1969): 40–44.

Rich, Dorothy, and Cynthia Jones. *A Family Affair: Education.* Washington, D.C.: Home and School Institute, 1977.

Shutz, Richard. "The Nature of Educational Development." *Journal of Research and Development in Education* 3, no. 2 (Winter 1970): 39–64.

Southwest Educational Development Laboratory. *A Development Process.* Austin, Texas: Southwest Educational Development Laboratory, 1970.

Stufflebeam, Daniel, et al. *Educational Evaluation and Decision Making.* Itasca, Ill.: F. E. Peacock, 1971.

Wheeler, Doris, and Hanna Henderson. *Reading Improvement through Home Help: A Program for Parents and Their Children.* A paper presented at the annual meeting of the International Reading Association, Anaheim, Calif., May 1976.

6 Developing a Program

We've all had the experience of going to a meeting that sounded as though it would be very interesting but turned out to be boring or disorganized. The speaker's presentation was unclear and the audience was frustrated and irritated at this waste of time. As teachers move from planning to carrying out the involvement program, they should be aware of and learn to use techniques that will help them work effectively with adults. Designing the program plan and selecting goals, objectives, and instructional strategies are extremely important tasks, but once these are completed, attention must turn to developing interesting activities.

We are going to review some important considerations in developing parent involvement program activities. Teachers are responsible for selecting presentation techniques and interaction strategies and designing ways to motivate and hold the interest of adults so that objectives can be achieved. Finally, teachers must evaluate the effectiveness of what has been tried. Just as there are many options in planning activities for parents, there are also different techniques that can be used to evaluate the activities. This chapter will present some ideas for consideration during the stage of program development.

CHARACTERISTICS OF PARENT GROUPS

Within every group of parents there is a wide range of individual differences. Teachers should be sensitive to these differences and be aware of the areas in which the differences will be most evident. Brim (1965) describes six factors that affect parental behavior: ability factors, unconscious factors, cultural values, interpersonal and social controls, group structural determinants, and ecological or physical factors. We will review how each of these causes specific behaviors or attitudes that teachers can learn to identify and respond to in program planning.

Abilities

Within every group of people there are variations in physical strength, size, weight, general health, and intelligence that should be taken into account as a program is planned. Variations in the abilities of parents affect the objectives, materials, methods of presentation, and the length of program activities teachers should select.

If most of the parents in a group did not finish high school, it is reasonable to assume that the literacy level or reading ability of this group is limited. In planning program activities, teachers should respond to the unique charac-teristics of this group by presenting basic information through group discus-sions and lectures. Printed materials could be used to reinforce or extend information introduced in other ways. If, on the other hand, most of the parents are college graduates, teachers might distribute printed information to them before a meeting and use meeting time to expand on ideas already introduced in the readings. While it will never be possible to respond to every ability found in a group, efforts should be made to consider these characteristics as the program is developed.

Unconscious Factors

Past experiences influence our adult behavior and attitudes. Many of these experiences remain below the level of conscious awareness but continue to affect our reactions in certain situations. I have noticed that whenever I walk into an elementary school building I feel very positive toward the environment. I suspect that this reaction is related to my own pleasant experiences as a student. In contrast, I tend to become anxious whenever I walk onto a tennis court. I suspect that this reaction is from my unpleasant experiences as a child trying to master different sports. Likewise, in any group of adults, certain topics such as discipline or sex education are likely to arouse almost irrational reac-tions. As teachers develop activities for the parent involvement program they should use the advisory group to help them select topics that parents can deal with rationally.

Cultural Values

Parent values or attitudes are another area in which teachers will find many group differences. Effective program development cannot occur without some examination of the cultural values held by parents. These values must be discussed and related to the goals of the program. What if most parents in the group value rather submissive behavior on the part of women in the family? A discussion leader might have been planning to emphasize the equality of the sexes and the unlimited potential for growth that exists for both men and women. These differences in value judgments should be discussed and some mutual resolution must evolve as program goals and activities are selected. Perhaps the parents will modify their position after some discussion, or teachers might have to modify their own behavior so as to be more consistent with the values of the community.

Interpersonal and Social Controls

Many people influence the behavior of parents. We often forget these other influences and the way they can interfere with the achievement of program goals. Teachers should try to be sensitive to the influence of a spouse, siblings, grandparents, neighbors, or other relatives. For example, differences can be reflected in the way decisions are made within a family. Who makes the decisions? How are these decisions carried out? Situations could easily be created that lead to conflict between school and home if the program developer is unaware of the social controls that operate within a particular group.

Suppose a teacher was developing a series of activities dealing with the ineffectiveness of using physical punishment with young children and did not know that families in the community believe strongly in this method of discipline. While the teacher might strongly disagree with this position, he will be much more effective working with these parents if he is aware of these attitudes and plans activities that reflect this knowledge. There is not much point in citing the latest research on child rearing when this particular approach might be totally meaningless to the parents. Strategies such as role-playing of discipline situations, films followed by discussions, and classroom observations might be appropriate ways of dealing with this topic.

Structural Characteristics of the Family Group

The number of relatives or adults in the home, the number of children, their ages, and their sex will all influence the interactions between members of a family. Parents of an only child will have different concerns than parents with four or five chidren. Structural factors should be considered in planning program activities that will accommodate the special concerns of parents.

Those parents whose child is the oldest in the family will be more likely to share common concerns than those whose child is the youngest in the family. Parents of the oldest child tend to be more anxious about the teacher's expectations and their child's chances for success at school. Parents of the youngest child might be more relaxed about these things because of experiences they have had with their other children. Information about family characteristics can be very helpful as groups with common interests are formed or discussion groups organized.

Ecological or Physical Factors

The behaviors and concerns of parents are also influenced by ecological factors. Do they have sufficient income to take care of basic needs? Do the mother and father work? Have they been able to get adequate medical care for both themselves and their children? Do they live in a home large enough for the entire family? Is child care available? Each of these factors and many others have a direct impact on the parents' behavior and can make the difference between a parent who wants to participate in an involvement program and one who simply does not have the time or energy. It is always easy to criticize the parent who chooses not to become involved, but very often the reasons for this choice are related to pressures that prevent any further commitment of time.

As teachers develop their parent involvement program, they should try to consider all of these factors and their potential influences on the behavior of parents. While there will be times when they will be able to accommodate specific characteristics of parents and plan a responsive program, at other times this will be much more difficult. Teachers cannot change the economic factors in a family's life or undo unpleasant experiences that might have occurred earlier. But if they can understand the possible causes of parent behavior, they should be able to develop more relevant and effective involvement activities.

SOME PRINCIPLES FOR WORKING WITH ADULTS

Build on Strengths

Effective teachers will reinforce parents for their accomplishments. Teachers can bring the culture of the community into the classroom by using parents as resources for sharing ethnic folktales, dances, songs, and special foods. Regardless of the kinds of problems a family might have, most parents are trying to do the best possible job in raising their children. Teachers should identify the positive factors in the parent-child relationship and build on these as the program is developed.

Watch Parent Reactions

Parent involvement leaders should be alert to signs of negative or indifferent reactions at meetings or other activities. Parents are not a captive audience and are not obligated to attend meetings or participate in the program. Once parents withdraw, it is usually very difficult to get them back into a program. Teachers might miss the unobtrusive signals communicated through body language. Do the facial expressions of parents show signs of boredom? Are they restless and moving around in their seats? Are they listening to what is being said? Do they seem to be irritated by comments of others in the group? Teachers must also listen to the comments parents make and the questions they ask. Do they want to discuss areas of disagreement or extend suggestions made by others? Are they politely agreeing with each other because they find the discussions uninteresting or irrelevant? Very often the substance of the comments will tell a great deal about how parents are reacting to the program.

Select Content Carefully

After analyzing information from a needs assessment, teachers should be able to develop a program based on identified goals and interests. Suppose the needs assessment indicated that parents want to know more about child rearing. Since there are any number of topics that could be included, more information must be gathered in order to identify specific topics. Teachers might ask the parents if they are interested in any of of sixteen child-rearing concerns identified in a recent national survey of parents whose oldest child was twelve years or younger (Gallup, 1977). These were:

1. What to do about drugs, smoking, use of alcohol.
2. How to help the child set high achievement goals.
3. How to develop good work habits.
4. How to improve the child's school behavior.
5. How to improve the child's thinking and observation abilities.
6. How to deal with the child's emotional problems.
7. How to increase interest in school and school subjects.
8. How to help the child organize his homework.
9. How to improve parent-child relationships.
10. How to help the child choose a career.
11. How to use family activities to help the child do better in school.
12. How to encourage reading.
13. How to help the child get along with other children.
14. How to reduce television viewing.
15. How to deal with dating problems.
16. How to improve health habits.

The key to effective program development is to find out what parents want and then respond by designing activities responsive to their interests.

Make Content Relevant

Parents should see the activities as relevant to their lives. Adults, like children, need to have opportunities to act on or use information, so whenever possible, planned activities should draw on their experiences. In a program on discipline, teachers can take parents beyond the step of talking about discipline by planning for and encouraging them to engage in role-playing and discussions to share special problems. Discussions should avoid jargon, abstract, and theoretical concepts and be as concrete as possible in the examples and suggestions given for dealing with problems.

Organize the Information

The teacher is responsible for organizing information in a meaningful way. This implies study and preparation before any activity ever takes place. If a teacher does not have the background or is unable to find information for a particular program activity, she should identify an appropriate resource person. Nobody expects a teacher or parent involvement resource person to be an expert in every area and there will be times when outside help is needed. When, however, a teacher is responsible for planning a meeting, workshop, training session, or discussion group, he must be clear on the points he will make, how he will make them, and whether or not supplementary materials will be needed to reinforce the objective. The process is identical with preparing lesson plans for children, so at least the same amount of effort should be given.

Use Repetition as Needed

As teachers work with parents, they should emphasize and repeat some of the important points they are trying to make. Much of this information may be new to parents, and it is never easy to assimilate unfamiliar material. Repetition in one form or another is always necessary before concepts can be internalized. The leader might present information at the beginning of an activity and then reinforce it in different ways, such as through a film, discussion, reading material, or demonstration. The reaction of parents and the comments they make will tell whether or not they are ready to move on to other kinds of experiences.

Generalize and Apply Information

The program leader should plan ways to help parents generalize and apply information or skills. The group could give examples of how they might use what they have learned with their own children at home. They should see how they can apply what they have learned to their role as a parent or teacher of their own child. If there has been a discussion about helping children develop good work habits, parents can discuss ways to encourage this at home or in the classroom. The perceived usefulness of these involvement activities will be an important criterion for parents. If they cannot see how the information or skills can be used in their own lives, they will be much more likely to drop out of the program.

DEVELOPING PROGRAM ACTIVITIES

Planning activities such as workshops, discussion groups, and training sessions requires time and thought. The substance or content of an activity is directly tied to the selected program objectives. There are, in addition, other procedural concerns that must be considered in developing a program. These are often ignored or seen as unimportant, but without attention to these details, many activities will end in apparent failure.

General Considerations

The first question to consider is how many people will participate in an activity. The number of people will determine the space needed, the amount of materials to be prepared, and the number of resource people needed to work wih parents.

Once an estimate has been made of the number who will attend, the leader can make arrangements for a room that is large enough to accommodate the group and suitable for the kind of activity that is planned. Good lighting, tables and chairs, and possibly a sink will be needed for a workshop. When role-playing is planned, it is essential to have space for moving around.

In order to help parents feel comfortable, the leader should review the background of the parents who will attend—their educational level, the kinds of experiences they have had, their cultural background, values, and attitudes. Should there be some refreshments before the meeting begins? Should there be time for informal visiting? Would some parents be willing to serve as hosts and hostesses? Will some parents need transportation or child care? Many of these arrangements can be handled by the parent advisory group and, whenever possible, should be delegated to parent volunteers.

There are other details to remember in developing activities.

Schedule the Meeting Reserve time for the activity or meeting on the school or center calendar. There should be no conflicting activities. The teacher might also block out the dates on the calendars of the center director, school principal, and any other administrators who need to be informed.

Reserve Space and Equipment Analyze space and equipment requirements. Will the group need a room with shades at the window, worktables, a television set, or a film projector? Will parents need paper and pencils or other materials for the activity? These should be collected ahead of time.

Prepare Advance Organizers Should any reading materials be distributed before the activity? Should an agenda be mailed out? A statement of goals and objectives for the meeting? Should parents read an article or newspaper clipping? Any advance organizers (reading materials or questions to think about) should be duplicated and distributed before the day of the scheduled activity.

Notify Participants   As soon as firm dates have been selected, notification should be sent to parents and any others who will be involved in the activity. Include a description of what will happen, who will work with the group, and any anticipated outcomes as a result of the activity.

Prepare the Environment   Consider the total environment. Is the room set up in such a way that people will feel comfortable with each other? The environment and the way it is prepared will often determine whether or not positive interactions can occur. The program organizer should work with the environment to create the informal groupings necessary to support the goals and objectives of the program activities.

Duplicate Materials   Prepare ahead of time any handouts, worksheets, special forms, and other materials that will be needed during the activity. The leader should not have to fumble for materials in the middle of the activity. This will make her look unprepared and interrupt the flow of the activity.

Plan the Activity   Every detail of the activity must be carefully planned. After the content has been selected, the available time can be divided into segments. For each segment of time, there should be an outline of what will be happening—the topic, goal, specific objectives to be achieved, the techniques to help the parents meet these objectives, the necessary materials or equipment, and any reading materials that should be reviewed by the parents before or after the meeting. Consider the following.

- What will be done?
- How this will be done?
- Who will be responsible?
- How much time will be needed?

If the group leader is well prepared, the learning experience will be most effective for the parents.

A Sample Plan

Topic: Working with children in small groups

Goal: To familiarize parents with instructional techniques for working with children in learning center activities.

Objectives: The parents will be able to name and discuss the purpose of the classroom learning centers. When given a card describing a learning activity, each parent will be able to role-play the appropriate instructional techniques.

Instructional techniques:

1. Introduction to working with children in small groups, teacher lecture (10 minutes).

2. Tour of the classroom and learning centers (10 minutes). Discussion of the purpose of learning centers (5 minutes).

3. Videotape of the teacher working with small groups demonstrating (20 minutes):

    a. Reading a story.

    b. Playing a lotto language game.

    c. Classifying objects by color.

4. Role-play activities (30 minutes): Parents working in small groups will simulate working with small groups of children in an instructional activity.

5. Wrap-up discussion and summary (15 minutes).

Equipment and materials:

1. List of classroom learning centers.

2. Outline of basic instructional techniques.

3. Videotape and video playback unit.

4. Activity cards for role-playing.

Total time: 90 minutes

PACING AND SPACING CONSIDERATIONS

In developing activities, the program leader should choose instructional strategies that can help achieve specific program goals. There are many pacing and spacing techniques to hold the interest of the adult audience. These techniques can be matched to the goals and objectives of a particular activity as well as to the characteristics of the parents. Unfortunately, few teachers have been trained in this area. Since there is not a great deal of research available on when to use different methods, the choice must often be based on trial and error or the availability of resources. As teachers gain experience in working with adults and experiment with different techniques, they will see which are most effective in holding the interest of the parents.

Presenting Information

Lectures   Very often the most effective way to present information is through a carefully researched, interesting lecture. When the program leader is not qualified to lecture on a topic, arrangements can be made for an outside speaker. Every community has resource people who are usually willing to meet with parent groups. Speakers should be provided with information about the parents, their interests, and the activities they enjoy, as well as specific objectives for the lecture.

Printed Materials   Another effective way to present information is through the use of printed materials. A useful resource file for teachers would include possible topics for parent activities, books and journals available in the school or local library, and magazine articles of special interest. Materials in the file will be handy and can be used as needed for special activities.

Films   Special films are available through the school district, the Head Start office, and the public library. Many excellent films have been produced that deal with topics of child rearing, development, and family living. The program leader should preview the films to know how the information relates to the goals and objectives of the activity.

Videotapes   Videotapes can also be effective in presenting information to parents. Parents who are being trained to work as classroom instructional aides could watch a videotape of adults demonstrating teaching techniques with the children. Videotapes can also be used to present information on discipline, child management and ways of fostering language development. Again, these videotapes should be carefully prepared and reviewed before the activity takes place.

Television   There are some excellent programs on public and commercial television stations. Sometimes it may be possible to plan a meeting at a time when the teacher and the parents can view a program together. This can be an effective technique for presenting important information to parents followed by group discussions.

Demonstrations   Planned demonstrations offer another way to present information. A resource person or a parent volunteer can demonstrate different ways to carry out an activity with children. These demonstrations could focus on teaching strategies, how to make materials, using the toy lending library, reading a story, or classroom management skills. Parents usually find demonstrations interesting, and the teacher is able to act as a model without applying any direct pressure.

Observations or Field Trips   Sometimes it is possible to schedule activities outside of a formal meeting setting. The school is not the only available setting for learning. Whenever possible, the program leader should vary the settings used by scheduling activities outside of the school or center building. Perhaps the parents would benefit from observing a librarian conduct a story time for children. What about a trip to the kitchen of the public service home economist, a museum, a toy store, or a walk in the neighborhood? Every community has places of special interest that can be used for parent involvement activities.

The effective program leader will incorporate all of these techniques into the program for sharing information with parents and vary them so as to maintain interest.

Using Information

Once basic information has been presented, there should be opportunities for parents to practice using this information. This is the step most often ignored when planning programs for adults. Just as there are many techniques for sharing information, there are also many different ways of providing opportunities for practicing skills.

Small Group Interactions   In small group activities, parents can work with each other and actually use information by practicing related skills. The leader might want to structure these small group sessions by telling or modeling for the parents what they are to do. Perhaps they can read stories to each other as they try to develop story-telling abilities. They could pretend to be involved in daily housekeeping chores and explore different kinds of questions they might ask their children.

Projects   Another technique for practicing skills is to develop group or individual projects that require the parents to construct or design a product using information previously presented. They might make toys to use at home with their own children or materials for classroom learning centers. Other projects might be of a more extended nature, such as planning the program for a special back-to-school activity or carrying out a school immunization program.

Games, Demonstrations, and Role-Playing   Other ways to give parents a chance to practice skills based on information presented through the program are games, demonstrations, and role-playing. These activities must be carefully designed so that they relate to the goals and objectives of the program. Charades can be an effective way to reinforce child-rearing principles such as praising positive behavior or modeling problem-solving skills. How about Twenty Questions to identify first-aid techniques for different situations? Why not role-play a trip to the grocery store, stressing the educational benefits to be gained by both the child and the parents?

Workshops   A workshop format lends itself to practicing skills. An appealing benefit of this technique is the product the parent makes. The workshop should be planned to capitalize on information that has been shared so that opportunities are built in to practice new skills. The leader is an important model for the parents. He or she should be enthusiastic and encourage parents to practice the skills introduced through the program.

Solving Problems

There will be times when the objectives for an activity will go beyond presenting or practicing skills. A reasonable goal for any involvement program would be to encourage parents to develop and use problem-solving abilities to resolve issues or concerns. A number of instructional strategies lend themselves to these sorts of objectives.

Group Discussion One very effective technique is the use of group discussions. This strategy gives the leader opportunities to model problem-solving behavior for the parents. Very often those parents who are hesitant to speak out can listen to the leader or other parents who feel more confident about their ability to resolve different kinds of problems.

Panel Discussions Panel discussions offer the opportunity to talk about problems and solutions. Parents can volunteer to serve on a panel planned as part of an activity. Sometimes they will want to do some preliminary research in order to gather information before taking part in the discussion. This technique gives the responsibility for problem solving to the parents rather than the teacher or involvement leader.

Small Group Problem Solving Small groups can be organized for achieving problem-solving goals. Each of the groups can meet separately, explore issues, reach some resolution, and then select a spokesperson to report back to the larger group. Very often, each of the groups will come up with different kinds of solutions. The point can be made quite dramatically that often there is more than one appropriate answer to a problem. Another benefit of this strategy is that parents can begin to see how they can use each other as resources in finding answers to questions or problems.

Games and Role-Playing A game format can also promote problem-solving objectives. A teacher might design a series of cards that describe common child-rearing dilemmas. Each of the parents can pick a card and role-play a solution while the other parents discuss whether or not they agree. Another idea for a game is to describe an educational or learning need of a child and ask parents to pick a home learning activity geared to these special needs. The game format allows the program leader to place the problem-solving activity in an informal context, relieving the anxiety that certain parents might feel.

Activities involving role-playing dramatizations can also be used for problem solving. The leader or parent volunteers can actually act out different solutions to problems. This can be done in a relaxed and informal manner that encourages the group to explore alternative solutions.

LEADING A DISCUSSION GROUP

Sooner or later, every teacher has to lead a discussion group. Effective discussions are sometimes difficult to achieve. Too many meetings or discussion groups end up as a waste of everyone's time because the leader was unprepared or those attending were not prepared. There are a number of ways to avoid these problems as the teacher plans discussion activities.

Before the Discussion

In planning a discussion, the leader must be totally familiar with the subject matter. The topic should relate directly to the parent group or local community. An effective discussion group leader puts in the necessary time to research the topic and learn as much as possible about the issues.

When a particular topic is to be discussed at a meeting, necessary materials should be mailed to the parents ahead of time. They should know the purpose of the meeting, the topic of the discussion, how they might prepare, and the expected outcomes.

The advance materials could include articles that will give parents an outline of basic information. These printed materials should be readable (geared to the appropriate literacy level) and interesting. They may have to be rewritten in order to address the interests of the parents who will be attending. It may be helpful to outline key points for the parents to look for as they read, to develop a list of questions, and to ask the parents to think about how the issues relate to their particular family situations.

Parents will get more out of the reading materials if they are asked to jot down and think about related examples of things that have occurred in their homes. If they prepare these examples, there must be time at the group meeting for sharing this information. Encouraging parents to reflect on advance discussion points (examples of family incidents, questions, key concepts) is an effective way to get them actively involved during the meeting. The leader should tell the parents that there are no right or wrong answers and that the goal is for them to consider these concepts and feel comfortable in discussing and asking questions about these ideas.

Conducting the Discussion

Every parent should really understand the material under discussion. One very useful technique is to encourage parents to define terms in their own words and to share examples with each other. They could relate the topic to their own family for relevance. The value of any discussion session cannot be measured by the amount of information presented, but by the extent to which the behavior of parents will be affected. Behavior changes will not come about unless the activity has been planned so that outcomes are discussed and applications to family situations are studied.

It is important for the discussion leader to monitor group participation. The leader should try to refer questions back to the parents and avoid turning the meeting into a sermon. The best questions are open-ended, for example:

- Would you like to carry that idea a little further?

- Does anyone have another idea?
- Could you explain that?

The leader can restate or paraphrase points and ask:

- Is that what you have in mind?
- Are we in agreement?
- Have I missed the point you wanted to make?
- Does anyone have a different idea?

Parents must have time to talk about the questions shared beforehand and to answer new questions raised during the meeting. The leader helps them relate the topic to their own home and to ways they might apply what they have learned to their own family situations.

EVALUATING THE PROGRAM

When you consider all the time and effort that go into planning and developing a program, it is important to determine whether the program's goals and objectives have been achieved. An evaluation plan can provide the information needed to improve the program.

One of the reasons people tend to avoid evaluating program activities is that they often equate evaluation with value judgments (passing or failing). Teachers in particular seem to set up standards of performance that are often totally unrealistic. Before a teacher even begins an involvement program, he or she must accept the idea that many aspects of the program will not be especially effective or appropriate. This does not indicate a failure but rather demonstrates a need to examine the data and see how the program can be improved. Developing a successful involvement program takes time, effort, and an openness to self-criticism as well as a commitment to the idea that improvement is a gradual process.

Getting Feedback

Questionnaires   There are many ways to get information on improving a parent involvement program. One of the most obvious is to develop a form that can be distributed at the end of each activity. (See Figures 6.1 and 6.2.) These forms can be filled out by parents when they attend meetings, discussion groups, in-service training, workshops, or any other type of planned group experience. Questions can relate to the effectiveness of the presentation, the appropriateness of the setting, instructional materials used, the relevance of the content, clarity of the discussion, or anything else that will help in evaluating and revising that particular activity.

Figure 6.1

GROUP DISCUSSION--REACTION SHEET

Instructions: Check the point on these scales that represents your
                opinion. Do not sign your name.

                    ----

1. How effective do you feel the discussion was?

    Poor   Average   Excellent

2. How productive was the discussion in generating new ideas?

    Very valuable   Moderately valuable   Waste of time

3. How satisfied are you with any conclusions or decisions that were
    reached?

    Very satisfied   Moderately satisfied   Very dissatisfied

4. Was your point of view considered adequately?

    Ignored   Acceptably   Entirely

5. Did the group atmosphere support good communication?

    Too cooperative   Just right   Too competitive

6. How effective was the leader in keeping the discussion moving?

    Poor   Average   Excellent

7. What percent of the audience took part in the discussion?

    20%   40%   60%   80%   100%

8. How prepared were you for the discussion?

    No preparation   Some   Completely

9. How prepared were the other members of the group?

    No preparation   Some   Completely

Figure 6.2

CLASSROOM TRAINING--REACTION SHEET

In order to make our involvement program effective, we need your honest evaluation of the training activities. Please answer the following questions and return.

How many training meetings did you attend? _____

What were your reasons for not attending?

What two or three things about the training sessions were most useful to you?

Why?

What suggestions do you have for changing the training activities?

Informal Discussions   Another way to get evaluation information is through informal discussions with parents. If parents are working in the classroom, the teacher can ask them how the day went, if they feel comfortable with their role, and whether the teacher should be offering more assistance or support. These same informal techniques can be used to assess program activities when teachers work with parents at home.

Monthly Meetings   A related strategy is to plan monthly meetings where all parents can talk about their experiences in the involvement program. Sometimes a specific planned activity could have been totally ineffective, but when that activity is examined within the context of other experiences that were offered during the month, the parents might find the original activity to have been very helpful. The teacher should vary the time period (one month, three months, the school year) for collecting information in order to get a clear perspective of the parents' reactions to what has been done.

Records   Simple record keeping can also provide useful evaluation data. The teacher could keep attendance records of every group meeting; ask the school library to maintain records on books checked out by parents dealing with aspects of the involvement program; try to note when parents stop by with questions either before or after school; and set up a system for recording the amount of time volunteers are giving to the program. All of these records will provide important information that can be used to measure the impact and effectiveness of the programs.

Structured Interviews   There are other techniques to elicit more specific information. The teacher might select a sample of parents and conduct structured interviews designed to gather specific kinds of information about the program. Some of the items might include:

1. Can you tell me three ideas you learned at the monthly parent meetings?

2. How have you used these ideas at home?

3. Do you think an involvement program is important? Why?

Observations   If time permits, the teacher might observe parents working with children or participating in group meetings and develop some simple rating scales that reflect key behaviors or skills (see Figure 6.3).

These observations should be done as unobtrusively as possible at the beginning and end of the school year. The data will show whether any behavioral changes have taken place.

End-of-the Year Questionnaire   At the end of the school year parents should fill out an extensive questionnaire. They should be encouraged to make

Figure 6.3
Rating Scale

	Always	Sometimes	Never
1. The parent reinforces efforts made by the children to answer questions or solve problems			
2. The parent listens to others in the group without interrupting			
3. The parent generates new ways to use familiar materials			

suggestions about changes in the program. The teacher should encourage the parents to be honest as well as critical and assure them that their anonymity will be protected.

Analyzing the Data

It will take time to study all the information that has been gathered. It might be helpful to organize the comments into categories that are useful for making program decisions. For example:

- How many parents said that the training programs for classroom volunteers prepared them for their role?

- How many parents said that meeting times should be changed?

- What was the most successful planned family activity?

The program leader may want to discuss certain identified problems with the advisory group, center director, and principal. Perhaps they can give suggestions for improving the program or resolving the problems. There will always be one or two parents who are very unhappy or dissatisfied with the program; a goal of 100 percent support is an unrealistic criterion for success.

In looking back over the school year, the teacher should review some of the positive changes that have come about, what has been learned, and how the program can be improved during the next school year. Short- and long-range goals should be evaluated in light of the year's progress.

SUMMARY

No one can give a set of simple rules for interacting effectively with adults, but there are a number of suggestions to help you to be more effective in your leadership role.

Take the time to understand the kinds of parents with whom you are working. Each group has unique characteristics, and the program offered should reflect the cultural background and interests of the parents. Always be thoroughly prepared for any activity so that you are able to listen and respond to the parents. If you are clear on what is going to happen, the material to be covered, the instructional techniques to be used, and the practical applications of the activity, you will be comfortable enough to listen, watch, and respond to every person in the group.

A large part of your role is to model and reinforce appropriate behaviors and responses. By using reinforcement techniques (such as smiling, encouraging, agreeing), you will be able to prompt more parents to speak out and become actively involved. If a parent says something that is controversial or reflects a very personal value judgment, encourage the group to discuss the issues. Help the parents to critically examine their position so that they might be willing to accept other approaches to resolving problems.

Try to use pacing principles by varying the instructional techniques used within any one activity. Alternate active and quiet kinds of experiences, those that require serious concentration with others demanding less concentration. A film might be followed by small group discussions, or a lecture followed by role-playing activities. Use the same strategies in planning and scheduling for adults that you consider when planning and scheduling for children. Put yourself in the position of your audience and ask whether you would be able to sit and remain interested throughout the planned activity. Learn to be your own critic and revise your plans as necessary.

Always be sure that you have built-in opportunities for parents to practice a skill or act upon the information introduced. Explore applications of concepts, and at the end of every activity allow time for the parents to synthesize the material that has been covered.

Evaluate your program and try to improve the effectiveness of all the involvement activities. Feedback can be gathered in informal and formal ways. Study the information carefully and revise the program to reflect the suggestions given by the parent participants.

FOR DISCUSSION AND FURTHER STUDY

1. Interview three teachers who work with parents and have them describe some of the unique characteristics of these parents. How do they consider this information in developing program activities?

2. Assume that you are a parent resource person planning a discussion group activity dealing with children's attitudes towards school achievement. What factors or parent characteristics should be considered? How might these factors influence the activity?

3. Attend a parent involvement meeting. Observe the participants carefully and note their reactions and levels of interest. Discuss these reactions and any suggestions you might have for the group leader for improving subsequent activities.

4. Describe three concepts you consider most important for working effectively with adults. Why do you think these principles are important?

5. Prepare instructions that parents might use when they observe in the classroom. Define the purpose of the observation and relate the observation guidelines to that purpose.

6. Prepare a checklist to be followed in planning a parent activity or meeting.

7. Role-play three different ways to present information to parents on the topic of encouraging children to read.

8. Develop a list of places in the community that could be used for parent field trips. What sorts of goals or objectives could be met through these activities?

9. Create a game that could be used by parents to achieve a specific program objective. Define the objective and develop all the materials needed for carrying out the activity.

10. Design three different questionnaires to evaluate a parent involvement program at the end of a school year. The questionnaires should deal with the following:
    a. A home-based approach.
    b. A home-school cooperative approach.
    c. A parent as classroom volunteer approach.

BIBLIOGRAPHY

Auerbach, Aline. *Parents Learn through Discussion.* New York: Wiley, 1968.

Brim, Orville. *Education for Child Rearing.* New York: Free Press, 1965.

Brophy, Jere, Thomas Good, and Shari Nedler. *Teaching in the Preschool.* New York: Harper & Row, 1975.

Gallagher, James, Richard Surles, and Andrew Hayes. *Program Planning and Evaluation.* Chapel Hill, N.C.: Technical Assistance Development System, 1973.

Gallup, George. "Ninth Annual Gallup Poll of the Public's Attitudes toward the Public Schools." *Phi Delta Kappan,* September 1977, pp. 33–47.

Good, Thomas, and Jere Brophy. *Looking in Classrooms.* New York: Harper & Row, 1973.

Honig, Alice. *Parent Involvement in Early Childhood Education.* Washington, D.C.: National Association for the Education of Young Children, 1975.

Horvat, John. *Focus on the Problems of Diffusion.* College Station, Texas: Innovative Resources, Inc., 1968.

National Advisory Council on Adult Education. *The Roles and Responsibilities of Adult Education within Parent/Early Childhood Education.* Washington, D.C., 1975.

Pickarts, Evelyn, and Jean Fargo. *Parent Education.* New York: Appleton-Century-Crofts, 1971.

PART THREE
Program Approaches and Applications

In this part, we will describe and tell how to implement parent involvement in five situations: the home, the school or center, a combination of school and home, parent education, and citizen/parent advising and policy making. To help you organize and analyze ways of involving parents in their children's education, we have developed a consistent way of looking at the basic characteristics of the major approaches. These characteristics are settings, goals, roles of parents and teachers, content, and methods. Our purpose is to help teachers look beyond parent activities to the underlying assumptions, goals, and limitations of those activities. Only then can school personnel and parents choose and develop the approaches best suited for a particular school community.

In the how-to portions of Chapters 8–11, we suggest a three-phase process of advance planning and preparation, implementation, and review to help make parent involvement successful. We apply the process to the different types and settings of involvement so you can see how to modify and adapt them to meet varying needs.

We assume that teachers will take an active leadership role in all these activities. The role of the modern teacher includes working with parents in many ways, and this section guides teachers as they assume that role.

7 Approaches to Parent Involvement

OVERVIEW

There are so many different ways of involving parents in their children's schooling that we must have a way to organize them, look at their similarities and differences, and analyze their basic approaches before we can discuss the specifics of implementing a given approach. In this chapter we will look at five characteristics of parent involvement programs: settings, goals, parent and teacher roles, content, and methods. We will use these characteristics to analyze some actual programs. By doing this, we hope to give you some tools to look beneath the surface activities of any program. The basic purposes and procedures of a program are more important than the particular film or discussion topic selected.

WAYS OF LOOKING AT PARENT INVOLVEMENT

Trying to figure out what parent involvement is, consolidating the many approaches to it, and identifying the similarities and differences in programs are like slicing a watermelon. Slicing it in half lengthwise is neat, clean, and attractive but hides much below the surface. Slicing crosswise reveals a different aspect of the fruit. Cutting the melon into bite-size wedges or balls makes it easier to eat and perhaps more attractive, but misses certain realities of a watermelon—seeds, rind, and underripe or overripe portions.

To avoid losing the knowledge and understanding of parent involvement that come from "slicing" only one way, we will present several ways of looking at programs and their implementation. In this way we can analyze existing approaches and look at the process of developing a parent program for a specific situation. Our discussion revolves around five questions about parent programs:

1. What are the settings?

2. What are the goals?

3. What are the roles of parents and teachers?

4. What is the content?

5. What methods are used?

Settings

Parent involvement can be carried out in one of three settings: school or center,[1] home, or a combination of the two. In a school setting, children are brought together in a classroom in a public school, parent-cooperative preschool, day care center, private nursery school, or parent-child development center. In some programs, parents come to stay and learn with the children. In other school-based programs, parents are not in the classroom, but attend periodic workshops or meetings, participate in social or educational activities for parents, or support the school by giving time and service.

In the home, a teacher or visitor works with the family in familiar surroundings. Families that have very young children or live a long distance from a center often choose a home-based program. Examples of such programs are Home Start, a home-based variation of Head Start, which was described in Chapter 1; the Portage Project for handicapped children and their families; and the Mother-Child Home Program, which is described later in this chapter.

A combination of the two settings, home and school, has some of the advantages of both. Children have an opportunity to develop socially by being with other children in a planned learning situation; in addition, their parents are taught how to be better parents. Some programs combine the two settings by linking a classroom and a home visitor program, sending instructional materials home from school with children, or conducting parent workshops while the children attend school.

In Chapters 8–10, we will describe specific programs in each of these settings, and tell how to plan, organize, and implement them. Let's look now at some of the reasons people choose a particular setting. These include the ages of their children; the location of the program; cost; and the relative importance attached to working with parents, children, or the entire family.

Ages of the Children   Society's age-related expectations for children, families, and schools influence the choices people make about the settings for parent involvement. We expect children over six years old to be in school most of the day and five-year-olds to be in kindergarten for at least a half day. Home-based programs are seldom even considered for these children unless they are severely handicapped or their families are quite isolated. On the other hand, children younger than three years are usually expected to be at home during the day, being cared for by their parents. Although this pattern is changing, the expectation is still that families will select home-based programs for children under three years old. Three- and four-year-old children who are in nursery schools or day care are likely to be involved in a center or combination program.

Location   People in rural and isolated areas frequently choose home-based programs. If families are spread out over great distances or isolated because of physical barriers such as mountains and lakes, the programs must quite logically go to them. Urban families often choose to have their children in a center so they have space and freedom to play and learn with other children their own age.

Cost   Home-based and center-based programs of comparable quality cost about the same. However, home-based programs that do not offer medical, psychological, and social services may be less expensive, especially if center-based facilities have to be rented and equipped. The home visitors in home-based programs are usually not professionally trained teachers, so their salaries are low, which helps to keep costs low. The cost of a combination center/home visitor program is higher than either of the two separately. However, other types of combination center/home programs, such as sending instructional materials home, can be implemented with little cost beyond that of the classroom itself.

Relative Importance of Working with Parents and Children   Families and program developers may have strong convictions about whether children, parents, or both should be the focus of an educational program. These convictions affect the choice of setting. Some parents, for example, may not want anyone coming to their homes but are eager to have their children go to school. Others may like the idea of home visits but want their children to be in school, too. Program developers may be convinced that they should work directly with children in a group setting, with outside parent involvement in addition to, rather than instead of, a children's program.

Goals

Another way to look at parent involvement programs is through their goals: What is supposed to happen as a result of the program? Of course, all programs want parents and children to have a better, happier life; they want to enhance understanding between home and school, parent and teacher; and they hope that society as a whole will benefit. If those lofty purposes seem remote from a bake sale, a parent conference, and a class on parliamentary procedure or toilet training, remember that our day-to-day experiences combine to make up such things as learning, enjoyment, understanding, and happiness.

Parent goals are also similar in their ultimate aim for children, which is to "produce intelligent, well-adjusted, academically successful children" (Goodson and Hess, 1975, p. 4). Most parents share this aim regardless of income level, culture, or place of residence.

Finally, program goals seek particular parental behaviors. Talking and playing with children, reading to them, listening and responding to them, understanding their needs, becoming involved in their education, providing healthful food, making sure children come to school rested, and attending school or center functions are specific examples of the general behavioral goals. We can group these goals into four general areas (Goodson and Hess, 1975):

1. To help parents be more effective teachers of their children.

2. To help parents understand and support the school's educational program.

3. To help parents be better parents and family members.

4. To help parents exert more control over their own and their children's lives.

Although these goals overlap, they are distinct enough to help us organize the different approaches to parent involvement.

To Help Parents Be More Effective Teachers of Their Children   Parents are children's first teachers. Under their parents' care, children learn the language that is spoken in the home and the social patterns of the home and immediate neighborhood; they learn who they are and how others perceive them; they begin to learn about and understand the world around them; and they develop patterns of living, talking, and seeking answers to problems. Parents need to be aware that they are doing this kind of teaching and know how important it is to children's development. They need to learn how to do it enjoyably, easily, and skillfully.

Fortunately, it is relatively easy to teach parents to talk with children about what they are doing, to name and describe food items, to count fingers and toes, and to give children a chance to explore the environment. Such behaviors are specific, concrete, and usually enjoyable for both parent and child. Even better, most parents are eager to learn. They can see the connection between what they are doing and school tasks, and their child's pleasure in learning is strong reinforcement. Since this goal is often directly related to school performance, teachers and schools usually support it. Parents can even learn how to be teachers by helping in the classroom as volunteers, mother or father helpers, or paid assistants.

To Help Parents Understand and Support the School's Educational Program   Many parents have little or no idea of what their children do in school or at a center. Children's reports are notoriously incomplete and inaccurate. Schools and homes have tried to establish communication and understanding in many ways, for example, back-to-school nights, newsletters, visiting days, and parent conferences. Interested and motivated parents become involved in supportive activities through the PTA, parent councils, booster clubs, and fund-raising drives.

Current efforts to help parents understand and support the school use all these traditional means, but also bring parents into the school as instructional assistants and volunteers in the regular school program. This type of parent involvement has been found in parent-cooperative nursery schools for a long time, as we discussed in Chapter 1, but is relatively new in public schools. An added benefit of parents working as school aides is that parents who have been involved in school activities are almost always understanding and supportive of the teacher and school activities.

To Help Parents Be Better Parents and Family Members   Being a family member and parent requires a wide range of knowledge and skill. Most of us receive little preparation for the enormity, difficulty, and persistence of these tasks. The goal of helping parents to be better parents and family members is much more comprehensive than helping parents to be teachers. It is also more difficult, more emotional, and more remote from traditional school concerns. It may involve basic conflicts between what seems best for the child and what the parents value. Cultural and local patterns of family life may resist change. Often the basic conditions for a stable, supportive family life are not within the school's power to supply—a steady job, health, a decent place to live, and something to live for. Yet many parents need to have these very basic life skills before they can do anything else to help their children. In some cases, help from several sources may be needed. The school, center, or home visitor may refer the parent to other people or institutions, such as public or private welfare services, marriage counselors, mental health clinics, financial advisors, and sources of basic education.

We sometimes associate the need for comprehensive parent and family education with low-income families. It is true that all the demands of family life are made more difficult by poverty; there is less money, less food, less space, and sometimes more children. Yet most families could benefit from some help in problem areas, particularly in child rearing. Few parents know how children grow and develop and what behavior is natural and to be expected. Even fewer know what they as parents can and should do to help their children grow and develop normally and happily. Support and some basic information give many parents the confidence they need.

Teachers and schools have always been involved in family life, if only through the child. Divorce, death, illness, hunger, unemployment, and family quarrels come to school with the children as surely as celebrations, vacations, nine hours of sleep, and a good breakfast. The goal of supporting parents in their family responsibilities recognizes this involvement.

To Help Parents Exert More Control over Their Own and Their Children's Lives   Parents who make or advise on school policy are trying to exert more control over their own and their children's experiences with school. We can list several reasons for having such a goal and for trying to reach it by involving parents in school decisions.

People act differently when they know that what they say and do has some effect. Many parents in our modern society feel powerless, particularly in dealing with today's schools and child care centers, which are often large, highly organized, and impersonal. Even the strongest parents are likely to feel like schoolchildren again as they enter; the timid seldom do. Perhaps if parents had more say about what goes on in schools, they would feel differently about them.

If parents have some control over school or center policy, the programs might better meet the needs of the children and the community. For example, the school might give more consideration to the different cultures in the community and thereby lessen the distance between school and home. If mothers and fathers see the school as responsive and interested in them and their children's welfare, they may become more supportive, with positive benefits to their children, themselves, and the schools.

Parents have always had a lot to say about educational policy in the United States. Lay (nonprofessional) school boards, school committees, and parent committees have either made or guided school policy since public school began, and of course parents have the final say in voting on taxes. However, this process has often been dominated by well-established, prominent people in the community. Since the 1960s there has been a systematic effort to involve poor and minority parents in the decision-making process.

The teacher's role in this approach to parent involvement makes many teachers uncomfortable. Their training has not prepared them for it. School boards, parent boards, policy, and politics seem remote from their primary interests. The division of authority between policy and implementation is often unclear. Teachers' unions may suspiciously regard lay boards and administrators as "management." Yet parents can be powerful allies of the school.

Parent and Teacher Roles

Parents and teachers take on different roles in different kinds of parent involvement. For example, a parent acting as a volunteer or paid aide in the classroom assumes the role of a teacher. A teacher or home visitor listening to a mother pour out her grief and resentment about a handicapped child assumes the role of friend and listener. Some excellent teachers are uncomfortable with parents in the classroom because they do not like the role of parent educator.

Basic to the roles of parents and teachers in parent involvement programs is the individual, the self. Each of us relates to other people in different ways. We assume a slightly different role with brothers and sisters than we do with our mothers and fathers. Our close friends know us in a role that is different from the one an employer or teacher sees. But there is always the basic "I" that remains the same. Personal strengths, needs, idiosyncrasies, motivations, and styles of living do not change much in different roles. In dealing with each other, parents and teachers tend to see roles rather than individuals. Little children express this well in their amazement when they see their teacher at the grocery store with spouse and children in tow. They can't quite believe that this is the same person they see in the classroom.

In times past, communities expected teachers always to play the role of "school marm" or "school master." They were to have no personal life at all. Parents are still somewhat surprised when they find that teachers have concerns and uncertainties, that they too need help and understanding. When teachers look beyond the parent role to the person who is filling it, they are less likely to expect the impossible, and more likely to respect and appreciate the whole person. This discussion of parent and teacher roles assumes that we look at individuals first and always.

We can understand parent and teacher roles best by using the four basic goal areas discussed earlier as reference points (see page 121). Figure 7.1 shows the relationship between them.

Figure 7.1
Relationship of Parent Goals to Parent and Teacher Roles

Goals for Parents	Roles of Parents	Roles of Teachers and Other School Personnel
Help parents to be more effective teachers of their children	Teachers of their children Learners from the teacher/parent educator	Teacher/parent educators Demonstrators Home visitors
Help parents understand and support the school's educational program	Home partners of the teacher and school Volunteers Paid aides or assistants and co-workers	School partners of the parent and home Leaders and facilitators Supervisors, instructors, and co-workers
Help parents be better parents and family members	Family members and parents Students and learners	Teacher/parent educators Group leaders Facilitators within the family or outside the family (referring family to other agencies)
Help parents exert more control over their own and their children's lives (by advising the schools)	Citizens and representatives Patrons of school or center Advisors and policy makers	Citizens Policy implementers Advisees

Parents as Teachers   In parent involvement programs that emphasize parents as teachers of their own children, parents assume the roles of teachers and learners. In this model, teachers assume the role of parent educators, helping parents learn some of the attitudes and skills essential for teaching.

Parents as Partners and Supportive Resources   Parents who are learning to understand and support the school's education program usually have one of three roles: home partners of the teacher and the school, volunteers, and paid aides or assistants.

As home partners of the teacher and the school, mothers and fathers are expected to make sure children are at school regularly and on time, attend parent conferences and meetings, share information and personal insights about their youngsters, and be interested in and supportive of their children's progress in school. As volunteers in support of the school, parents might be in the classroom as tutors and assistants, but more often they are volunteers outside the classroom. They may raise money, help make instructional materials or costumes for special programs, serve as officers or members of parent-teacher organizations, or supervise field trips. As paid aides or assistants, parents help in the classroom or throughout the school or center. They may be bus drivers, lunch room supervisors, cooks, or library aides.

To have parent partners in children's schooling, teachers must be partners, respecting parent ideas and concerns as well as sharing school triumphs and problems. When parents serve as paid assistants, school personnel become supervisors, instructors, and co-workers.

Parents as Better Parents and Family Members   In programs that emphasize the comprehensive family member goal, parents become students and learners. They learn about child development, nutrition, time and money management, and child guidance. Parents who participate in study and discussion groups have a different relationship to the group leader than most learners. They share experiences and problems they have had with their own children, and may use these as the beginning point for learning how to solve child-rearing problems. Parents also assume the role of guiding and supporting each other.

School personnel help with child and family life education by teaching, leading discussion groups, and referring parents to information or help.

Parents as Advisors and Policy Makers   Programs that involve parents as advisors and policy makers ask them to assume the roles of concerned citizens and representatives for their children and the larger community. The exact way in which these roles are carried out varies with the traditions, regulations, and delegated authority of the institution or agency involved. Parent councils in public schools may be primarily advisory, since state laws and regulations place the authority and responsibility for policy on elected boards of education, on which parents also serve.

Parent boards in an independent cooperative nursery school may make all policy decisions. Parent advisory councils in federally funded programs such as Head Start and Title I must follow guidelines in both federal and local rules and regulations.

Teachers and other school personnel have even more variable roles in their relationships to these advisory or policy boards. In large schools, they may have little or no direct contact; a parent coordinator or administrator may act as liaison. The teacher/director of a small school may work actively with the policy board and may even be a member.

Content

We can look at the content of parent involvement programs as the subject matter actually being learned. For example, parents might learn how to make toys and games and play them with their children.They might learn to organize and conduct their own meetings using the rules of parliamentary procedure. They might learn how to select books appropriate to their child's age level, set up a budget, or reinforce desired behavior. The content of parent involvement programs is closely linked to the goals of the program and the methods that are used, but there is more leeway than we might think.

Let's look at some examples of how content can be varied to meet the needs and interests of a particular parent or group of parents, yet still be linked to the goal of a given program. Suppose the general goal is to help parents be better parents; specifically, to be more sensitive to and understanding of the growing child's strengths, needs, limitations, and problems. What are some of the possibilities for content? Most obvious, of course, is child growth and development. Parents need to know that four-year-old children have difficulty taking anyone else's point of view; that it is normal for two- to three-year-old children to eat less than they did when they were younger; and that children in the second grade are usually able to think through certain problems in their heads.

But there are options. A teacher might start with "tender topics," those troublesome areas of human life that parents find so hard to discuss with their children: Why did Grandma die? Where do babies come from? How come Daddy doesn't live here anymore? Discussions of these questions help parents understand the children's points of view, fears, uncertainties, and strengths, and in the process foster an awareness of child development.

Parents can also discover more about their growing children by learning to understand and be sensitive to all people regardless of age, learning specific guidance and discipline techniques, or analyzing their own family relationships as they were growing up. Parents learning to be advisors and policy makers might study such things as group dynamics, organizational and parliamentary procedures, the history of effective lobbying, research and preparation of background material on an issue, organization and structure of schools and centers, and how to debate and decide on policy issues. Any one of these topics or processes could form the content of a parent involvement program to increase parent participation in decision making.

Just as content is linked to goals, it should be planned to be linked to outcomes. Parents who participate in making policy may or may not become better teachers of their children. Parents who learn to understand themselves and their developing child may acquire no skills in persuading the school board to retain or drop a particular program. The content of the parent involvement program determines much of what parents and teachers learn and should be thoughtfully selected to achieve the stated goals.

Methods

Methods refer to all the ways information and ideas are shared: such techniques as discussions, lectures, films, reading materials, demonstrations, workshops, on-the-job training, and role-playing.

Sometimes developers choose certain methods because of philosophical convictions about how people learn. A teacher who is convinced that people learn through experience and doing is unlikely to use lectures, films, and readings extensively. Sometimes, however, we use methods simply because they are known, familiar, and easy, not because they best suit the content and the people who are learning. All too often we use only a few—a talk and a discussion, a film and a discussion, parent conferences, or an open house—with the result that both parents and teachers become bored.

Some program leaders choose a particular method because it seems best suited to the attitudes, understandings, and behaviors they want parents to have with their children. Programs that want parents to use behavior modification techniques with their children usually give direct instruction in the principles of behavior modification, followed by careful practice in applying those principles with their own children. Programs that want parents to understand and ✓ have insight into their children's psychological development often discuss and share insights into their own feelings as well as their children's. Programs that use toys, books, and games to increase the quantity and quality of verbal and social interaction between parents and children often use methods that directly involve parents with the materials they will use with the children.

We do not have much evidence about which methods work best, although one study of parent involvement found that parents changed more if the training methods involved demonstrations, modeling of the desired behavior, and active participation, rather than simply telling parents what they should know and do (Lazar and Chapman, 1972).

Looking at parent involvement programs in a systematic way using the five characteristics of settings, goals, parent and teacher roles, content, and methods helps us organize and think about programs in broad terms, rather than trying to remember a multitude of variations. In the next section we examine examples of four approaches to parent involvement, looking for these characteristics.

EXAMPLES OF PARENT INVOLVEMENT PROGRAMS

The programs described below are representative of the various types of parent involvement. We have chosen a home visitor program, a parent-cooperative nursery school, a parent-child center, and a public school parent involvement program not because they are the best known or most effective programs, but because they have different settings, goals, degrees and types of parent involvement, and wide-ranging content, methods, and procedures.

The Mother-Child Home Program, Verbal Interaction Project

The Mother-Child Home Program, directed by Phyllis Levenstein, was a unique example of a home-based program. First field tested in 1967 with low-income families, the program offered a distinct, clearly structured approach to home visits. Every two weeks trained "toy demonstrators" visited participating homes for an average of half an hour. These volunteers or paid paraprofessionals demonstrated desired verbal and social interaction techniques through tasks structured around carefully selected books and educational toys. Verbal interaction stimulus materials (VISM) provided both the immediate and continuing stimulus for mother-child verbal interaction. The books and toys, which were given to the family, provided a focus and guide for the mother's efforts to teach her own child. Parents with children between two and three years of age, in the stage of rapid language development, were the initial target group. They participated in the program for two years.

Several elaborate and systematic evaluations of this program are available. They indicate that the Mother-Child Home Program was highly effective in raising general and verbal intelligence. Children with two full years of treatment retained IQ gains at least into first grade. Mothers were generally supportive of the program and reported improvement in the verbal and social interactions within the family. The stimulus materials (toys and books) without the training of the mothers did not produce the desired results.

Setting   The Mother-Child Home Program took place in homes and involved two- to five-year-old children and their mothers, with program emphasis gradually shifting to the mother.

Goals   Parents were to become better teachers of their own children by increasing concept-rich verbal interaction between parent and child. This interaction was to become an integral part of the mother-child relationship.

Parent and Teacher Roles   Parents were to be teachers of their own children and learners of more effective interaction patterns. Teachers were to be demonstrators, models, and colleagues of the mother.

Content   The content of the program consisted of the verbal, cognitive, social, and motivational techniques necessary to help parents teach their children. The specific content was the verbal interaction surrounding carefully selected books and educational toys that were given to the family. These materials were selected to promote perceptual-motor skills, imaginative play, problem solving, and social concepts as well as language and concept development.

Methods   Modeling and demonstrating the desired parent behaviors were the methods used by the toy demonstrators. Mothers were gradually drawn into the play sessions, which emphasized play and conversation focused on toys and books. Giving the toys and books to the family encouraged continuing home education of the child between visits and after the program was over. The toy demonstrators used social reinforcement to encourage both parents and children.

Parent-Cooperative Nursery Schools

Parent cooperatives are examples of center-based parent involvement programs in which parents make and advise on school policy. Parent cooperatives typically are started and continued by an interested group of parents who want their children to go to nursery school and who want to learn more about being parents. The parents elect representatives to the parent board. These representatives write a constitution and bylaws, and agree on general operating procedures. They hire the staff, locate a facility (often a church classroom), recruit children, and do all the organization. The teacher plans the educational program for the children, using mothers and fathers as assistants. The parents work on a rotating basis; their involvement as assistants supplements the relatively low tuition and teaches them about children in general and their own child in particular. Another component of the program is parent meetings, which usually focus on child-rearing or family problems of concern to a particular group of parents.

No formal evaluation of the effectiveness of these programs is available. Their widespread incidence and persistence are the only evidence that they seem to be meeting the needs of children and families, and that parent organized and operated groups are feasible.

Setting   Parent cooperatives involve both children and parents in a center-based program. The children are usually three, four, and five years old, although cooperative primary schools are occasionally operated by parents.

Goals   Parent cooperatives aim to increase parents' understanding of children's growth and development and to enhance their child guidance techniques. They also educate parents through having them serve on advisory and policy boards, which are often in complete control of the school.

Parent and Teacher Roles   Parents act as volunteer assistants in the classroom, learning how to teach young children and about their needs and behavior. Another parent role is that of student in group or individual meetings. The third parent role is in school governance, serving on the parent board or committee to make center policy.

The teacher acts as instructor, model, and supervisor of the volunteers; planner and leader of the parent meetings; and implementer of school policies. Sometimes the teacher is an active participant on the advisory and policy board.

Content   The content of the program is usually child guidance and interaction techniques, particularly relating to problems of the center and home life. Principles of child development, human development, and human relations are included in the information presented to parents. Parents learn how to organize and run programs that reflect their own values for their children.

Methods   Because of the many facets of parent involvement in these programs, several methods are used. The teacher in the classroom uses demonstration, modeling, direct instruction, and reinforcement. In parent meetings, the teacher may use films, lectures, discussions, and role-playing. In policy board meetings, parents set their own tasks, assign committees, research and debate issues, and come to a consensus on policy and procedures.

Birmingham Parent-Child Development Center

The founders of the Birmingham Parent-Child Development Center, Thomas Lasater and Paul Malone, worked out an elaborate and unique parent education program based on parent and child involvement in a child development center. Mothers and children progressed through a series of age-graded nurseries, staying together in the first one (Nursery I) from entrance (infants three-and-a-half to five months old) until the infant was six months old. Mother-child attachment and interaction were planned and encouraged. Nursery II, with children ages six to eighteen months, kept mothers with their children until the child was one year old, continuing to encourage normal attachment and interaction, including secondary attachments to the other mothers. Children from eighteen to thirty-six months old were in Nursery III with mothers other than their own. In the nurseries for the older children, the program stressed concept and language development, motor and perceptual development, and self-awareness.

Mothers also progressed through a definite sequence based on the age of their children and their own abilities and interests. The mothers decided if they wanted to assume positions of greater responsibility in the program. We will describe this sequence below in discussing the role of the mother; it is shown in Figure 7.2.

Figure 7.2
Relationship of Mother's Role to Age of Child and Her Own Interests

Role of Mother	Age of Child	Responsibilities and Learnings
Participating mother	3½–15 months	Adjusting to center, encouraging attachment and interaction, assuming responsibility.
Senior participating mother (15–25 months)	15–25 months	Learning about curriculum in nursery, child development principles, outside classes in home management, and interpersonal skills. Apprenticing to model mothers, helping in classroom.
Model mother I and II	12–36 months	Increasing responsibility in the nurseries and training other mothers; receiving stipend or pay. Attending classes to help her teach other mothers and to learn better home management and greater interpersonal skills.
Senior participating mother (30–36 months)	30–36 months	Teaching other mothers, often specializing in one aspect of the center program, such as health education or health care.

The division of the mothers' time (60 percent on learning to teach their own children and 40 percent on personal growth) and the sequences of responsibilities and expectations are indicative of the Birmingham Center's stress on helping mothers to grow as persons and family members as well as mothers and teachers.

The available information on program results is positive in that mothers and children appeared to be moving in the direction of stated goals.

Setting   The Birmingham Center brought parents and very young children into a center-based program.

Goals   The program attempted a comprehensive upgrading of the mothers' abilities as teachers, parents, homemakers, and family members. It expected mothers to acquire increased appreciation of the mothering role, increased ability to encourage children's growth and development, and better home management skills. Personal and interpersonal goals for the mothers included increasing their self-esteem, increasing their ability to cope with outside demands, and improving their interactions with other adults.

Parent and Teacher Roles   The mothers' roles varied as they progressed through the several levels of this complex program. A "participating mother" learned how to work with her own child and the other adults in the center. A "senior participating mother" apprenticed to a "model mother," learning on the job the many skills involved in running the nurseries in the center. "Model mothers" were both teachers and learners. They taught groups of mothers and mother-child pairs, managed the classroom, and continued to learn both in the center and in outside classes.

Content   The content of the parent component included child development, nursery school curriculum, child care and guidance, homemaking information classes, and personal development classes, as well as much social learning from each other.

Methods   The parent-child center used informal, nondidactic approaches such as demonstrations, guided interactions, simple written materials, films, and group discussions.

Project Early Push

The public schools of Buffalo, New York, began Project Early Push in 1966 to help children and families with educational needs. Three- and four-year-old children participated in a half-day center program that was carefully planned to develop children's physical, social, emotional, cognitive, and communication competence. Parents were involved in almost every aspect of the program. Parents maintained records of their own participation in a workbook that included observation guides, parent tasks, outlines for parent/teacher conferences, and a system for tracking their use of the book and toy lending library. The program received federal grants to help other school districts replicate its approach.

This program was typical of many well-organized, responsive, goal-oriented nursery schools for children, with parents involved as partners and supporting resources of the school. It had the type of parental involvement likely to occur in many public school preprimary and primary programs. It was distinctive in the wide variety of approaches used to obtain that support.

Results indicate that the program was successful in improving children's readiness for school and their cognitive development. High parent participation, particularly in the toy and book lending library, was associated with high gains for children. The program also increased parent participation in the classroom, PTA, parent-teacher conferences, and other activities designed for parents.

Setting   The Early Push program brought three- and four-year-old children to classrooms in the Buffalo public schools. Some parents came to the center, while others participated in their homes and the community in a wide variety of ways.

Goals   The program tried to increase communication and understanding between home and school. Parents were to become more supportive of their children's work in school and of the school as a whole, and to participate in the educational system. The program also helped parents become better teachers both at home and in school.

Parent and Teacher Roles   One of the strengths of the Early Push program was the variety of roles available for parents. Parents acted as partners with the school, participating, sharing information, attending parent conferences and workshops, working with their children at home, and contributing to the Parent Corner and to "Parent News," a monthly newsletter. A parent council acted as an advisory body. Parents were also volunteers in and out of the classroom. Teachers and other school personnel assumed the roles of partners, leaders, and resource people.

Content   The content of the program for parents included information on child development, teaching techniques, activities at school and in the community, and their own child's development and progress in the program. In addition, some content was based on parent suggestions and requests.

Methods   The Early Push program used a wide variety of methods to meet the needs and interests of its varied parent population. These included parent-teacher conferences; classroom participation; workshops; discussions following teacher demonstrations, slides, film strips, movies, or other stimulus materials; a toy and book lending library; a monthly newsletter; a center "corner" to share information; and discussion and involvement in the parent council.

SUMMARY

In this chapter we set forth a systematic way of looking at five aspects of parent involvement programs: settings, goals, parent and teacher roles, content or subject matter, and methods. We related the setting—home, school, or a combination of home and school—to the ages of the children involved, the geographic location of the program, cost, and the relative importance attached to working with parents, children, or both.

We grouped goals and roles into four broad, related areas:

- To help parents be more effective teachers of their own children (parent role: teacher).

- To help parents understand and support the school's educational program (parent roles: home partner, volunteer, paid assistant, supportive resource).

- To help parents be better parents and family members (parent role: better parent).

- To help parents exert more control over their own and their children's lives (parent roles: school advisor, policy maker).

We then discussed curriculum content and the methods used to achieve these goals.

The five aspects of involvement programs were used to study four actual parent programs—a home visiting program, a parent-cooperative nursery school, a parent-child center, and a public school program.

FOR DISCUSSION AND FURTHER STUDY

1. Locate a parent involvement program in your community and analyze it using the five key questions suggested in this chapter.

2. What are some advantages to having many types of parent involvement? What are some disadvantages?

3. Pretend that you are a parent with a young child and you have an opportunity to participate in one of the four models we described—the Mother-Child Home Program, a parent cooperative, the Birmingham Parent-Child Center, or Project Early Push. Which would you choose? In small groups, share and discuss with your fellow students the choice you made.

4. Now pretend you are a young child. Which program would you prefer? Why?

5. Do you think the present types of parent involvement programs meet the needs of many of today's parents, such as working parents, solo parents, and parents who have remarried and have two sets of children? If not, how could these programs be modified or new programs developed to meet those needs?

BIBLIOGRAPHY

Auerbach, Aline B. *Parents Learn through Discussion: Principles and Practices of Parent Group Education.* New York: Wiley, 1968.

Becker, Wesley C, and Janis W. Becker. *Successful Parenthood.* Chicago: Follett, 1974.

Birmingham Parent-Child Development Center. *Birmingham Parent-Child Development Center Progress Report.* Birmingham, Ala., 1974.

Dreikurs, Rudolph, and L. Grey. *Parent Guide to Child Discipline.* New York: Hawthorn Books, 1970.

Ginott, Haim G. *Between Parent & Child.* Riverside, N.J.: Macmillan, 1965.

Goodson, Barbara D., and Robert D. Hess. *Parents as Teachers of Young Children: An Evaluative Review of Some Contemporary Concepts and Programs.* Stanford, Calif.: Stanford University Press, 1975.

Gordon, Ira J. *Baby Learning through Baby Play: A Parent's Guide for the First Two Years.* New York: St. Martin's, 1970.

Gordon, Ira J., B. Guignagh, and R. E. Jester. *Child Learning through Child Play: Learning Activities for Two- and Three-Year-Olds.* New York: St. Martin's, 1972.

Gordon, Ira J., Michael Hanes, Linda Lamme, Patricia Schlenker, and Harvey Barnett. *Research Report of Parent Oriented Home Based Early Childhood Education Program.* Gainesville: Institute for Development of Human Resources, University of Florida, 1975.

Gray, Susan W. *Home Visiting Programs for Parents of Young Children.* Nashville, Tenn.: George Peabody College for Teachers, 1971.

Lazar, Joyce B. and Judith E. Chapman. *A Review of the Present Status and Future Research Needs of Programs to Develop Parenting Skills.* Washington, D.C.: George Washington University, 1972.

Levenstein, Phyllis. "Learning through (and from) Mothers." *Childhood Education* 48 (December 1971): 130–34.

Levenstein, Phyllis. *Verbal Interaction Project: Aiding Cognitive Growth in Disadvantaged Preschoolers through the Mother-Child Home Program.* New York: Family Service Association of Nassau County, February 1971.

Lillie, David L., and Pascal L. Trohanis. *Teaching Parents to Teach.* New York: Walker and Co., 1976.

Office of Child Development. *Head Start Program Performance Standards.* Washington, D.C.: U.S. Department of Health, Education, and Welfare, July 1975 (OCD notice N-30-364-4).

Parent Education and Preschool Department. *Student Aide Handbook.* Denver: Denver Public Schools, n.d.

Project Early Push. *Project Early Push: Preschool Program in Compensatory Education.* Buffalo, N.Y.: American Institute for Research in Behavioral Sciences, 1969.

U.S. Office of Education. *Educational Programs That Work.* San Francisco: Far West Laboratory for Educational Research and Development, 1976.

NOTE

[1] The terms *school* and *center* are used interchangeably to indicate a group setting for children.

8 Home-Based Parent Involvement Programs

Home intervention was begun in the 1960s to see whether education in the home would help children from low-income families make and sustain educational gains. Susan Gray (1971, p. 106) describes the way home visiting came about in the Nashville Early Training Project.

We provided for the children with whom we were working, an intensive program for ten weeks during the summer. This program was planned to extend through three summers beginning at age 3½. Because we were well aware that much forgetting could take place when the child was sent back for 9½ months to the limited environment from which he came, we planned a bridge from one summer to the next. We met with the children once a month on Saturday mornings; we sent monthly newsletters to the parents. Our most important step, however, was the introduction of a home visiting program. In this endeavor, a skilled individual, with preschool and social-work training, met in the home with each mother for approximately an hour a week. She brought materials, and showed the mother how to use them effectively with the child.

Other programs tested the feasibility of home-based programs in other settings, expanded the concept, and evaluated various approaches. As a result, programs began to concentrate more on parents and families than on children alone, and this emphasis has become one of the big advantages of a home-based program.

In this chapter we will first describe a home-based program in terms of the setting, goals, parent and teacher roles, content, and method. To help you weigh the merits of a home-based program as opposed to other settings and approaches, we will discuss its advantages and disadvantages.

The second part of the chapter will explain how to implement a home visit program. The process takes place in three phases: advance planning and preparation, implementation, and review. Each of these phases has several steps. Because of the unique nature of a home-based program, we will spend some time describing the home visit, and include a section on educational activities for home-based programs.

We will use the organization outlined in this chapter whenever possible in the chapters that follow, departing from it only when the nature of the program dictates. We believe this consistent approach will help you learn about and understand the many ways of involving parents in their children's learning.

HOME VISIT PROGRAMS: A DESCRIPTION

A Look at One Program

Gayle Timons was reflecting on the seven months she had been in charge of Lawson County's Home Teaching Program. It began last July, when the school district designated that money from a federal grant and local funds should be used for a home teaching approach. Now, in her role as combination home teacher and supervisor of paraprofessional home visitors, Gayle was driving to her first home appointment of the day—the Murphy family.

Gayle had thought a long time before she made the move from classroom kindergarten teacher to this new position. After all, she had been trained to be a classroom teacher, not a home teacher. Since the program was new, everyone was unsure about whether or not families would even let a school representative into their homes, even though they indicated strong support and interest as the program proposal was being written. Gayle had been particularly uneasy about the responsibility of organizing and supervising the entire program, which included three paraprofessional home visitors.

But Gayle was intrigued with the idea of being able to work with families, to reach the younger brothers and sisters of children she had seen come to kindergarten so inadequately prepared for school work. She knew from her own experience that the families and the children could benefit. The school district's federal projects supervisor clinched her decision by showing her the wealth of printed material available for guidance. Most of it was the result of large federal research and development projects—the Appalachia Educational Laboratory's *Home Visitor's Handbook*; a resource book entitled *Home Visitor's Kit* (Gotts, 1977); *Building Effective Home-School Relations* (Gordon and Breivogel, 1976); *The Portage Guide to Home Teaching* (1975); a whole stack of materials on planning and operating home-based child development programs from the national office of the Administration for Children, Youth, and Families; a textbook entitled *Parents and Teachers: A Resource Book for Home, School, and Community Relations* (Croft, 1979); and many shorter guides and pamphlets.

From these guides, sample forms, training suggestions, and her own experience and knowledge of the rural area in which she lived, Gayle got the program under way. Working with three sensitive, conscientious paraprofessional home visitors, she had been able to involve all but five of the target families in the program—but it hadn't been easy!

Gayle turned into the Murphy's gate. On the seat beside her was a basket of home learning activities, including carefully selected, simple toys and books that she would encourage Mrs. Murphy and Michael to play with and talk about. Her goals were realistic and attainable. She wanted Michael to sort the interesting toys in several different ways and tell *why* he sorted them that way. She wanted Mrs. Murphy to give Michael specific directions, supply descriptive words when Michael needed them, and find other things around the house that Michael could sort. The books were a follow-up to last week's activities that were designed to encourage and help Mrs. Murphy read to Michael. They were also preparation for a field trip to the county library's bookmobiles for *all* parents and children in the program.

Gayle felt again the uneasy mixture of anticipation and apprehension that came with every home visit. Would they be home or would Mrs. Murphy have "forgotten"? Would Michael be interested in the toys and books she had brought? Would she be able to help Mrs. Murphy take on more of the role of parent-teacher this time? Gayle knew she had to fight the tendency to teach Michael directly instead of also teaching Mrs. Murphy.

Would the leaflet on buying and preparing food for nutritious meals help Mrs. Murphy get away from the "junk food" diet that she, Michael, and the younger children lived on? Maybe they could turn preparing a simple dish into a learning experience to help teach nutrition as well as language and concepts.

Apprehension and reflection were forgotten for the moment. Michael was standing in the door watching for her car, and he ran to get his mom as Gayle drove up.

Distinguishing Characteristics

Setting If a family has children younger than school age who are not enrolled in a nursery school or day care center, they might be involved in an educational program that takes place exclusively in the home. In such programs, parents may or may not get together for occasional meetings.

Goals Home-based programs emphasize two of the four goals discussed in Chapter 7: to help parents be better parents and family members and to help them be better teachers of their own children. Gordon et al. (1975) group these goals into three categories: (1) improving parent skills in teaching the child, (2) improving parent responsiveness and sensitivity to the child, and (3) improving the home environment, with special emphasis on the child's health and nutrition.

Since we cannot know which parenting practices are "best," most programs combine local preferences and needs with research findings, established and approved practices, the experience of other programs, and the implications of one or more theoretical orientations to arrive at specific parenting goals. Goals are often stated quite broadly, such as fostering in the child a "sound value system," or helping the parent take an "active role in promoting the welfare of the family" (Karnes and Zehrbach, 1977, p. 78). Goals that help parents be better teachers may be stated more specifically, such as: "manages discipline without scolding . . . ; (gives) positive reinforcement of desirable activities . . . ; gives information; converses wih child" (Levenstein, 1977, p. 36).

Sometimes programs state goals for the parent-child system, for the emotional, social, and verbal interaction between mother and child. These goals emphasize that the mother and child are not to be considered separately, but together. Goals such as helping the mother be sensitive to her own child's needs and adapting activities to the child emphasize the importance of parent and child working together.

Parent and Teacher Roles   Parents and teachers involved in home-based early childhood education have different roles and responsibilities from those in classrooms. In addition to their roles as family members and parents, parents are expected to be learners. They learn how to use household items and activities to teach their children, how to talk with children to help them understand the world around them, and other teaching behaviors. They also learn how to be better home managers, more knowledgeable consumers, and more active family and community members.

Teachers take on the role of parent educators, either directly through actually conducting home visits, or indirectly through training another person to be a home visitor.

Typically, a home visitor or home teacher—almost always a woman—comes to the home once a week, brings a variety of activities for parent and child, discusses and demonstrates their use, and listens and responds to parent concerns. If necessary, she refers the family to other community resources or services, such as a medical or dental clinic or a place to get information on raising food or securing other needs. During the course of a week, the home visitor will work with ten or twelve families, follow up on the referrals she made, attend training and staff meetings, prepare for and report on home visits, and perhaps attend a group parent meeting. She will learn to know the families she works with better than any classroom teacher ever does.

Content   The exact content of home visiting programs is quite varied, but in most programs there are three types: content to build rapport and trust between the mother and the home visitor, content to improve home management and family life, and content to improve mother-child interaction and teaching. Home visitors usually set aside a short time for greetings, informal conversation, and discussion of whatever is on the mother's mind in order to establish a rapport and trust. Content to improve home management and family life is selected to meet a particular family's need, and may include information on such things as food selection, preparation, and storage; home health and safety; and finances. Content to improve mother-child interaction and teaching usually focuses on teaching behaviors using informal situations that arise daily in the home, such as cooking, eating, cleaning, and shopping, plus some structured school-like activities that the home visitor brings, demonstrates, and encourages the mother to do with her child.

Figure 8.1 illustrates the content of home activities in the Home Start program. Note that time was divided about evenly between parent and child and between education and other family and child concerns.

These figures indicate only the way time *was actually* spent, *not* the way it

Figure 8.1
Focus of Home Visit Activities in Home Start (National
Home Start Evaluation, adapted from the Administration for
Children, Youth, and Families, formerly the Office of Child
Development)

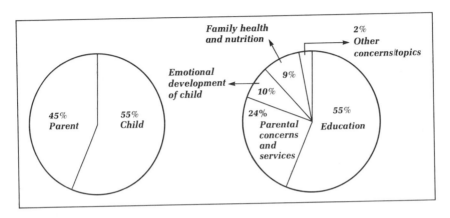

necessarily should be spent. Programs with different goals might well have home teachers spend their visiting time in different ways. For example, if the home is quite disorganized, initial home visits might concentrate on helping the mother bring some order and organization into her life and the home (Gray, 1971). Behavior modification is used in some programs, particularly those that work with handicapped children. In these cases the content consists of behavior modification and precision teaching principles, including how to specify a desired child behavior; do a task analysis to specify the teaching steps; and teach, tally, and reinforce the desired behaviors (Shearer, 1976). The best-known example of this approach is the Portage Project, funded by the Bureau of Education for the Handicapped, and developed at Portage, Wisconsin, for handicapped children and their parents.

Method Home-based programs use one primary method—a home visit by a parent educator, home teacher, or home visitor (these titles are interchangeable). The home teacher or home visitor teaches more by example, demonstration, and involvement than by direct instruction. Like all good teachers, she is tuned to the learners—sensitive to their responses and feelings and encouraging them to contribute their own ideas and skills and become independent learners. The families she works with often have special needs, so she must be able to individualize what she does. She may not work with the parent at all, but with the grandparent, baby-sitter, or older brother and sister. She may work not with a mother and one child, but with a mother and several children. Many home visitor programs deliberately place "complete responsibility for the selection of activities, sequencing, and their style of delivery upon the home visitor" (Gordon et al., 1975, pp. II–6).

Advantages and Disadvantages

Advantages   Home-based programs implemented through home visitors have four advantages over other types of parent involvement programs: (1) the school reaches out to the home, (2) parents are likely to participate, (3) the program can be individualized to each family, and (4) the program benefits all family members.

In home-based programs, the school reaches out to the parent and family, rather than requiring the parent to come to the school. The school seeks out those families that can benefit from home visits and, in most cases, successfully maintains their involvement. The school can do this even when distance or inaccessibility might prohibit other types of programs.

Because of this outreach, parental participation is more likely. If a parent cancels, the home visitor just reschedules the appointment. Not every family will participate even then, but a persistent and persuasive home visitor can involve almost every family.

Home visiting programs are individualized to meet the needs of each mother, child, and family in a way that a group program never can. Each separate home visit has activities and materials selected specifically for that family.

There are likely to be benefits for all family members. Improved nutrition, health, and home management practices benefit everyone. One of the early experimental home visit programs found that the younger brothers and sisters of the target child also showed improvement in IQ scores (Gray, 1971). This "vertical diffusion" may be evidence of a more pervasive change in the mother and family.

Disadvantages   Home-based programs have these disadvantages: (1) the difficulty of supervising and training visitors, (2) the undeveloped state of materials and procedures to use, and (3) the questionable appropriateness of these programs for all families.

Paraprofessional home visitors need extensive training and supervision. Unlike classroom aides, who receive on-the-job training and supervision working in the classroom with a teacher, home visitors are on their own much of the time. They have to learn how to teach both parents and children; plan, prepare, and organize materials and time; keep records; and a host of other things before they can begin. Because home visitors spend much time in the field, supervision is more difficult than in center-based programs, but it is even more essential. Real problems can arise unless everyone knows from the beginning of the program what the supervision will consist of, who will do it, and how it will take place. Because home visitors work on their own so much of the time, they need encouragement, support, and a sustained exchange of ideas and information as part of regular supervision and training.

The materials and procedures for home-based programs have all been developed since the mid-1960s, so there are still some basic problems. We can identify two recurring criticisms: (1) many programs tend to teach the child rather than the parent, and (2) materials and procedures used in homes are too much like group nursery school activities. Programs can overcome these problems by careful training and supervision and by thoughtful selection of activities. Suggestions for home activities are given at the end of this chapter.

Home-based programs may not be appropriate for all families. The experience and research to date have been concerned with families and children that have special needs such as low incomes and educational problems. Programs have worked with the parent and family on whatever is needed to make a supportive home environment for the child. Few programs have experience and information on whether this high level of support is appropriate or can be modified for families that do not need this sustained and intensive contact to help them with child-rearing and family problems.

In addition, home-based programs may not be able to meet some needs specific to the very families they were designed to serve, for example, social and nutritional needs. Since home-based programs are often located in rural and isolated areas, the family's need for social contact with other families may not be met. Some programs have followed the example of the Appalachia Educational Laboratory's Home Oriented Preschool Education (HOPE) program and moved a mobile nursery school classroom from one area to another, giving children a chance to play and learn together at regular intervals. Most home-based programs also have periodic parent meetings and social events. Center-based programs for low-income families almost always serve a meal and a snack. Home-based programs are unable to do this and must rely on the family to provide all the child's nutritional needs.

HOME VISIT PROGRAMS: A GUIDE FOR IMPLEMENTATION

In Part Two, we outlined five general steps in planning parent involvement: identifying needs, selecting goals, developing objectives, planning activities, and evaluating. These steps are a preliminary phase we call advance planning and preparation. We will now add two more phases: implementation and review.

Implementation is the phase that actually puts the plans into action. It involves recruiting participants, orienting them to the program and its expectations, and getting started. Review is the phase that looks at how the program is progressing. The actions and feelings of the people involved as well as the program itself are monitored so that necessary modifications can be made. It involves reflection on and review of what is going on, recognition of people's contributions, sharing of information, and formal evaluation if one is planned.

These three phases and the steps within them are not discrete, nor do they necessarily follow each other in a linear sequence. For example, recognition of parents' contributions is discussed in the review phase because most formal recognition occurs near the end of the program. However, informal recognition of parents' contributions should occur throughout the program.

In this chapter and the ones that follow, we will elaborate on each of the steps in these phases as they apply to the specific approach to parent involvement under consideration. If, in reading, it seems as if you have been through a certain step before, you are probably correct. However, our purpose is to show

how the same basic processes are used and varied to fit different approaches. Where no variation is necessary for a given approach, we will indicate that and proceed to the next step.

Advance Planning and Preparation

Many of the problems that arise in home-based programs can be avoided (or at least lessened) by thorough advance planning. Assess parent and community needs to determine if the home delivery is actually what parents want. Involve parents early and throughout the planning stages to avoid misunderstandings, anticipate problems, and keep the program close to the families it will serve. All parents do not have to be involved in this process, but representatives can alert planners to what is on parents' minds.

A year or two is a short amount of time. You will not be able to do everything to benefit both families and children, so set reasonable, attainable goals and objectives. Because a home-based program is individualized for each family, you can set objectives separately for each family, or even for each child. If you are implementing a behaviorally oriented approach, you are likely to state objectives quite precisely, as in these examples taken from *The Portage Guide to Home Teaching* (1975, p. 107): "Mother will tell Jill which of two like objects is big and which is little, five minutes each day, minimum." Even objectives that are somewhat more broadly stated, such as "Someone in the family will read to the child regularly (at least three times a week)," should be specific enough to put into action and have some chance of being reached.

In planning evaluation strategies, there are several choices, depending upon the program emphasis. You may want to use either standardized or criterion-referenced child assessment measures. Home environment and mother-child interaction scales are also available (Gordon et al., 1975). If objectives for parents lend themselves to it, you can develop checklists or observation forms to follow parents' as well as children's progress. You should also simply track the progress of the program. Careful record keeping from the beginning of home visiting will show how many home visits were scheduled and how many were kept; how many books, toys, and other instructional materials went to the homes; how many parents obtained library cards; how many parents purchased or made educational materials; and how many parents dropped out and why.

Begin preparing for the actual operation of the program. In the Bibliography of this chapter, we list several guides that give detailed information on training and supervising home visitors, record-keeping procedures, activities, and helpful hints. One or more of these guides will supplement the suggestions in this chapter.

Training is geared to the needs of the home visitors, of course, but should include training in professional ethics, teaching children and adults, selecting and using instructional activities for the home, and keeping records. Home teachers must maintain the same professional standards as classroom teachers. The confidentiality of teacher-family communications must be even more rigidly maintained when teachers go to homes.

Implementation

Recruiting   Sometimes home-based programs have a family population identified when the program begins. For example, you might focus on the preschool children in specific families identified because the older children are in remedial reading classes. If not, you will need to go through a recruitment process. Because the families you want to reach may not be easily identified through normal channels such as school, church, and community announcements, talk to county or regional public health nurses, doctors, school personnel, and social workers. In addition, you will probably need to go out into the community for some door-to-door identification of families you may have heard about from other sources. Plan to make personal calls to explain the program fully to each family, preferably to both parents if possible. Leave written information giving a brief, but complete, explanation of the program: who sponsors it, its length, benefits, responsibilities, and obligations. Give the families time to think about and discuss their participation before expecting a decision. You may have to go back several times.

Orientation   You can orient parents to the program either individually or in a group meeting. Make sure parents understand what will be expected of them and their children. Most programs, for example, expect parents to do the following.

1. Be present during the home visits.
2. Participate with their child and the home visitor.
3. Do the suggested activities with their children during the week.
4. Turn off the television set during the visit.
5. Take reasonable care of instructional materials left in the home.
6. Save household discards and natural materials to use for teaching.
7. Attend parent meetings.

If you plan to use any evaluation procedures other than record keeping, tell parents what those procedures will be and the purpose.

Demonstrate some of the activities and procedures that you will use in the program, and then role-play (with another home visitor) a shortened version of a home visit. Allow plenty of time for questions and discussion and make sure that everyone is clear about home visit appointment times.

Getting Started: The Home Visit   Home visits usually involve a mother, a child or two, and the home teacher working together for an hour and a half once a week. The home teacher works with the child part of the time, the mother part of the time, and both of them together part of the time. During the home visit, the teacher may help a child decide which books he wants to keep for the next week, discuss the procedure for getting immunizations from the public health clinic, try out healthful substitutes for soda pop, or practice positive discipline techniques. On another day, the entire visit may consist of a trip to the local library or bookmobile to get acquainted, get a library card, and learn how to check out books.

The home visitor plans the visit, considering all the information she has about the child, the parent and available program, home, and community resources. She puts the plan in writing so that important materials and processes will not be forgotten. A sample planning guide is given in Figure 8.2.

The home visitor or the program may establish some sort of routine or framework for the visit. For example, the visit might start with an opener or ice-breaker to put everyone at ease and begin to focus on the day's activities, progress to activities for all participants, something for the parent alone, a time for sharing concerns, and end with a review of what was done and the plan for the coming week.

An ice-breaker will help ensure a welcome and quick lead-in to the day's activities. It might be a favorite finger play or song, a book to read together, or a "child charmer." Child charmers are the little games with which parents and grandparents have amused and enchanted children through the years; examples are given on pages 157–159.

The activities for mother, children, and home visitor help the home visitor show the mother and children how to work and talk together while they are engaged in a task. For example, they may read and discuss a book together, with the home visitor helping the mother ask questions to get the child talking. They may make play-dough, with the home visitor modeling a way to talk with the youngster to help focus her attention on the measuring, mixing, and changing that is going on. During this time, both adults may practice positive guidance techniques to deal with some persistent discipline problems in the home.

Activities for the mother alone may include arrangements for getting to an immunization clinic at a nearby school, discussion of the parents' meeting next week, and explanation of a short booklet on child guidance that the home visitor has brought. The booklet may lead to a discussion of the mother's concern about guiding and helping her active children "mind."

The end of every home visit should be a quick review of what the parent and child are going to work on during the week—arrived at by joint agreement between home visitor and parent—and a look ahead to next week.

The order of these parts of the home visit can be varied; for example, the home visitor may prefer to begin by talking with the mother alone, then involve the child. But the same elements appear to be basic to a successful home visit.

The home visit is completed when the visitor cleans and checks back in toys, books, and materials from the resource library. She then makes two kinds of reports. The first covers the home visit itself: who was there, what materials were taken, evidence of progress of both parent and child, and notes about what should be planned for the next visit. A sample is given in Figure 8.3. The other is a time and mileage report.

Figure 8.2

```
                        HOME VISIT PLANNING GUIDE


                                          Family_____
                                          Date_____
                                          Home visitor_____

General goals
   Parent:

   Child:

Specific objectives
   Parent:

   Child:

Opener:

Discuss week's accomplishments:


Child/Parent/Visitor time:


   Points to emphasize:


Parent/Visitor time:


Planning for next week:


Conclusion:



                              REMINDERS

Materials needed:


Notes:
```

Figure 8.3
(*Administration for Children,
Youth, and Families, 1974*)

HOME VISIT REPORT

Date of visit_____

Home visitor_____ Time_____ to_____
Other children's
Name (child) _____ Age_____ Ages_____

1. Materials taken:_____

   _____

   _____
   (Starred materials left in the home for the week.)

2. Objectives/plans for this visit:

   _____

   _____

   _____

3. People present during visit:_____

   _____

4. Factors affecting accomplishment of the plans/objectives:_____

   _____

5. Progress made:_____

   _____

6. Problems identified:_____

   _____

7. Objectives/plans to be included for next visit:_____

   _____

   _____

   _____

(If more space is needed, continue on other side. Be sure to identify
continuations by item numbers.)

Review

The review phase consists of monitoring the program's operations, recognizing the contributions of parent participants, conducting formal and informal evaluations, and sharing information.

Monitoring   Weekly staff meetings, frequent review of all records, control of time and mileage, and open discussion of problems are ways of monitoring the program. Programs that have several home visitors sometimes pair them up so they can help each other improve. The supervising teacher should also accompany home visitors periodically. Cancelled or forgotten appointments, sketchy plans, short visits, or overuse of a few activities may indicate problems. Sometimes a home visitor makes parents dependent on her, rather than teaching them how to be independent. This will often show up in records or discussion. Careful monitoring will enable the program to maintain its focus.

Recognizing Parents' Contributions   Praise parents' progress in every visit. If they contribute an idea or material, make sure their names are on it. In addition, acknowledge parents' contributions in group parent meetings, thank-you letters, and newsletters.

Evaluating the Program   Collect the evaluation information the program decided on during the planning period. Compile and study it to see what progress you made, what the problems were, and how to do better next year. In addition, ask parents what they thought about the program: what they liked and what they would like to have done differently another time. Along with some good suggestions for improvement, you will probably get lots of encouragement from parents.

Sharing Information   Share information collected about the program, its effectiveness, and the parents' response with people who are interested and need to know, such as the director, principal, superintendent, school boards, parent boards, and, of course, the parents themselves. Select items that will be interesting and will show progress toward meeting the goals of the program. A feature story in the local newspaper or school newsletter can let the larger community know what has been going on, and stimulate interest and support for the coming year.

EDUCATIONAL ACTIVITIES FOR HOME-BASED PROGRAMS

Home visitors take books, toys, games, crayons, scissors, paper, and a wide variety of other materials to each home. Some are given to the family to keep, some are consumed, and others are loaned on a rotating basis. Much of the educational program for both children and parents revolves around these curriculum materials, which home visitors use to foster both child and parent development. Ideally, the activities encourage the child to grow physically, socially, emotionally, and intellectually, as well as encourage the desired parent-child relationships. That is a lot to ask of an activity. Of course, it is not the toy, book, or game that does this, but rather talking about it, playing with it, enjoying the activity, and being together.

Parents and children may need to learn how to take care of books, toys, and other materials. A sturdy cardboard box, a special shelf, containers from ice cream stores, and drawstring bags made from drapery and upholstery remnants will all help. Personalize these by adding the child's and parent's names. Help parents establish reasonable rules about where crayons are used, how books are handled, and sharing the responsibility for clean-up. Teaching children to value and care for learning materials is a desired parent behavior and one that must be brought about early if the program is to work.

Purchased or collected material should be safe, durable, have more than one use, and be appropriate for the child's age and developmental level. Since they will be going into a number of homes, toys and equipment will last longer if they have few parts that will get lost and parts that can be easily replaced and can still be used if some of the pieces are gone. Beads, small blocks, and pegboards and pegs are toys that meet the last two criteria.

Almost all programs have some type of curriculum guide, activities file, worksheet file, or other resource for home teachers and families to use. In Phyllis Levenstein's Mother-Child Home Program (1971), the carefully selected toys and books, called verbal interaction stimulus materials (VISM), were the stimuli for the verbal and social interaction between mother and child.

Other curriculum guides simply bring together many activities from which home visitors can choose. Usually these are organized around concepts, skills, and curriculum areas for the children, such as sizes and shapes of things, how many and how much, music, art, or health activities. After formal and informal assessment of the children, activities are selected and organized to meet each child's needs. Some of the Home Start demonstration projects used weekly or monthly themes, topics, or units, such as All About Me, which had subthemes of My Home, Getting to Know My Family, The Five Senses, and The Community (Grogan et al., 1976). These themes integrated social, emotional, intellectual, health, and nutrition studies. Home visitors could vary some of the specific activities for each home, but were expected to stay with the theme.

Ideally, of course, each home visitor assesses family needs and develops activities and plans specifically for that family. In actuality, some kind of organizing guide saves time, avoids duplication of efforts, and enables home visitors to operate independently more quickly. In addition, a curriculum guide or file can become a way of acknowledging and sharing ideas from other families in the program. It is an excellent way to build parents' confidence and pride. Using the format of other activities (see the examples on pages 153–156), the home visitor and parent can write their idea so that others can use it. They can note on the bottom "Contributed by Arlene and Joe Berman, 1978" and share it both that year and in the years to come. Family contributions may be excellent sources of activities appropriate to a particular culture, community, or location.

Characteristics of a Home Learning Activity

Home learning activities are not very different from center learning activities in some respects. In both settings, activities should be appropriate to the age, developmental level, and interests of the children, and should promote the goals and objectives of the program. They should encourage talking, thinking, and experimenting with different ways of doing things for both adults and children. When the activity is completed, adult and child should know that they have accomplished something and should feel good about it (Gordon, 1969). All equipment should be safe, sturdy, durable, attractive, and appropriate for both sexes and all ethnic groups.

But home learning activities and the material used in them require some additional characteristics quite different from those necessary in a center. Whenever possible, materials should be readily available and acceptable to the family, activities should promote both parent and child development, and materials should be adaptable to the particular needs of a home visit.

Use Materials Available and Acceptable to the Family

Use Materials Available and Acceptable to the Family   Activities should use materials readily available to the family so that parents realize they do not need a lot of special equipment to help their children learn, but can simply use the ongoing tasks of daily living. The home visitor might involve herself, mother, and child in making a salad, folding clothes, or putting away toys to show all the things that children can learn from sharing these tasks with parents.

Unfortunately, many home-based programs have simply transplanted to the home materials and activities that are used in preprimary classrooms. Lotto games, letter and numeral games, flannel boards, number and shape puzzles, sound and smell cans, and other classroom materials are widely used. It may be that teachers and program developers were simply familiar with these materials and saw that they could be used to focus attention on the desired studies. Another and more important reason why these school activities are used may be so that parents and home visitors know that they are doing something educationally important. Attractive, colorful, well-made equipment, nice books, and alphabet and number games may bestow status and importance on an activity or program in a way that sorting buttons or matching socks never could.

So, in addition to being available, activities should be accepted by the family. The messiness of finger painting, clay, play-dough, or even felt-tip pens may be too much for some parents to manage. Respect that and take crayons, pencils, chalk, and an individual chalkboard. No single activity or group of actvities is important enough to jeopardize a parent's participation in the program.

Use Activities That Promote Both Parent and Child Development

Use Activities That Promote Both Parent and Child Development   The activity should help bring about desired *parent* behaviors, as well as child behaviors. Few of the curriculum materials for home-based programs make this second check on appropriateness. Let's look at an example to clarify the point.

A desired parent goal might be to get books for parents to read to children in the home, either through borrowing them from the library or buying them at the grocery or discount store. Programs should buy books with a durable library binding. Programs should also include some books that were actually bought at the local stores, and home visitors should tell parents where they bought them and give some tips on selecting the best books.

Use Materials You Can Adapt to the Needs of the Home Visit   Ideally, home visit activities expand to include other family members who happen to be around, for example, younger or older children, grandparents, and fathers. At the least, the activity should expand from one adult and child to two adults and child, so that the home visitor modeling the way to play a game with a child can include the mother, then gradually leave the game so that the mother and child play alone. Examples of such activities are singing games and action rhymes, books, and small manipulative toys such as wooden cubes and beads.

Activities should also promote increasing complexity in both child and adult behaviors. If an early task for a child was to sort beads according to color, size, or shape, a later task might be to sort small blocks according to color, size, *and* shape. The activities should also promote and support increasingly complex adult-child interactions. For example, the home activities for a particular family might start with simply getting parents to talk and play with their children, and then progress to helping parents to ask questions that encourage children to think, see relationships, and use descriptive words.

Activities should also encourage parents to take on more responsibility for the independent teaching that should continue after the home visit program is over. Early in the year the home teacher will probably plan most of the lesson, select the activities, and bring the materials. Gradually the parent will assume more responsibility, be expected to make suggestions, help with planning, and take a more active role (Millville Home Start, 1977). The home visitor may discuss what activities they will do together on the next visit and have the parent and child collect and have the materials ready. Or she may leave some materials and have the parent and child show her next week the games they have discovered how to play.

Preparing Home Learning Activities and Guides

Home teachers need to develop lesson plans and learning activities, just as classroom teachers do. The plans will be individualized for a family rather than for a group of children, but they should reflect the same care and thought. In addition, professional teachers in home-based programs are often curriculum and instruction leaders for a team of professional and paraprofessional home teachers, and they have the responsibility for teaching others how to plan. We have developed a sample way of organizing parent/child activities and some examples of the way you can use them to help home visitors and parents communicate with each other about the activities (pages 153–156). Whether you use this or another way of organizing home activities, you should use the following basic guides.

Link to Goals and Objectives   Link most activities to the goals and objectives of the program. This seemingly obvious reminder is often overlooked when people decide on toys, games, and other activities. Of course, there should always be room for a few things just for fun, but unless you can say how an activity is furthering the progress of the families, you should probably reconsider it.

Include Several Program Goals   Whenever possible, activities should incorporate several program goals—nutrition, health, motivation, social and physical development, as well as intellectual and language development. For example, a cooking activity that involves mother, child, and home visitor in preparing and eating a low-cost, healthful snack includes all the goals mentioned above. The home visitor acts as a model and discusses good nutrition and safety in the use of kitchen tools as they work and eat together. Health and physical development are directly related to adequate nutrition. Cutting, rolling, spreading, and other actions involved in the preparation of food help develop the child's motor skills. The love, fellowship, and sharing involved in preparing and eating food together build strong bonds between parent, child, and home visitor. Reward is immediate and tangible, and language flows throughout the entire task. In addition, the activity is clearly linked to daily living in the home.

An activity promoting a goal in one area of development should definitely not detract from another. Many times the food prepared by home teachers, parents, and children consists of treats, such as cookies, candy, or sweet desserts that detract from the health of the entire family. Parent and child may learn about the rich language-learning possibilities in cooking and eating together, but they are also learning that sweets are to be desired.

Include Many Materials and Approaches to Learning   People learn in many ways, and we should take advantage of all of these: doing, listening, talking, seeing an example or demonstration, reading, and discovering for themselves. Using a variety of these in each home visit will make it more interesting to everyone, and by example will help mothers learn a variety of ways to teach their children. We almost always tell and discuss too much.

Use Simple, Clearly Understood Language   There is no reason for parents to learn many of the technical terms used by educators. Simple, everyday language can communicate all the ideas parents need to know in working with their children. Technical language can sometimes communicate the wrong things, too. Ira Gordon and his associates at Florida originally included a "criterion item" in home visiting activities to tell when a child successfully completed an activity. They changed it to "aim of the game" when they found it was being used for testing rather than teaching (Gordon et al., 1977). We suggest avoiding such terms as "behavioral objective," "procedures," "adaptation," and "extension" in favor of words everyone knows.

Be Explicit about What Home Visitors Are to Do   Home learning activities are often developed and written in terms of what the parent, child, or both are supposed to do. The role of the home visitor should be made clear also. Sometimes instructions for the home visitor in helping the parent learn are covered in a training session, but if they are written out in the form of a guide and attached to the home visitor's copies of the home activities, they will serve as a helpful reminder.

SAMPLE PARENT/CHILD ACTIVITIES

A consistent way of organizing parent/child activities makes writing and doing them easier. The following elements should be included.

Name: An interesting and distinctive name will help everyone remember which activity is being discussed.

Why do it?   A clearly stated reason for the activity and the objective for the child will help keep the activity focused.

What you will need: List all the necessary materials.

How you do it: Give directions (not too many) for doing the activity.

What to look for: List some ways of knowing when the purpose of the activity is being achieved.

Other things to do: Include some different things to do with this activity, as well as other related activities around the home.

Examples of some activities are given to show both how the organization works and the kinds of activities that are appropriate for home visits.

Let's Count Fingers, Let's Count Toes

Why do it?   Help your child learn to count things correctly.

What you will need: Your fingers and your child's fingers and toes.

How you do it: Say to the child: "Let's see how many fingers you have. You help me count. One, two, three . . ." Count with him several times, showing him how to use the other hand to point to each finger in turn. Then say: "Now you try it." If he hesitates, get him started by saying: "One, two . . .," and let him go ahead. If he can't, count together a couple of times more, stop, and do it again another day. If he counts up to five correctly and without hesitation, then count to ten. Older children can often count to fifteen or twenty, using your hands or their toes. However, learning to say the eleven, twelve, and the teens is difficult and takes a long time, so be patient. Do this a few minutes every day—in the car, getting your child dressed or undressed, and at other times, and he'll soon learn how to count. Count other things, too, such as people in the family, the sections in an orange, the raisins in a handful, pegs on a pegboard, and the steps to the basement. Show him how to point to each one or move the things he's counted so that he will be able to help keep track of them. Show the child you like to see him trying to count with a hug, a smile, or a pat on the shoulder.

What to look for: When your child catches on to the idea that she is to point to a finger each time she says a number and she can say the numbers in order, she is learning. After that she just needs to learn more numbers.

Other things to do: Teach your child some counting songs and games, such as this one adapted from "Ten Little Indians": "One little, two little, three little fingers; four little, five little, six little fingers; seven little, eight little, nine little fingers; ten little fingers, *hide*." Show the child how to hide his fingers and thumb in his fist. Another is the nursery rhyme: "One, two, buckle my shoe; three, four, shut the door; five, six, pick up sticks; seven, eight, shut the gate; nine, ten, a big fat hen."

To the home visitor: Begin counting activities early in the year: the process is simple, clear-cut, requires no elaborate equipment, and usually has quick success for both parent and child. The main things to stress to parents are:

- Count a few minutes every day, rather than a long time once or twice a week.
- Be patient; it takes a long time for the child to learn all those number names.
- It's all right to just count, but count things, too.
- Say the numbers *with* the child until she learns them (demonstrate).
- Show the child you like to see him trying to count.

Sandwich Special

Why do it: Letting your child help you make sandwiches can help him learn the meaning of the words we use to describe the process. Your child can learn words such as "top," "bottom," "middle," "spread," and "half."

What you will need: Sandwich makings of any kind—bread slices, biscuits, crackers, hamburger buns, or apple slices; a filling that is easy to use; and a knife.

How you do it: Let the child kneel on a kitchen chair or stand on a stool or box so she can use the kitchen table for a work space. Have all materials within reach. *Show* and *tell* her what to do; the telling helps her learn the words. Say: *Spread* the peanut butter on one slice of bread, *sprinkle* this chopped lettuce *on top*, and put the other slice of bread *on top of* the lettuce." Demonstrate if you need to. After your child has made sandwiches a few times, let her tell you what she is doing. Try lots of different kinds of sandwiches to teach your child the names of different foods, add variety and interest, and teach good nutrition. Here are a few suggestions:

- Cottage cheese and shredded carrots on whole wheat raisin bread.
- Peanut butter between apple rings.
- Honey butter (mix equal parts of honey and soft butter) between graham crackers (*much* better for a snack or dessert than cookies).
- Chopped leftover meat (moisten with mayonnaise) and a lettuce slice.
- Peanut butter and alfalfa sprouts or tomato slices on whole wheat bread.

What to look for: At the beginning, just watch to see that your child is following the directions. If not, repeat them (one step at a time), demonstrate, and let him try again. After he has learned the words, listen to see if he is using them correctly.

Other things to do: After the sandwich has been made, the filling that was *on top of* the bottom slice becomes *in the middle.* Talking about this and teaching your child those words will help her learn that the relative position of things changes. Under close supervision, let her cut the sandwiches (except the crackers!) in half or in fourths; this is a good way to begin to learn fractions. Let your child help mix some sandwich spreads, such as honey and butter, peanut butter and pickle relish, and others.

To the home visitor: Either bring the needed materials or ask the parent to have them ready. Find out what things they usually have around and decide together what you will use to make the sandwiches next week. Encourage healthful, nutritious foods; these are as important to children's growth as language. Use whole-grain breads, protein, and fruit and vegetable fillings. Avoid sweets. Work with the parent and child the first time, showing the parent how to:

- Set up the food preparation area so the child can comfortably and safely reach the work surface.
- Make acceptable behavior clear; the child works at the table or counter and keeps the knife and food there.
- Give the directions one at a time instead of all at once, and demonstrate the meaning as she does so.
- Use the important words; for example, "Put the lettuce *on top of* the peanut butter" instead of "Put that stuff on there."
- Eat some and tell the child what a good cook he is.

The Button Box

Why do it? Children love to sort things, particularly if they can do it their own way. This game encourages children to *decide how a group of objects should be sorted, do it, and tell you why.*

What you will need: A collection of common objects that can be sorted. Buttons are ideal, but jar lids, bottle caps, old keys, rocks, seashells, and evergreen cones can be used. Be sure to have enough to make it interesting. Put them in a flat can or cardboard box.

How you do it: Set up a work space so the child can work without having to move. The kitchen table or the corner of a room is fine. Say, "Here are a lot of buttons (jar lids, keys, or whatever you and your child have collected) for you to sort. Just put them in piles the way you think they ought to go." Let the child work for a while and then tell you about the groupings. Remember, there is no right or wrong. You can help by supplying words if you need to, but don't feel that every pile has to be thoroughly described.

What to look for: If the child sorts the objects in some way that makes sense and then tells you how the groups are alike or different, he understands.

Other things to do: After he has sorted the objects for a while, mix them up again and say: "This time, see if you can sort them a different way."

To the home visitor: The week before you do this activity, take some examples of collections and ask the mother to have one ready next week. If she doesn't have any of the items suggested, help her decide on another collection. As you discuss the activity, point out that:

- The game can be played by the child while the mother is doing something else. She does need to talk with him about what he is doing. The activity is good any time, but especially for a rainy day, a hot afternoon, or for a child who is not feeling well.

- There is no end. Many children group and regroup the objects, coming back to them again and again.

- She should encourage lots of different ways of grouping. Writing them down and keeping track of the different ways of sorting will do this. For example, buttons can be grouped according to size, color, shape, number of holes, the material they are made of (plastic, wood, metal), the ones the child does and does not like, the way they attach to the fabric (shank or no shank), and so forth.

- Being able to see how things go together or don't go together is important in school and in life.

- She has taught the child words to describe things, and this gives him a chance to use them.

Child Charmers

Use these activities to capture children's attention, have a little fun at the beginning of a visit, and demonstrate to parents some ways to amuse a restless or bored child.

Babies in a Basket   Ask the parent to have a handkerchief or a large square of soft cloth (from an old sheet is ideal) ready for the next visit. You bring one, too. Make the babies once, as shown, then demonstrate each step, having the parent follow using the square of cloth. Older children can fold and roll the babies also.

Fold the square diagonally.

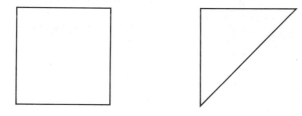

Roll the points tightly inward. Let the child hold one while you finish rolling the other.

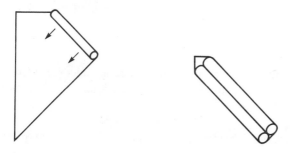

Gently tug on the two loose protruding points, turning them inside out so that the "babies" are enclosed in the rest of the square. Swing or fold back one corner to make a bed.

Marchers in a Row   Symmetry, pattern, and repetition appear as if by magic as the marchers unfold. Use newspaper pages, a large clothing sack, or any other thin paper. The process offers rich opportunity for language development. (Note the italicized words in the directions below.) With a little help, older children will be able to make these marchers.

Cut the paper to approximately 12 by 4 inches. *Fold* the paper accordion style, so it is 6 by 4 inches, then 3 by 4, then 1½ by 4. *Crease* the edges by rubbing them with your hand. Then *draw* half of a figure, with the hand extending to the edge of the paper. Cut out the marchers, being careful not to cut apart the hands. With a little practice you can cut them out without drawing. *Unfold.*

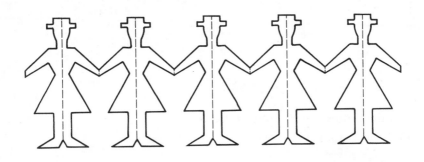

Puppets from Nature   Elaborate puppets are not at all necessary for puppeteering. Flowers, acorns, a hand, and a few daubs with a pen are all it takes to create a puppet. Try one of these suggestions.

Use the "caps" from acorns as hats for puppets painted directly on fingers.

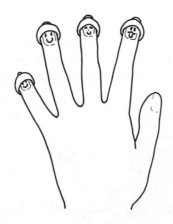

Snapdragon blossoms will "talk" if you squeeze the sides of the flower.

Paint a mouth and eyes on the side of your hand to make a puppet. Practice moving your thumb to make the puppet talk.

Finger Plays   Finger plays are great fun and also help develop language, finger and hand dexterity, and a sense for the rhythm, rhyme, and fun of language. Any finger play will be enjoyed, but some seem to have more appeal than others. Each teacher, parent, and child has favorites. Whenever possible, use some from the cultural heritage of the family.

Nursery Rhymes   Nursery rhymes also are excellent for playing with words, rhymes, and the way word meanings change. Phrases such as "hickety pickety" invite a child to repeat them; "muffet" and "tuffet" and other rhymes heighten the awareness of sounds and the meaning of the word *rhyme*.

Any of these suggestions—child charmers, home activities, toys and games taken to the homes—will help fulfill the basic purpose of a home-based parent involvement program, which is increasing parents' and children's verbal and social interaction, their enjoyment of each other, and their mutual pleasure in growing and learning together in the family.

SUMMARY

Parent involvement through home visits takes place in a home with children below the age of school entrance. Frequently, but not always, the programs are in rural or less accessible areas. These programs concentrate on two goals: helping parents to be better teachers and helping parents to be better parents and homemakers. Teachers take on the role of parent educators, home visitors, and home teachers; they often work as part of a home visiting team, working with and supervising paraprofessional home visitors.

The typical home visit is an hour and a half long, once a week, and involves mother, children, and home visitor. Home visitors usually work with ten or twelve families.

The advantages of home-based programs lie in their outreach to the family, which makes for greater parent participation; in the changes that occur in the parent so that the whole family benefits; and in the way the program can be individualized to the family. Disadvantages are the difficulty of supervision and training, the preponderance of school activities, and the lack of knowledge about the appropriateness of home visits for families other than those with special needs.

Careful planning and implementation of home-based programs are essential. Three phases are involved: advance planning and preparation, implementation, and review. Educational activities for home-based programs should use materials that are available and acceptable to the families, promote both parent and child development, are adaptable, work to accomplish one or more program goals, include many materials and approaches to learning, and use simple, clearly understood language. In particular, they should be explicit about what the home visitor is to do to accomplish her primary task: help the mother be a better parent and teacher.

FOR DISCUSSION AND FURTHER STUDY

1. Research some of the early demonstration home visiting programs and compare and contrast them to current ones (see Schaefer, 1972; Schwartz et al., 1965; Weikart and Lambie, 1968).

2. Develop and write some parent/child home learning activities using the format and guidelines on page 153. Role-play these with your classmates.

3. Every family has its favorite child charmers. As a class project, make up a booklet of these, with one from each family represented in your class. Use one you remember from your own childhood, one you might use with your own children, or one you have observed someone using.

4. Most home visiting programs are for families with special needs. Discuss how the program might be successful with middle-income families with no special needs. Would it need to be varied?

5. Many parents prefer that their children be in a center-based program. What might be their reasons?

6. Pretend you are calling on such a parent and explain the advantages of a home-based program.

BIBLIOGRAPHY

Appalachia Educational Laboratory, Inc. *Home-Oriented Preschool Education: Program Overview and Requirements.* Charleston, W. Va.: Appalachia Educational Laboratory, 1972.

Appalachia Educational Laboratory, Inc. *Home Visitor's Handbook.* Charleston, W.Va.: Appalachia Educational Laboratory, 1972.

Croft, Doreen. *Parents and Teachers: A Resource Book for Home, School, and Community Relations.* Belmont, Calif.: Wadsworth, 1979.

Gordon, Ira. "Early Childhood Stimulation through Parent Education" (mimeographed). Gainesville, Fla.: Institute for Development of Human Resources, 1969 (ERIC-ECE. ED-038-166).

Gordon, Ira J., Barry Guinagh, and R. Emile Jester. "The Florida Parent Education Infant and Toddler Programs." In *The Preschool in Action: Exploring Early Childhood Programs,* ed. Mary Carol Day and Ronald K. Parker. Boston: Allyn and Bacon, 1977, pp. 97–127.

Gordon, Ira J., M. Hanes, L. Lamme, P. Schlenker, and H. Barnett. *Parent Oriented Home-Based Early Childhood Education Programs.* Research report to the U.S. Office of Education, contract from Region IV, P.L. 90-35, Title V, Part D, COP Grant. Gainesville, Fla.: Institute for Development of Human Resources, May 1975.

Gordon, Ira J., and William F. Breivogel. *Building Effective Home-School Relationships.* Boston: Allyn and Bacon, 1976.

Gotts, Edward E., ed. *The Home Visitor's Kit: Training and Practitioner Materials for Paraprofessionals in Family Settings.* New York: Human Sciences Press, 1977 (contains home visitor's notebook, parent's notebook, and home visitor's resource materials).

Gray, Susan W. "Home Visiting Programs for Parents of Young Children." *Peabody Journal of Education* 41, no. 2 (1971): 106–11.

Gray, Susan W., and Rupert A. Klaus. The Early Training Project: A Seventh Year Report. *Child Development* 41 (1970): 909–24.

Grogan, Marian, Kathryn Hewett, Marritt Nauta, Ann D. Rubin, and Mora Stein. *The Homesbook: What Home-Based Programs Can Do with Children and Families.* Cambridge, Mass.: Abt Associates, 1976 (prepared for the Office of Child Development, Early Childhood Research and Evaluation Branch, HEW Contract No. HEW-105-72-1100).

Hess, Robert D., and Virginia C. Shipman. "Early Experience and the Socialization of Cognitive Modes in Children." *Child Development,* 36, no. 4 (December 1965): 869–86.

Karnes, M. B., J. A. Teska, A. S. Hodgins, and E. D. Badger. "Educational Intervention at Home by Mothers of Disadvantaged Infants." *Child Development* 41 (1970): 925–35.

Karnes, Merle B., and R. Reid Zehrbach. "Educational Intervention at Home." In *The Preschool in Action: Exploring Early Childhood Programs*, ed. Mary Carol Day and Ronald K. Parker. Boston: Allyn and Bacon, 1977, pp. 75–94.

Levenstein, Phyllis. "Cognitive Growth in Preschoolers through Verbal Interaction with Their Mothers." *American Journal of Orthopsychiatry* 40 (1970): 426–32.

Levenstein, Phyllis. "The Mother-Child Home Program." In *The Preschool in Action: Exploring Early Childhood Programs*, 2nd ed., ed. Mary Carol Day and Ronald K. Parker. Boston: Allyn and Bacon, 1977, pp. 27–49.

Levenstein, Phyllis, Helen Roth, and Arlene Kochman. "Manual for Replication of the Mother-Child Home Program" (mimeographed, for field testing). Freeport, N.Y.: Verbal Interaction Project, 1971.

Millville Home Start. "*The Developmental Nature of Home Visits*" (mimeographed). Millville, Utah, 1977.

Office of Child Development. *A Guide for Planning and Operating Home-Based Child Development Programs*. Washington, D.C., 1974 (DHEW Publication No. OHD 74-1080).

The Portage Guide to Home Teaching. Portage, Wisc.: The Portage Project, 1975.

Schaefer, Earl S. "Parents as Educators: Evidence from Cross-Sectional, Longitudinal and Intervention Research." *Young Children* 27, no. 4 (April 1972): 227–39.

Schaefer, Earl S., and May Aaronson. "Infant Education Research Project: Implementation and Implications of a Home Tutoring Program." In *The Preschool in Action: Exploring Early Childhood Programs*, ed. R. K. Parker. Boston: Allyn and Bacon, 1972, pp. 51–72.

Schwartz, A. N., L. W. Phillips, and M. B. Smith. *REACH: Raising Educational Aspirations of the Culturally Handicapped*. Cooperative Research Project 5-8072-12-1, State University of New York at Plattsburgh, 1965.

Shearer, Marsha S. "A Home-Based Parent Training Model." In *Teaching Parents to Teach*, ed. David L. Lillie and Pascal L. Trohanis. New York: Walker and Co., 1976.

Shearer, M., and D. Shearer. "The Portage Project: A Model for Early Childhood Education. *Exceptional Children* 36(1972): 210–17.

Weikart, David R., and Delores A. Lambie. "Preschool Intervention through a Home Teaching Program." In *Disadvantaged Child. Volume 2: Head Start and Early Intervention*, ed. J. Hellmuth. New York: Bruner/Mazel, 1968.

9 School- and Center-Based Parent Involvement Programs

In this chapter, we will describe and tell how to implement school-based parent involvement programs. The goal of such programs is to have parents become supporting resources for the school through active participation in the daily operations. In the first part of the chapter, we will describe such a program and analyze its distinctive characteristics along with its advantages and disadvantages. In the second part, we will specify how to put a program into action.

Schools and centers can involve parents in other ways, too, such as helping them become better teachers of their own children or asking their advice on school policy. These topics are covered in other chapters. Many parents are teacher or school aides, hired by the school and treated as employees. Although the procedures we suggest are helpful in working with aides, our primary focus is on working with volunteers.

PARENT PARTICIPATION IN SCHOOLS: A DESCRIPTION

A Look at One Program

Nancy Baker teaches at Jefferson Elementary, an older school in a suburban community. Each school day, she and her aide work with 28 children from diverse cultural and socioeconomic backgrounds in a half-day kindergarten program. Nancy is quite aware that the community has high expectations for its children and its schools. Several years ago, a group of parents, teachers, and administrators specified goals and objectives for the school district's kindergarten program. Each year, Nancy and her aide assess what each child knows and can do in relation to those goals, and Nancy consults with the parents to decide on specific objectives for each child as well as for the group. But even with an aide, Nancy found it difficult to operate the individualized, flexibly organized kindergarten that seems most appropriate for helping her pupils achieve the objectives. There was no point in asking for another paid aide. The school district had budget problems and was very unlikely to finance smaller classes or additional instructors. So Nancy, the other teachers, and the principal turned to the parents of the children in the school. Response was slow at first, but when parents found they were wanted, needed, and appreciated, they provided dependable and sustained support. In fact, many of them welcomed it as a chance to get to know more about that part of their children's lives, since the schools were large and impersonal.

In Nancy's classroom, different parent volunteers come every day for the full three hours. They work directly with individuals or small groups of children on tasks that Nancy has planned for them, perhaps language development games, classification activities, and creative dramatics or art. When a special need arises, such as a field trip, a cooking or art activity that requires extra hands, or preparation of some specific instructional materials at home, Nancy goes to her file of parent resources and finds someone who can help. Parents who cannot participate in the classroom contribute by making or saving needed materials at home, arranging special events, or keeping younger children of parents who are helping at school.

Parents help in the general school program, too. One parent comes monthly to repair books and other instructional materials; others help conduct vision and hearing tests for all children; another shares her considerable knowledge of the county's rich history; another records high-interest books on cassette tapes so children can listen independently; and three or four music lovers repair, file, and maintain the school's growing music library. The Jefferson Parents Association, formed when the school first opened, works with the school staff to set up and maintain the volunteer program as part of their other school support functions, which include regular meetings on topics of special interest, fund raising, and advising on school matters.

Although all parents are not involved, those who are enrich and enhance the school's programs. They know the satisfaction of having made a worthwhile contribution to their own and other children's education, as well as having learned a great deal about teaching young children.

Nancy Baker's kindergarten in Jefferson Elementary is typical of parent participation programs in many schools and centers. Even though programs differ in exactly what parents do, how often they participate, and how the program is organized, they are alike in that parents supplement and support school activities through volunteer and paid assistance.

Distinguishing Characteristics

Settings   School-based parent involvement can take place anywhere young children go to school—private and church-sponsored nursery schools, independent parent-cooperative nursery schools, Head Start, public kindergarten and primary schools, day care centers, and schools for special purposes, such as university child development centers and centers for children with special needs. The setting affects the way in which parents supplement and support the school.

In public schools, the National Congress of Parents and Teachers (PTA) has been the focus of many parent volunteer programs. It is, in fact, the largest volunteer organization in the United States. Its effectiveness and functions at the local level vary, but its goals and approaches were the models for many other parent organizations.

In parent-cooperative nursery schools, parents take turns being assistant teachers or aides. They participate for one full session every week or two weeks, depending on the number of children in the group and the number of parent helpers that participate each day. A parent committee works with the teacher to schedule the regular parent assistants, extra help for special events, and a backup system in case a parent gets sick or has an emergency. This committee also keeps track of each family's other contributions to the school, such as serving on committees, arranging programs, typing, telephoning, and tending to all the other details involved in running a small school. Participation, including classroom participation, is required if parents want their children to attend the school.

In the Head Start program, mother volunteers work in the classroom with a trained teacher as the first step on a "career ladder." With experience and training, the mother could become a paid aide and later a teacher. Almost one-third of all Head Start teachers used this entry into teaching (International Training Consultants, 1978). Also, because Head Start was begun as a way to provide jobs for parents as well as services for children, parents may drive buses, cook, clean, and repair the center and equipment, and any other paid or volunteer tasks.

Working parents whose children are enrolled in day care centers usually do not participate in the daily center activities, except for brief periods of time at the beginning or end of the day. However, they are sometimes involved in weekend or evening social and work activities such as fixing up the playground, repairing equipment, and altering used clothing to brighten and rejuvenate the dress-up areas.

The degree of parent participation in other settings—schools sponsored by private organizations, universities, or churches—varies with the interest and enthusiasm of school personnel, particularly the teacher.

Goals   School-based parent involvement programs usually concentrate on the two broad goals of helping parents understand and support the school. Parents are also supposed to learn how to be better teachers of their own children, but that goal is usually secondary or incidental, as shown in the National Education Association's summary of goals (1972, pp. 7–8):

1. Meet the needs of individual children through increased personal attention and assistance.

2. Develop cooperation and communication between parent and teacher for the benefit of the child.

3. Increase parent cooperation, support, and understanding of the school and its programs, and school understanding of the community.

4. Help teachers be more effective by giving them more time for professional activities, including the use of new learning materials and techniques.

5. Encourage parents to contribute to the welfare of their children, schools, and community.

Most schools have additional local goals that reflect community priorities. For example, a community that wants its children to know and respect a particular cultural heritage may involve parents and grandparents to help teachers know and teach the culture. These local goals may change from year to year.

Parent and Teacher Roles   Teachers who are working with parents and children in the classroom fulfill several roles, all of them demanding. They instruct both children and adults. They plan the overall instructional program, organize the classroom, decide what activities will be available, assess children's progress, and perform all the other tasks of teaching. In addition, they plan what the other adults will be doing, teach them how to perform any tasks that are unfamiliar, and guide and supervise their work. As co-workers, they share with parents both the pleasures and difficulties of teaching a group of children. As skilled professionals, they lead and direct other members of the teaching team.

When volunteer and paid aides first began to assist trained teachers in elementary schools, some professional associations, government agencies, and school systems attempted to distinguish between the role of the professional and that of the paraprofessional or nonprofessional assistant. The U.S. Office of Education, for example, suggested that only professional teachers should diagnose student needs, prescribe instructional programs, select appropriate materials, present content, and counsel and evaluate students. Many school people were concerned that untrained personnel might displace trained teachers, so their tasks were seen as clerical and supportive: running dittos, typing, filing, preparing art materials, repairing books, and supervising lunch and recess. As teachers and administrators became more familiar with paid aides and volunteers, however, they seldom tried to make a sharp distinction between teaching and nonteaching responsibilities. A variety of roles are shared by all the adults involved in the school or classroom. Under the direction of the teacher, the volunteers, teachers, and aides divide up the work according to the difficulty of the task, competency of the individuals involved, characteristics of the children, size of the group, and other considerations. With supervision and guidance, most nonprofessionals become a valued part of the instructional team.

Content   The content of parent involvement depends on whether the parent is directly involved with in-school instructional and supervisory tasks or with out-of-school supportive services. When they are working in the classroom, parents learn to do almost all the teaching and interacting with children that the regular teacher does. Outside the classroom, parents may raise money, make costumes, or build a playground. The content that is always present is understanding and support of the school.

Method   Although parents learn some of the desired skills and attitudes through direct instruction, most are taught by demonstration and example. Teachers model the desired instructional behavior and parents are expected to follow their example.

Advantages and Disadvantages

Parent participation in schools has three major advantages: (1) it expands the available resources, (2) it brings about closer and more sustained contact between parents and teachers, and (3) it enables parents to make a direct contribution to their children's education. The disadvantages are: (1) the additional work teachers must do if the program is to be successful, (2) the inconsistencies and problems inherent in any volunteer work, and (3) some particular problems with the parent-child relationship.

Advantages   The most obvious advantage of having parent aides and volunteers is that extra resources (people) permit a more personalized, individualized program for children. Individualization has long been a goal of education; but with the inclusion of handicapped children in regular classrooms, the emphasis on having children with different backgrounds in classes together as a means of achieving educational equality, and the trend toward individual educational plans for each child, individualization has become a necessity. The extra resources mean that teachers are able to spend more time on the instructional tasks they have been trained for and less on routine tasks that anyone can do. Parents' skills and interests become additional resources for the classroom. Parents bring in fresh ideas and often follow through with whatever is needed to implement them. Such experiences enrich not only the curriculum, but all concerned.

The advantages to home and family through this direct contribution and contact may be less dramatic, but just as real. Parents who are volunteering or working at school have an opportunity to learn what their children are doing and ways to help them at home. They see their own children more clearly and in a broader context, particularly when the teacher discusses and interprets their child's and the group's progress. The realization that the school values and respects what parents know and can do may help parents value and use their knowledge for the benefit of their children at home as well.

Young children are usually delighted to have their parents helping at school. Many mothers who are at home with their children enjoy the opportunity to get out of the house, meet some new people, and do some creative work that contributes to the education of their children.

Perhaps the least tangible benefit, but no less real and important, is the love and affection that flows between children and adults as they get to know each other. A small community is established, and parents begin to know other families through the children.

Disadvantages   There are, of course, some disadvantages to having parents involved in the daily operation of the school as either paid aides or volunteers. Teachers must plan what they are to do, train and supervise them, discuss any problems, and recognize their contributions. All this adds up to extra work, even if it does ultimately result in a better program for children. In addition, many teachers are not trained to teach other adults how to teach children.

Any volunteer program is likely to have problems with absenteeism, inconsistencies, and unprofessional behavior. Parents who do not come when the teacher is counting on them may disrupt the whole day's plans as well as the teacher's commitment to parent involvement. It is difficult to get adults to be consistent with each other in discipline, expectations, and approaches to instruction. Not all this is inevitable when including adults or other volunteers in the school, but problems may result when school and teacher do not make clear what is expected of both children and parents.

Parents may not know or may have difficulty remembering the professional ethics that must guide their behavior. They may discuss a child or situation away from the classroom, play favorites, or be unwilling or unable to adapt to the discipline and guidance techniques used by the teacher. Problems that may result because of the unique nature of the parent-child relationship are another disadvantage. Some children may cause problems on the days their parents are there, particularly at the beginning of the year. Some parents may have difficulty being objective about their own children. Also, since many parents will be unable or unwilling to participate, their children may feel left out.

PARENT PARTICIPATION IN SCHOOLS: A GUIDE FOR IMPLEMENTATION

School districts, schools, centers, and individual classroom teachers all go through similar steps to achieve successful parent participation. We will group these steps into three phases: advance planning and preparation, implementation, and review, emphasizing the practical things that school personnel can do to make volunteers welcome and successful.

Advance Planning and Preparation

Most schools and centers have some parent involvement that leads to understanding and support of the school. Parent meetings, fund-raising drives, booster clubs, PTA activities, and work days are examples of ways in which schools have solicited and obtained parent support. Before bringing parents into the schools as volunteers and aides, however, a school must assess carefully whether or not the school and community support it.

Parent participation seems to work best in schools and centers that (1) have classroom programs flexible and varied enough to let several people share in

Figure 9.1

TEACHER AND STAFF INQUIRY

Dear Colleague:

   We have discussed having a systematic parent volunteer program at
Pueblo School and have a committee to get people's opinions, feelings,
and suggestions. Please take a few minutes to fill out the questionnaire below, so that we have your thinking and experience. Your replies
will be confidential. Return the questionnaire to the box marked
"Volunteer Program" on the secretary's desk, and the committee will
pick them up, compile them, and let you know the results. Thanks.

1. Do you think Pueblo School should begin a systematic parent
    volunteer program? Yes_____No_____

    Why?

2. What are some tasks a parent could do in the classroom that would
    help you?

3. What are some tasks a parent could do outside the classroom that
    would help you?

4. What can teachers, aides, and administrators do to encourage
    parents to volunteer?

    Teachers:

    Aides:

    Administrators:

5. What are some goals you think a parent volunteer program could
    accomplish for the school, children, parents, and teachers?

6. What other additional comments, suggestions, or questions do you
    have regarding parent volunteers in the school?

the instruction; (2) provide for many different kinds of satisfying participation by parent volunteers and employees; (3) provide training and consultation for participants related to what they are expected to do; (4) provide leadership and organization to assure that essential planning and administration are done; and (5) have strong administrative support to facilitate the operation and integration of the program into the overall school program (Elliott, 1972).

Preliminary investigation and discussion can determine if these conditions exist or can be brought about. If not, then traditional types of involvement may be more appropriate.

Assessing Needs   Plan to assess the needs, concerns, and interests of school personnel as well as parents. Involve and consult the director, principal, superintendent, and other administrators so that you have the necessary support and approval. They will know school law and policy relating to parents as volunteers, and they can give good advice on many other matters. For example, does school insurance cover volunteers? Are there school policies that limit or encourage anything that is being discussed?

Teachers and administrators also need to discuss in-house concerns, such as fears teachers may have about their positions or their responsibility for instruction, increased work load, or possible disruptions because of discipline problems. Early and frank discussions will help eliminate problems later on and will also point up topics that may need further study or emphasis in a training session. A questionnaire such as the one in Figure 9.1 can either precede or follow general discussion. Only when school support is strong should you meet with other interested and concerned groups, including the existing parent organization, citizen advisory groups, and, of course, parents.

Well-announced open meetings, workshops, study and discussion groups, and written inquiry and reaction sheets give everyone a chance to express their views, concerns, and questions. Parents and school personnel must honestly and openly address questions and doubts, such as: Are parents needed and wanted in the school or center? What will such a program mean to teacher and children in the classroom? What will parents do? Isn't teaching the school's job?

If necessary, follow these meetings with fact-finding sessions or visits to other programs already using volunteers, so that you start off with a common understanding of what the program is about.

Goals and Objectives   Parents and teachers will make many suggestions about goals during preliminary discussions and on the inquiry sheets. They may not be stated as goals, but if you listen and read carefully, goals begin to emerge. Teachers may say, "I just don't feel that I'm giving each child the individual attention he or she deserves." Parents may say, "I don't see how you manage all those kids." These kinds of statements soon add up to a goal such as: Meet the needs of individual children through increased personal attention and assistance. A committee can use those suggestions for preliminary planning, solicit more ideas if needed, and pull together the goals and specific objectives that seem most appropriate for their situation.

Set reasonable and attainable goals and objectives to keep expectations realistic and help avoid discouragement. Expecting *every* parent to spend a minimum of five hours in volunteer work is unrealistic, but someone in every family can be given an opportunity to assist in some way. Expecting IQ changes in children is unrealistic, but attitude changes in participating adults can be expected.

Program Procedures and Guidelines   Procedures and guidelines for the program give the practical framework for accomplishing the goals. You will need to consider how and where parents will be assigned, how records of participation will be maintained, what modifications in school facilities and procedures will be needed, and any other questions that may have been raised during preliminary discussions. Some examples related to each of these areas will show why guidelines are necessary.

The school administration, advisory committee, volunteer committee, or teacher will have to decide where parents will work and what they will do. Some schools discourage or even prohibit parents from working with their own children, yet parent cooperatives and many individual classroom teachers expect and want parents in their own children's class. These groups and individuals think that the advantages of having a parent share a child's experiences, of teacher and parent working together and getting to know each other, and of each relating to the child outweigh the disadvantages. School and program policies regarding these and other decisions must be made clear to everyone. For example, if teachers do not make assignments of volunteers to classrooms, who does and what is the procedure? Is participation by teachers voluntary or required? What if an assignment of a volunteer to a classroom isn't working out?

Some schools and centers have a staff member whose duties are to coordinate parent activities. Other schools successfully use parent volunteers as coordinators, particularly those who cannot participate at school. Like the parent committee in the cooperative nursery school, this person maintains the volunteer schedule and is the liaison between the volunteers and the teacher. If a parent cannot come on the day agreed upon, he or she takes the responsibility for getting a substitute and notifying the coordinator. Parents soon learn that the school and teacher are depending on them to assume this responsibility.

Look at your school's facilities to see if any modifications are needed to help parents feel welcome and be effective. Can parents easily find their way to where they are going, or are some additional signs needed? If volunteers are to make and repair instructional materials, do they have a pleasant place to work with all necessary supplies readily available? Can you find space for a "parent place," as described in Chapter 6? If so, make a spot there for books and articles about volunteer work, parent-school relationships, and other topics of interest.

If you are just beginning a program, have an initial trial phase and then make necessary modifications. Parents who find they do not have enough time can lessen their hours, assignments can be adjusted, and parents who are not comfortable in a particular situation can be transferred.

A simple record-keeping system will help keep track of parent interests and availability and who has done what. Ongoing records can be kept up to date by parents. If the school is large, parents will need to sign in and sign out so that school personnel know where they are in the school. In a classroom, library, or resource center, volunteers can fill out a card such as the one in Figure 9.2 and drop it in their file. Teachers can fill out the forms for parents who contribute in ways other than volunteering in the school. These forms help teachers remember what parents have done, so they can be assigned a variety of tasks in line with their interests and abilities. They also help the school keep track of the number of parents who participated, what they did, and their reactions. Records of this type help monitor the program as it is in progress, as well as evaluate it at the end of the year. The system should be set up and ready to go before implementation begins.

Figure 9.2
Volunteer Parent Record Form

```
Name                          Teacher: Baker

Date

        Arrived_____Left_____

        Total hours:

What I did:


Comments:
```

Implementation

The implementation phase consists of recruiting parents, orienting them to the school and program, and actually getting started.

Recruiting   You can recuit parents in several ways, such as by letter, by a questionnaire sent home with children, by telephone, or at a regular parent organization meeting. One of the most effective ways to generate enthusiasm and commitment is a workshop planned by teachers, administrators, and parents to introduce volunteers to the kinds of things they will be doing. Use posters, flyers, and features in local newspapers to generate interest, along with regular communications from the school and the parent organization.

In the workshop, focus on the children, what parent volunteers will do for them, and what the volunteers will learn that will help them work with their own children. Use slides or materials from other programs to show how a system actually works. Explain the various kinds of participation that are possible and the amount of time necessary to do each. Allow plenty of time for discussion, sharing with participants the information and understanding that were generated during the planning steps, but also allowing for their insights and concerns.

After this general background, involve parents in the kinds of activities they will be doing both in and out of the classroom. Have workshop centers where they actually make puppets, books, bulletin boards, instructional games, and other materials. Let them play with blocks, geo-boards, Montessori apparatus, science and math manipulatives, and reading games with the help of a teacher, so they learn how they would be using these with the children. If possible, have some parents who have already shared a skill or hobby with the children show other parents what they did. This hands-on experience generates interest, helps parents understand what they will be doing, and makes it easier for them to sign up to participate.

Have interest and availability questionnaires, such as the one in Figure 9.3, at a center with someone nearby to answer questions and collect the sheets. You will want to send letters and questionnaires to parents who were not there in order to make sure everyone has the opportunity to respond. Some programs make two inquiries— one to determine if parents are interested, and another to see what they are interested in doing and when they can participate. The questionnaire in Figure 9.3 combines the two, listing examples of what volunteers do, so that parents have many options for participating. You may not even want to have a written questionnaire, but simply pass around a calendar at a meeting and ask people to sign up.

Figure 9.3 can be adapted to suit your own situation and preferences. It is designed so that each parent fills one out, rather than just one per family. Even though few fathers can work in the classroom, they should be given the opportunity to contribute. As with any other message, if parents speak a language other than English, the questionnaire should be available in that language as well.

Organize responses into logical categories such as classroom volunteers; at-home volunteers; special skill categories such as music, foreign languages, arts, carpentry, typing, and sewing; and resources related to units of study such as transportation, career education, pioneers, and animals. Study the responses to make assignments and to help prepare for orienting those parents who said they would help.

Orientation   Plan an orientation of everyone concerned to help get the program off to a good start. Consult with support personnel (secretaries, custodians, cafeteria staff) about the program and brief them on what they will be expected to do. If the program is not school-wide, principals or directors should know exactly what will be taking place. If other teachers are affected, they should know what is planned, even if the volunteers will not be working directly in their classrooms.

Most of your efforts will involve orienting parents and children. Parents need to be familiar with the school and its policies, the classroom or area they

Figure 9.3

INTEREST AND AVAILABILITY QUESTIONNAIRE FOR PARENTS

Dear Parents:

    We have talked with many of you about the parent volunteer program
at Pueblo School. Now we need to know who would like to be a volunteer
and what things the volunteers would be willing and able to do. Please
answer the questions below, so that we can go ahead with our plans to
support the school by volunteer work.

Would you be willing and able to be a parent volunteer at Pueblo School
this year? Yes_____No_____

If no, please explain why not.

If yes, please check where you would like to work.
          In a classroom   _____
          At school, but not in a classroom _____
          At home   _____
          Other   _____

We have listed below some of the kinds of things parent volunteers do.
Please check the ones you think you'd like to do.

_____   Tell the children something about your occupation, hobby, or a
               special interest (if you check this item, tell us what it is)

_____   Read a story to a small group of children

_____   Help a child write a story

_____   Play some instructional games with children, such as lotto,
               science, and math games.

_____   Help the children with drawing, painting, and other art work

_____   Teach a song or some other musical activity

_____   Supervise children on the playground

_____   Help in the library

_____   Make instructional materials, such as games, puppets, bulletin
               boards

_____   Save household and industrial discards for use in the classroom
               (if you check this, list the items you can save)

Figure 9.3 (continued)

_____ Go with us on field trips

_____ Help with vision/hearing screening, or with classroom
assessment

Note to Reader: We have left this list incomplete so that
you can add other items that are important to you. Add
enough for parents to have a representative selection from
several different types of volunteer work.

What are some special skills that you could share with the school and
the children, such as typing, cooking, woodworking, speaking a
language other than English, playing a musical instrument.

When can you help?

If you cannot help regularly, could you be a substitute when a regular
volunteer is sick or has an emergency? Yes_____No_____

Do you have any comments about the volunteer program?

Name _____

Address _____

Telephone _____

will be working in, their roles as parent participants, and the characteristics of the children they will work with. With such a large amount of information to cover, you may want to schedule several short meetings, supplemented by written guidelines. You may want to develop a handbook for parents.

A sample agenda for an orientation meeting is shown in Figure 9.4. Let's look at the types of things that might be included in each section of the meeting.

If at all possible, have assignments ready to hand out with name tags, so people will know where they will be working. Inform parents of any school policies and regulations that apply to their situation: regulations observed in the school and play yard, lines of responsibility, confidentiality of information, philosophy of discipline and guidance, and what to do if a situation arises with which they need help.

Parents will want to know more about their roles and responsibilities as volunteers. Discuss the attitudes and behaviors the school expects of them so there are no misunderstandings. For example, the brief time teachers have to consult with parents before and after class will be focused on classroom concerns, not on matters that belong in a parent conference.

Tell parents about the basic educational philosophy, the curriculum, and any special services such as a media center, speech therapy, or tutorial programs. Particularly if they will be working with one of these programs, they need to understand what it is and its relationship to the regular classrooms.

Parents will appreciate a written handout that summarizes the information for them. Give each parent a handbook or guide and place several in the parents' room at school. Even with orientation information pared down to absolute essentials, no parent can remember it all.

Take parents on a tour of the school facilities, pointing out things they need to know: the location of the principal's or director's office, nurse's office, rest rooms, entrance closest to the parking lot, fire alarms, emergency exits, and so forth. Include information on where to park, where to check in and out when they come to the school, use of the school phone, what to do about meals, and other necessary details.

Specific information is best given in the actual location in which parents will be working, so they can locate supplies, find directions, learn how to use any special equipment, and get acquainted with the schedule, preferences, and expectations of their co-workers.

Parents need to know the characteristics of the children they will be working with: what four-year-olds or seven-year-olds are like, what the children will be doing and learning, typical reactions, and helpful guidance techniques. Don't schedule a course in child development, but select information related to what the volunteers will actually be experiencing. For instance, many parents are concerned about children's behavior when their parents are acting as teachers in the classroom. You can explain that the youngsters know and relate to the *parent* primarily in the social context of the home. They know and relate to the *teacher* primarily in the context of the school. When a child's parent acts as a teacher in the classroom, the child becomes confused about his social role and may act inappropriately. It may take a while for him to get used to having to share mother equally with the other children or having dad enforce a school rule.

Figure 9.4
Sample Agenda for Orientation Meeting

```
  I.  Greetings, introduction, and assignments

      A.  Name tags and assignment of volunteer responsibilities
          for everyone; introduction of key people if group is large,
          of everyone if group is small

      B.  Purpose of orientation

 II.  Briefing on general guidelines and regulations

      A.  Oral briefing

      B.  Distribution of parents' handbook, with attention drawn to
          helpful features

      C.  Question and answer session on general guidelines

III.  Tour of school facilities

 IV.  "Job-alike" training:  Participants form small groups for
      training in the areas where they will be working

      A.  Guidelines, demonstrations, and practice related to
          specific tasks volunteers will be doing

      B.  Question and answer session

  V.  Conclusion:  Reconvene for refreshments, informal visiting
```

You can also help orient parents by preparing the classrooms or work areas for extra people. Post near the art or writing area a list of all the children's names printed in correct manuscript or cursive form. Post a neatly printed daily schedule and some simple rules to encourage consistency. Label instructional games and materials whenever possible, and attach instructions on how to use them. When you prepare instructions and questions for learning centers, prepare some for adults who will be stationed there. Attach directions for use to the record player, overhead projector, and other machines. Even if you had time to go through each of these procedures with the volunteers, the written procedures help them remember. These instructions do not detract from orderliness and beauty if they are neatly prepared and mounted.

Plan an orientation for the children, too, even the very young ones. Let them know parents will be coming, what they and the parents will be doing, how they are to behave, and how they can help parents feel welcome by introducing them to classmates, showing them where classroom supplies are kept, and expressing appreciation. Discuss with the children how they may feel when their parents are in the classroom, including feeling resentful at having to share a parent with other chidren, embarrassed, or other mixed feelings. With older children, there should be frank discussions of the problems that sometimes result when their parents are in the classroom and clear explanations of what is and is not allowed. Explain to the children any changes in procedures or in the classroom.

With this preparation and background, you, the children, the parents, and the school will be ready to get started on the actual volunteer program.

Getting Started   Parents are involved in classrooms for different lengths of time doing many different things, so the specific plans for getting parents started will vary. Training, supervision, feedback, and human elements are basic.

The first few days of parent involvement will require more of your time, so develop classroom plans to permit this. Have parents observe the total classroom the first time they come, to get acquainted with the children, the classroom schedule, and the sense of classroom procedures. You may prepare a one-page observation guide to focus their attention on different aspects of what is going on in the room. As soon as parents are confident, involve them in class activities. Start on activities that are informal and simple enough to guarantee success, then gradually increase the difficulty and complexity of what you ask them to do. For example, a parent can start with reading to one or two children, and gradually learn how to work with a larger group at a learning center or with an instructional game.

Ask parents to come early or during a free time so you can explain and demonstrate what they will be doing. Be specific about the procedures that should be followed closely, but also indicate where they can improvise. For instance, if an instructional game is designed to help children learn the meaning of the words "same" and "different," the teacher and children need to use those words in sentences. However, in discussing the pictures or objects that go with the game, there is more freedom. Anticipate and suggest ways to handle children's typical responses, including ones that are difficult. Give each parent the materials needed for that day. Be sure to include a small pad of paper and a pencil for taking notes.

Reassure parents that mistakes will not hurt anything, and that you will be close by to give them help if they need it. Stay where you can unobtrusively observe and supervise, keep parents from floundering if (or perhaps we should say *when*) children go too far, and look for strengths to compliment and build on and areas where training is needed. Communicate encouragement and reassurance to help the parents know they are successful.

Take a few minutes at the end of each day to discuss with the volunteers how it went. Objectively discuss and analyze some of your own mistakes and triumphs, but be sensitive to what parents are ready for. If in doubt, reassure and recognize all the excellent things they did, and leave suggestions for improvement to another day. Let parents have a chance to share with you interesting things that happened and any concerns they have.

Parents who serve as special resources, either at home or in school, will also need your help. Prepare complete directions for making any instructional materials you request and give parents a model, if possible. When parents come in to share a particular skill or make a presentation, meet ahead of time to help them adapt to the developmental level of the students and the material they are studying, find out what special materials or arrangements are needed and answer any questions.

Begin a volunteer record, such as the one in Figure 9.2, so that you know what activities a volunteer has done and where he or she feels comfortable. This begins the process of reviewing and monitoring the involvement, so that interest is maintained and maximum benefit results.

Review

In reviewing the program, you will monitor progress, recognize parents' contributions, assess and evaluate the program, and share this information with others.

Monitoring   As you, the parents, and the children work and learn together, you will want to monitor the parent involvement just as you keep track of the children's learning. Be sensitive to parents' needs for variety, challenge, and information in their work. No one likes to do the same task over and over again, even if he or she is very good at it. Parents who are ready can be given greater responsibility and more challenging tasks. You may have volunteers or aides who are trained teachers, ready to use those skills for the benefit of the children. Under your guidance, these and other highly competent parents can assume additional tasks. Proceed slowly, but avoid underutilizing the volunteers. Let parents know what things they are doing well and where they need improvement. Modeling the desired behavior helps but may not be sufficient. Give parents positive suggestions for ways to improve.

Watch for patterns indicating that you may not be making the most of the volunteer program. Are you calling on the same parents over and over again without trying to involve others who may now be ready? Do you have a tendency to always assign difficult children to a volunteer or aide? Have you let careful advance planning slide, so that you are hurriedly looking for something for the volunteer to do just before he is scheduled to come? Monitoring and correcting your own performances will help avoid these pitfalls.

Schedule some informal meetings with your volunteers so they can share experiences, exchange ideas, and make suggestions. Use these to strengthen the volunteer and school program in other ways also, by keeping parents informed on school affairs so they can become liaisons to the community, by recognizing parents' many contributions, and by providing in-service training to sharpen parents' teaching skills.

Recognizing Parents' Contributions   You can recognize volunteer efforts in many ways. The informal sharing meeting described in the preceding section is only one. Supplement the daily "thank you" from children with specific praise for contributions the volunteers made that day. Small gifts or notes from the children; a letter from the principal, director, or superintendent; a picture of the parent working with children; or any other small token of appreciation is appropriate.

Many schools give formal recognition in the spring at a tea, a potluck dinner, a PTA meeting, or a program presented by the older children. Share some of the interesting and rewarding incidents that happened in the volunteer program that year, as well as the number of teachers, parents, and children involved, so the parents can see what happened as a result of their combined efforts. This reporting is one part of the review phase of one year's operation, and the first step of next year's involvement.

Evaluating the Program   Take time periodically through the year, and certainly at the end of the year, to reflect on and review the volunteer program, to see what has been accomplished, what procedures are working, and which ones need to be modified. Compile or ask the parent committee to compile all the information the school has gathered on parent involvement. If you kept the cards suggested in Figure 9.2, the information will be collected. How many hours did parents work? What tasks did they perform? What were their, the children's, and the teachers' reactions? If your program has been at all successful, everyone will probably be amazed at the number of hours parents have logged and the wide variety of services they have performed.

Ask the children about their reactions to the other adults and the new classroom activities. Or you can simply observe whether they are happy and learning or perhaps confused and disruptive with parent volunteers in the room.

Ask both participating and nonparticipating parents what they think of the volunteer program and their role in it. You can use a questionnaire, but allow some space for parents simply to express their feelings. You may get some responses as rewarding as those to an individual kindergarten teacher's parent volunteer program.[1]

I believe that parents learn quite as much as the children over the year, and I believe it important that they have that chance.

To see [my child] in school with all his peers helped me to relate and realize some of the quirks I thought he had were not better or worse than some of the other children. He turned into more of a regular kid all the time.

I volunteered because I want to be active in my child's education and this is a way of observing him and his environment without having to question him and seem nosy or put him on the defensive. I really enjoy working with the kids.

I firmly believe that the reason [the] volunteer program is a success is that each mother is kept so busy—not with busywork or menial tasks, but actually helping the children.

In addition, ask parents if they got enough instruction and guidance, if they felt over- or underutilized, and what suggestions they have for improving the program next year.

Finally, assess your own feelings and reactions to having parents in the classroom. Were you comfortable directing and working with parents? Were you able to do the necessary planning to enable parents to function effectively as volunteers? Was instruction more individualized, or were there just more adults in the room? Was closer home-school cooperation really achieved, or were the parents just there? What will you do differently next year? What went wrong and what worked well?

If the program has not gone so well, look for causes and ways it can be modified, but remember that changes in established relationships between home and school are not going to happen in a year or even two, particularly if there has been distrust or indifference by either party. If it has gone well, look for the strengths of the program and build on them. One of those strengths is a committed, well-organized teacher who can teach both children and adults. The importance of the teacher has been well stated by a volunteer parent:

> I feel strongly that the success of a program such as this depends greatly on the teacher herself. She sets the mood for the day. Without her warmth and cheerfulness I doubt many mothers would be there—happily. Her ability to get along well with others is the cornerstone for any program involving volunteers.

Sharing Information   Let the community, school board, administrators, and especially other parents know about a successful parent volunteer program. Share the statistics compiled on people involved, number of hours contributed, and tasks accomplished, but also include some anecdotes and reactions from the parents. These will make it easier to get started another year.

ACTIVITIES FOR PARENT VOLUNTEERS

Some of the volunteer activities parents can do are listed in this section, organized by the services parents can perform at home, in the community, in the classroom, on the playground, and in general school operations. Pick and choose the ones that seem right for your situation and add more.

At Home

- Act as parent volunteer coordinator.
- Telephone other parents with messages and requests.
- Make puppets, costumes, and instructional materials that do not require special equipment to construct.
- Save household discards for school use. (Supply a list of things you can use—berry boxes, carpet and fabric scraps, nylon stockings, plastic tubs such as those for margarine and whipped topping, magazines, corks, cotton socks, and so forth.)
- Save, alter, and wash "dress-ups."
- Plan special events.
- Start plants for school and classroom beauty.

- Keep classroom animals over vacations.
- Cut out pictures from magazines.
- Baby-sit for parents who are volunteering at school.

In the Community

- Locate and contact sources for give-away supplies—computer cards and paper, wood scraps, boxes, print shop paper discards, spools, and industrial discards that can be used in the classroom.
- Explain school programs and needs to the larger community.
- Explain special needs of the community to teacher and school.
- Locate and investigate field trip possibilities.
- Serve as interpreter for non–English-speaking parents.
- Encourage other parents to get involved.
- Accompany the teacher on a home visit to a family the parent knows well.

In the Classroom

- Write or print a story as the children tell it.
- Read stories to and with the children.
- Serve as a resource person, sharing a special skill, hobby, collection, occupation, and so forth.
- Observe, record, and compile information on one child or the group's behavior, to help in instructional decisions.
- Help with tutoring, remedial work, or at learning centers.
- Supervise art projects, rest periods, snacks, or lunch.
- Prepare and execute a cooking activity.
- Help review math, phonics, spelling, and basic concepts.
- Lead small group discussions on special topics.
- Help with routines of toileting, hand washing, dressing, and clean-up.
- Work with small groups or individuals with educational games and materials of all kinds.

On the Playground

- Help children engage in constructive play.

- Set up and supervise outdoor learning centers, perhaps for several classes, for example, carpentry and water and sand experimentation.

- Teach children games you played as a child.

- Encourage language development by talking with children about what they are doing.

- Play Follow the Leader.

- Serve snacks outside.

- Encourage bystanders to actively engage in physical activity.

- Help children plant, tend, and harvest a garden.

- Share special knowledge of the outdoor environment—birds and bird calls, trees, clouds, bugs, and city sounds and smells.

Behind the Scenes

- Repair, paint, or make playground equipment.

- Make props and sets for dramatic productions.

- Raise money and support for school and class projects.

- Research the cultural and historical background of groups represented in school to make sure displays and presentations are accurate.

- Research the history and growth of the community to share with children at appropriate levels.

- Research and check the safety of playground equipment and ground cover.

- Help modify the playground for use by handicapped children.

In the General School Program

- Compile a booklet of community resources such as speakers, field trips, places of interest, and available displays.

- Prepare instructional materials of all kinds.

- Act as reader or story teller for the library.

- Repair books, flash cards, posters, games, and other materials.

- Operate audiovisual materials such as projectors, record players, and other special machines.

- Prepare cultural displays honoring the cultural heritage of families in the school.

- Make arrangements for open houses, meetings, receptions, and so forth.

- Duplicate materials to be sent home.

- Answer the telephone for routine inquires during a set time of the day or week.

- Act as host or hostess in the parent place or lounge.

SUMMARY

School or center-based parent involvement with the goal of having parents understand and support the school's educational program takes many forms. Traditionally, parent meetings, fund-raising events, PTA functions, and other noninstructional activities have been used. In recent years, parents have also been participating directly in the school's instructional program as volunteers and aides. This form of parent involvement has the advantage of expanding available resources, promoting closer contact between parents and teachers, and helping parents make a direct contribution to their children's education. However, it does make extra work for teachers, and there may be problems with absenteeism, inconsistencies, and maintaining professional standards. Also, there may be problems related to the parent-child relationship, such as children showing off when their parents are around.

Parent participation as volunteers works best when schools (1) have flexible and varied classroom instruction, (2) have many different kinds of tasks for volunteers, (3) train and supervise volunteers, (4) do essential planning and administration of the program, and (5) have strong administrative support (Elliott, 1972). In the second part of the chapter, we set forth some guidelines for starting volunteer programs, emphasizing the three phases of advance planning and preparation, implementation, and review.

Before starting a parent volunteer program, schools should assess the needs and interests of both parents and school personnel to make sure they are receptive. Likewise, both groups must be prepared and oriented for the roles and responsibilities they will have. Teachers and other school personnel are responsible for recruiting, orienting, training, supervising, and recognizing parents, as well as making sure that what parents do is of benefit to the chidren. Suggestions were given for the kinds of tasks parents can perform to support the school.

FOR DISCUSSION AND FURTHER STUDY

1. Get together with four or five other students and brainstorm to see how many additional parent volunteer activities you can think of. Take notes and exchange ideas with other groups in the class.

2. What are some ways that teachers can make parents feel wanted, needed, and welcome in the classroom?

3. Suppose that in one of your preliminary discussion meetings, a parent says: "The teachers are supposed to teach the children, not the parents. If teachers were doing their jobs we wouldn't be wasting our time at these meetings." What could you say or do?

4. We have mentioned that a parent volunteer handbook is helpful to everyone involved. If some of the schools in your community have a parent volunteer handbook, examine it to see what topics are covered, how it is written, and what important points may have been forgotten.

5. Outline a parent volunteer handbook, including the information you think is important for parents to have.

6. Write to the organizations listed below for additional general information on volunteers and volunteer programs:

National Center for Voluntary Action
1785 Massachusetts Avenue, N.W.
Washington, D.C. 20036

Director, Volunteers in Education
U.S. Office of Education
400 Maryland Avenue, S.W.
Washington, D.C. 20202

National Reading Center
1776 Massachusetts Avenue, N.W.
Washington, D.C. 20036

Retired Senior Volunteer Program (not parent resources, but grandparents)
ACTION
806 Connecticut Avenue, N.W.
Washington, D.C. 20525
or your local RSVP office

BIBLIOGRAPHY

Baruch, Dorothy W. *Parents and Children Go to School: Adventuring in Nursery School and Kindergarten.* Chicago: Scott, Foresman, 1939.

Brock, Henry C. III. *Parent Volunteer Programs in Early Childhood Education: A Practical Guide.* Hamden, Conn.: Shoe String Press, 1976.

Carter, Barbara, and Gloria Dapper. *School Volunteers: What They Do, How They Do It.* New York: Citation Press, 1972.

Community Cooperative Nursery School, Menlo Park, California. *A Preschool Program Involving Mothers as Organizers, Helpers and Decision-Makers.* Available from Superintendent of Documents, U.S. Government Printing Office, Washington, D.C., 1970 (HE 5.220:20161, ED 045 222).

Craft, Maurice, John Raynor, and Louis Cohen. *Linking Home and School.* London: Longman Group, 1972.

Elliott, David S. *Project 88: Parent Participation in the Elementary School*, 1972 (ED 071 751). Available from ERIC/ECE, 805 W. Pennsylvania Avenue, Urbana, Ill. 61801.

Gilmar, Sybil, and John Nelson. "Centering Resources for Learning: Parents Get into the Act." *Childhood Education* 51, no. 4 (February 1975): 208–10.

Hedges, Henry G. *Using Volunteers in Schools:* St. Catherine's, Ontario: Ontario Institute for Studies in Education, 1972 (ED 085 848).

Heffernan, Helen, and Vivian Edmiston Todd. *Elementary Teacher's Guide to Working with Parents.* West Nyack, N. Y.: Parker, 1969.

International Training Consultants. *Developmental Assessment Instruments: Survey and Identification of Head Start Practices and Needs. Final Report to the Administration for Children, Youth, and Families.* Denver: International Training Consultants, 1978.

McGeeney, Patrick. *Parents Are Welcome.* London: Longmans, Green & Co., 1969.

National Education Association. *Parent Involvement: A Key to Better Schools.* Washington, D.C.: NEA, 1972.

Parent Involvement: A *Workbook of Training Tips for Head Start Staff.* Washington, D.C.: Office of Economic Opportunity, OEO Pamphlet 6108–12, May 1969.

Points for Parents: 50 Suggestions for Parent Participation in Head Start Child Development Programs. Washington, D.C.: Office of Economic Opportunity, U.S. Government Printing Office, 1967 (0–247–832).

Robinson, Floyd, David Brison, Henry Hedges, Jane Hill, Cecilia Yau, and Lee Palmer. *Volunteer Helpers in Elementary Schools.* Ontario: Ontario Institute for Studies in Education, 1971.

Sayler, Mary Lou. *Parents: Active Partners in Education.* Washington, D.C.: American Association of Elementary/Kindergarten/Nursery Educators, 1971.

NOTES

[1] Comments from Sally Brandenburg's kindergarten parents, Jefferson County Public Schools, Jefferson County, Colorado.

10 School and Home: A Partnership

OVERVIEW

In Chapters 8 and 9, we described how to implement home-based and school or center-based parent involvement programs. This chapter is about approaches that try to establish a home-school partnership by helping parents become better teachers of their own children while those children are in school. In the first part of the chapter we will describe and analyze the distinguishing features of a home-school partnership, using the consistent method of looking at setting, goals, roles, content, methods, advantages, and disadvantages.

In the second part of the chapter, we will examine the processes for implementing the three major approaches to establishing a home-school partnership. The School Bag System has the child carry linking activities back and forth. The Make and Take Workshop brings parents to the school to make activities to teach their children. The Traveling Teacher works part of the day in the classroom and part of the day in children's homes. We will also discuss ways of planning, implementing, and reviewing these three programs.

SCHOOL AND HOME PARTNERSHIP: A DESCRIPTION

A Look at One Program

Ken Freeman firmly believed that the children in his first-grade class needed to be involved in a wide range of experiences—art, music, dance, literature, and science, as well as the basics of reading, writing, and arithmetic. Ken knew that some of the children could use more individual attention and tutoring in certain skills than he and the aide he had for an hour and a half a day were able to give. Some of the parents had asked him what they could do at home to make sure their children got off to a good start, and Ken knew the community well enough to know that many parents felt the same way. The school did give each parent a booklet of general advice on things they could do at home to help their children in school, such as make sure the youngsters get a good night's sleep and a nourishing breakfast, take them to the library, read to them, talk with them, and encourage them in their school work. But something more specific seemed to be needed to help parents become true home partners of the school.

Ken informally discussed his concerns with several parents, other teachers, and the principal, who helped confirm his feelings. Meetings with parent committees and then with the full group of parents gave enough support and direction to get the class, including parents, started on a Home Education and Learning Program, promptly dubbed HELP. After much discussion, an experimental period, and revision, they developed a system that worked.

Activities for parents to do with their children at home are sent home every Friday. The children return the materials on Thursday, to be checked in, repaired if needed, and replaced in the resource files by two volunteer mothers. They also remove any notes or special requests from home, set them aside for Ken, and note on a progress sheet in each child's file that the item was returned. Ken discusses with the children the HELP activities they have had that week, then on Thursday afternoon before he leaves the school, he goes through the HELP file on each child, reviews his own records about each child and his or her family, and decides what activity should be sent home. He prepares a list of these activities and any special instructions that are needed. On Friday, a parent volunteer comes in, pulls out the activities and materials Ken has designated, checks them out, and puts them in each child's cloth drawstring bag to take home.

With the exception of library books on loan from the school and city libraries, all the materials and activities are inexpensive. Most were donated or made by the parents themselves, who continue to meet periodically to develop and make new and challenging projects. The Parent Teacher Association helps by buying supplies and officially supporting the program.

The activities include alphabet and number games, language development work, problem-solving and thinking games, and plenty of ways to promote social, physical, and aesthetic development. Every week Ken shares with the parents a "recipe for learning"—an idea, poem, story, finger play, song, art or cooking recipe, or suggestion of something special to do with the children. He duplicates these on index cards so parents can use the idea, then file it for future reference. At the end of the year, parents will have a record of things their child has done and learned in first grade as well as an excellent resource to use over the summer or with younger children.

Before the program begins and periodically during the year, Ken meets informally with parents to discuss basic teaching techniques such as how to correct children's mistakes without hurting their feelings, how to encourage children to think through problems, how to give positive reinforcement, and how to ask questions that encourage many responses. He also uses this time to discuss anything parents have on their minds about the first-grade program or the HELP activities. Ken tries to maintain contact with those who do not come to these meetings through telephone calls and notes tucked in the HELP bag.

Ken is pleased with the way the program is going, and most parents and children are enthusiastic. Not all parents do all the activities, but Ken and the parent committee did not expect the impossible. Children whose parents work with them at home are benefiting, although Ken is not really able to separate the effect of that help from the school teaching. Perhaps the best indicator of the success of the program is the conscientious way the children bring their HELP bags back to school every Thursday and look forward to taking them home on Friday. Another positive indicator is the increase during the school year in the number of parents who stop by after school to ask questions about the program or share information about their child.

This first-grade system is a typical approach to involving parents by helping them become better teachers of their children and thus home partners of the school. We will discuss other ways this can be done later in the chapter.

Distinguishing Characteristics

Settings   In this shared approach, some programs place more emphasis on the home, some place more on the school, and some are fairly evenly balanced, but both home and school are considered essential to children's learning. Many programs are very similar to the one carried out in Ken Freeman's first-grade class. Others may have a home visitor who works as an aide in the school for part of the day and visits the homes of children in the class for the rest of the day to show parents how to teach their children at home. Programs for handicapped children often teach parents to use instructional techniques identical with those used in the center or school, so that a youngster who is having difficulty learning does not have to contend with two sets of rules. All the programs attempt to link the two settings into a coordinated, cooperative learning environment for the child. The approach is suitable for most early childhood programs, kindergartens, primary schools, Head Start, and nursery schools. It is probably least often used in full day care centers, where the primary link is the brief period of the child's transition from home to center and back again (Powell, 1977).

Current practices reflect the way in which early childhood education in the United States has been funded and sponsored, with certain ages and groups of children much more likely to be involved in this type of program than others. Centers that work with handicapped children usually try to help parents become home teachers because many of the self-help, language, and social skills that handicapped children need to learn require home involvement. Schools and centers funded to help children with educational needs resulting from poverty, discrimination, or language differences are also likely to involve parents as home partners, especially as the children approach public school age.

Goals   The goals of home-school partnership programs concentrate on three areas: the home-school relationship, parents as teachers of their own children, and children as learners. Almost all programs aim to accomplish the following:

1. Develop continuity and active cooperation between the individual home and the child's classroom, particularly in the day-to-day learning experiences of the child.

2. Expand children's opportunities for learning important school-related skills and attitudes even when they are not in school.

3. Enhance parents' skills as teachers of their own children by providing them with procedures and activities appropriate to their child's developmental level and need, and by encouraging them to use and expand upon those activities and instructing them how to do so.

4. Develop in parents positive attitudes relating to their role as teachers, especially helping them to feel more competent in teaching, helping them to recognize the importance of themselves as teachers, and helping them to be more confident in their children's ability to learn from them.

Within these broad goals, programs develop many different specific objectives, depending upon the needs of the children and parents, the program philosophy, and the way in which the program is implemented. For instance, a federally funded program working with children who need help in mastering basic concepts of space, time, position, size, and number might have an aide work with the children on these concepts in the classroom and then teach the parents in a home visit how to reinforce the concepts at home. On the other hand, a program working with children who need special help in the acquisition of language may set very specific behavioral objectives for the child and teach the parent behavior modification techniques to help the child achieve those objectives. Such specificity is rare, however, for in most programs the exact teaching skills that parents are to master and generalize to other situations are seldom specified or directly taught. Suggestions of some appropriate objectives for parents as teachers are given on pages 195–196.

Parent and Teacher Roles   Home-school partnership programs assume that parents can and should create an intellectually stimulating learning environment in the home, one that complements and supplements what children are learning in school. Parents can take on this role within any cultural, economic, or language setting; it is not necessary to change other aspects of the home in order to have parents become effective teachers of their children.

The teacher's role is primarily that of parent educator, but the teacher also takes on the role of developing and maintaining two-way communication between home and school. If the primary means of linking home and school is a home visitor who spends time both in the classroom and in homes, the teacher has still other roles to fulfill. She acts as team leader, supervising the work of home visitors in the classroom and helping them prepare and plan home visits.

The home visitor teaches the children in the classroom and then shifts her attention to teaching parents in the home. Home visitors often find it difficult to teach adults, so they tend to concentrate on the child. The shifting of roles that is necessary in these home-school programs is one of the reasons they are difficult to coordinate and implement successfully. But using the same people in teaching both at home and in school makes communication and coordination more direct and immediate.

Content   With few exceptions, the content of home-school partnership programs is school-related learning. Parents learn that they can help their children at home, and the specifics of how to do so. Gordon (1977) identified the things parents and children do that seem to make a difference in children's educational achievement. He found that effective parents (1) engaged in direct face-to-face instruction with the child; (2) modeled by reading and discussing materials; (3) engaged in dinner conversations that included planning; (4) had consistent expectations for behavior; (5) used the home, neighborhood, and community as resources for learning; (6) spent time with the child; and (7) provided a secure and orderly home. There was also some evidence that valuing and encouraging independence, thinking, and freedom of discussion are related to success in school. Most of the home-school partnership programs attempt to include these behaviors in their content and methods.

Method   The most widely used method is that of focused interaction around a joint task, usually books, toys, games, or some other type of structured activity. For example, parent and child may play games designed to teach the child the letters of the alphabet or to count to ten. The interaction around the game will teach the child, of course, but, even more important, parents learn how to teach, when to teach, and that they can and should teach. Teacher-parent interaction around the same activity or game is also used to teach parents how to enjoy playing and working with their children. Parents and teachers may make toys and games in a workshop, for example, with the teacher showing parents, and parents showing each other all the ways they can use the activity to help children learn. Focused interaction plus demonstrations and discussions are the predominant methods used.

Advantages and Disadvantages

Home-school partnerships have many advantages for children, parents, and teachers. Some of these are that children get additional focused attention and are likely to learn faster. The approach communicates trust and confidence in the family's ability to teach children. The advantages for schools are that this approach to parent education is less controversial than many others; it establishes an inexpensive, simple method of regular communication with homes and gives a way of varying attendance and staffing for children with special needs. The disadvantages are that parents and children may get too emotionally involved in the tasks, which are overly school-oriented. And, inevitably, there is additional work for the teacher.

Advantages   Children get more time and individual attention devoted to their learning than they ever could in a group program. In addition, all that attention is from people the child values most—parents and other family members. Children learn that their parents respect what is being taught in school, want them to learn it, and are willing to help them. The effect on learning of having children know that their parents value school learning cannot be easily documented but is very important.

In addition, the approach is adaptable to almost anything that children want or need to learn. For example, children can be given special help with skills they find difficult, so that they are not hampered in the next stage of the learning process. Schools can also help parents learn how to teach school-related behavior that is more appropriately taught at home than at school, such as the selection and limitation of television viewing, getting enough rest, sound eating habits, responsible use of materials, and reading for leisure enjoyment. Parents can also help children learn things that the school might not have the time to teach but that allow children to explore their own interests and abilities. Parents who know how to respond to their children's interests can enrich learning in these special areas. If parents do not respond, interest often fades.

We have known for a long time that increased time and emphasis given to a particular skill or knowledge help children learn. But there are only so many hours in the school day. Encouraging parents to help at home increases both the time and emphasis placed on a specific skill. As a result, children who are taught both at home and in school learn the material faster (Fredricks et al., 1976).

The optimistic view of home and family life that the home-school partnership assumes will never be true for all families, but the trust and confidence it reflects may mean a great deal to families who never felt they would be able to help their children with school work. Parents gain confidence and understanding of their role as teachers when the school and school learning are taken out of the realm of the mysterious and become part of everyday life.

Schools and centers are less likely to be criticized when they concentrate on that part of parent education that is clearly related to the school and do not try to change other customs and values of the home. School-home partnerships usually try for continuity and congruence between home and school in academic areas only and do not attempt to change work and buying habits, housekeeping, or relationships to other community agencies. Of course, a change in one area may result in other changes, but the school is not trying to do this directly.

Perhaps the biggest advantage from these programs is that a regular, frequent method of communication is set up that can be varied to meet many child, parent, and teacher needs. Except when home visitors are used, the system is inexpensive and relatively simple to operate. Most of the instructional materials can be easily made from cardboard, crayons, felt-tip markers, wood, and household discards. The approaches can be used with any kind of classroom organization or philosophy, and with minimal change in classroom procedures. This home-school partnership also makes possible varied attendance and staffing for children and families with special needs. For example, a disabled child might benefit from being mainstreamed into a program with nondisabled children once or twice a week, and receive home instruction from either the parents or a home visitor on the other days.

Disadvantages   Some parents may get too emotionally involved in teaching their own children, resulting in anger, frustration, and a sense of inadequacy for everyone. Of course, many teachers have those same feelings, so parents should not be criticized too harshly. The difference in the home is that emotional ties and the parents' identification with the child are so strong that objectivity is difficult, if not impossible.

Another limitation is that too often school activities are simply adapted to home use, rather than analyzed to find the appropriate home learning activity to support school learning. This is a limitation of many home visitation programs as well. Children learn a tremendous amount from the informal, incidental, and broad teaching that parents do in daily living, yet most current programs have a rather narrow view of the parent as teacher. They usually emphasize a set of academic skills and basic concepts that parents are to help children learn. School-home partnership programs need to give more thought to tapping the rich learning possibilities in family life. Also, we need to identify the school-related learnings that homes can do best, and encourage those. For example, instead of encouraging parents to teach rhyming sounds directly, perhaps we need to encourage parents to surround children with nursery rhymes, poetry, and song. Instead of teaching letter sounds, perhaps parents simply need to read to and with their children.

From a teacher's point of view, perhaps the biggest disadvantage of the home-school partnership is the additional time that will have to be spent in planning and coordinating the program. Even though some schools have a parent coordinator who assumes much of the responsibility of organizing the program and making sure things go smoothly, there is still extra work for the teacher, who must work closely with home visitors, volunteers, and extra personnel to decide which materials best suit each child's needs.

SCHOOL AND HOME PARTNERSHIP: A GUIDE FOR IMPLEMENTATION

Schools, homes and communities use many approaches to help parents be better teachers of their own children, for example, lending libraries of instructional materials and toys, meetings and workshops, weekly home activity sheets or cards, telephone tips, and home visitors who also work in the classroom. In this part of the chapter we will describe the various approaches and tell how to implement them, with examples of the activities.

Advance Planning and Preparation

You may get indications of the need for home-school partnership in teaching children from many sources. Parents may ask what they can do to help their children at home; teachers may realize that parents are not talking and playing enough with their children to give them the basic background needed for success in school; a teacher may have children who are learning but also need more time and attention than they can ever get in the classroom; or the school day may be so short that the necessary time to help children is not available. A formal assessment of needs, as outlined in Chapter 4, may result in further indications; for example, parents want to help their children, but don't know how; parents cannot come to the school often enough to participate in a parent volunteer program; or parents need an intermediate involvement step before volunteering at school. You may find home-school partnership the most feasible approach to parent involvement because it requires few changes in established expectations and school procedures.

Discussions with parent groups, teachers, principals, and others who will be involved with the program should revolve around the benefits that result when parents and schools work closely together to help children learn. The problems and advantages specific to having parents learn how to be better teachers of their own chidren, discussed earlier in this chapter, should also be addressed. Teachers may want to know how much additional time will be required to do the necessary coordination and where they will find that time. Some parents may object to someone attempting to get them to teach in addition to all the other things they have to do; some may object to the school telling them what they should do with their children. Administrators may well ask about direct costs, expected use of the building, and additional tasks for busy teachers.

You will need to investigate the various approaches to helping parents become home educators as they apply to your particular situation. Organize committees to do the necessary background work and present information and recommendations to the group. Since there are so many ways the school-home partnership can be carried out, a given community should be able to find one or a combination that fits its needs. If not, parents and teachers may want to modify an existing program or even devise their own approach. Once a decision has been made, the next step is to establish reasonable goals and guidelines for parents, children, and teachers.

Remember that even the most dedicated parents and teachers have many other obligations. Even if every parent did everything the school expected, school-related difficulties would not magically disappear. When materials are taken or sent to homes, not every parent will participate. A home/center-based program for handicapped children and their parents, who might be expected to be highly motivated, reported that "the average center will have about 50 percent of their parents actively [involved]" (Fredericks et al., 1976, p. 116). Few parents will spend an hour each evening working with a child on instructional activities, but many will spend ten minutes if they and the child are enjoying it. Few parents will read a treatise on instructional methods, but many will try out short, specific, practical ideas about helping children learn. Be fair in your expectations, and let parents who are interested do more.

Implementation

In this section, we will discuss recruiting, orientation, and some general principles of starting and maintaining a successful home-school partnership. In addition, we look at three major approaches to achieving that relationship and give some examples of the methods and materials they use.

Recruiting   Even though children are already enrolled in school, you cannot assume that their parents will automatically want to participate in the home activities, so plan recruiting and motivating activities as carefully as if you were recruiting "new" parents. Use whatever techniques are most effective in your community to get parents out to a preliminary meeting—a potluck supper, picnic, Sunday afternoon meeting, special program, or workshop. Plan to give a complete explanation of why the school is starting such a program, what the benefits and problems will be, how much time it will require, and the way the program will be organized. Demonstrate what parents and children will be expected to do. If a home visitor will be working as a classroom aide, role-play a discussion as the teacher and the home visitor plan the home visit, then role-play the visit to that child's home. If workshops for parents are used, role-play (or use an actual demonstration of) a parent and child playing with the material the parent has made, then have a short workshop so parents can actually make materials to use with their own children. A film, videotape, or slide show explaining the approach to be used also provides both explanation and motivation for parents. Allow plenty of time for discussion and be prepared to answer many practical questions: What if a youngster loses the material as he or she is bringing it home? Who pays for the workshop materials? Who decides what activities a child will do? What if the child doesn't want to play the games?

If possible, record the meeting on a cassette tape so that parents who were unable to come can share in what went on. If parents are uncertain whether they want to participate, suggest that they try out the partnership for a few weeks and then make a decision.

Orientation   Orientation can be combined with recruiting or conducted separately, but it should include general principles of effective home teaching, tips on the care and use of materials, and the specifics of the approach being used. Give parents a summary of desirable behaviors for parents as teachers, such as the following examples:

1. Get children to ask questions.

2. Ask questions that have more than one right answer.

3. Ask questions that require more than one or two words to answer.

4. Get children to talk about their answers.

5. Praise children when they do well, or when they take small steps in the right direction.

6. Let children know when their answers are wrong, but do it in a loving way.

7. Get children to back up answers with facts and evidence.

8. Give time to think about a problem.

9. Give time to look at the materials before starting work.

10. Explain what is going to happen before you start.[1]

Many programs develop parent/teacher guides to meet the needs of their own communities. Discuss and demonstrate these guides and other basic principles during orientation and give parents a chance to role-play and practice. You may want to add additional suggestions such as:

1. Stop when your child begins to lose interest, or even a little before.

2. Present new information a little at a time.

3. Repeat information as needed until children remember—once is usually not enough.

Show parents how the games and activities that will be used in the program will help children learn. A few tips on encouraging children to care for and put away toys and materials will not only help parents but also conserve the materials. Some examples are:

- Have a certain place to keep the materials and return them every time.

- Work with your child to put the materials away.

- Give positive, firm directions that can be followed a step at a time, such as "Put the buttons and little trucks in the box, close it, then we'll put everything in the envelope."

Getting Started   Certain elements seem to be essential to successful program implementation: coordination between home and classroom, regularity of contact, specificity of tasks, and inexpensive and readily available materials.

Coordination does not always require that home teachers and school teachers work on exactly the same tasks using the same instructional materials. Rather, home teaching and classroom teaching should complement each other. If the kindergarten class is learning beginning letter sounds using pictures of familiar objects, families can find objects at home that have names beginning with that sound.

Sometimes parent and child activities are not coordinated with the classroom, but concentrate instead on more general teaching behaviors and skills, such as giving positive reinforcement, responding to children's interests, and encouraging children to think for themselves. Probably the best known of these is the Parent/Child Toy-Lending Library (Nimnicht el al., 1972). Parents learn to use toys to help their children learn. Variations on this concept are frequently used in school settings to complement classroom learning.

However, regular, sustained contact between home and school helps parents maintain interest and motivation. Most programs see parents or send something home every week or two weeks. This regularity helps both parents and children establish habits of taking materials to and from school and sharing new materials and ideas.

Give short, simple, step-by-step directions about how to play and talk with children. Making materials available is not enough. You must explain and show how to play Concentration, Twenty Questions, or other similar games, rather than just saying, "This is played like Concentration." Even if parents know how to play that game, they may call it something else.

Use toys, games, and supplies that are available to most parents. If the materials have to be purchased through a school supply catalog, parents will not be able to continue teaching on their own after the program is over. With some parents, you may have to begin with purchased "educational" materials, but try to work toward the use of home discards, natural materials, supplies, and toys found at the local grocery or discount stores, and books available at the libary or local store.

Let's look now at the approaches you can use to achieve home-school partnership. We have called these three major types of programs the School Bag System, Make and Take Workshops, and Traveling Teacher. We will describe each major approach and discuss ways to implement it. Ways to monitor the programs and recognize parent contributions will be suggested under each approach and summarized at the end.

The School Bag System   Not too many years ago, a sturdy school bag with a handle, pockets for pencils, crayons, and a ruler, and compartments for papers and books was an essential part of growing up and going to school. The school bag, carried from home to school and back by the child, linked the two institutions that were concerned with his or her growth and learning. Many home-school partnership programs use the same system of linkage. Sometimes games, toys, books, and instructional supplies are checked out to the home to be used and returned. Other programs send home cards or one-page sheets with suggestions of things parents can do with their children.

Let's look at an example of how one school uses cards and other printed material to help parents become better teachers of their own children. To meet the needs of families in their Follow Through, Title I, and other special programs, the Chattanooga Public Schools in Chattanooga, Tennessee, developed a parent involvement system based on parent/child activity cards and sheets to help children with readiness skills, mathematics, and reading. Short booklets for parents summarize the recommended teaching and parenting behaviors, health and safety tips, and information on children's social and educational development.

The activity cards are designed to use materials found in the home and to be "home-fun, not home-work." They explain why the skill that is being developed is important to the child, encourage positive parenting behavior and parent-child interaction, and urge parents to think of other things they can do to help the child. Examples of the cards are shown in Figures 10.1, 10.2, and 10.3. Parents and teachers can develop similar cards to meet their own needs and interests.

The Chattanooga materials include guides for starting the program,

Figure 10.1
(© 1976 Chattanooga, Tennessee Public Schools)

SHOPPING SPREE

Each of us has had the experience of sending someone to the grocery store to get flour, milk, and eggs; and had that person return with the flour and milk—no eggs!

This happens to children at school, too. They are told to bring pencil, paper, and a storybook to the class. They show up with the book—not the one teacher asked for—no pencil, no paper.

Repeating aloud what they have been told helps some children remember better. Others get better at remembering by playing games that help build memory skills.

Each of the games described has a special twist to help build listening and remembering skills. Play a different game each night. Maybe they will remind you of other memory games you played when you were younger.

Front

SHOPPING SPREE. Memory games to play with your child:

PLAY STORE—Choose props from the cupboard for this game—about ten items. The purpose of the game is to have the child look at the items on the table, then turn his or her back and name the items. As you add each item to the "store," say, "In my store is butter and cereal." Then, "In my store is butter, cereal, and eggs." Go as far as your child can remember the items.

STOCK THE SHELVES—Begin with three items. Place them on the table (now the grocery shelf) and name them—butter, cereal, eggs. Have your child turn his or her back and name the items on the shelf. Can the child remember what item was the first? What came next? What was last? Change the groceries around—cereal, eggs, butter—and name them again.

GROCERY LIST—Pretend your mother is sending you to the store. The first person says, "Mother sent me to the store to buy an apple." The second person says, "Mother sent me to the store to buy an apple and an orange." Each time add something new to the list. The game ends when someone leaves an item out.

VEGETABLE SOUP—The first person says, "I made some vegetable soup. In my soup I put some tomatoes." The next person adds another vegetable to the soup, and so on. The game ends when someone leaves an item out.

FRUIT SALAD—Name some fruits that might be used in fruit salad. Play the same way as the vegetable soup game.

Back

Figure 10.2

(© 1976 Chattanooga, Tennessee Public Schools)

FIND THE LETTER

Parents of young children often ask, "Should I—or should I not—teach my child the alphabet?"

YES, do teach the names of the letters IF you can do it in a fun way. No harm can come from learning the names of letters unless you pressure your child. Knowing the names of letters gives the beginning reader a clue to the sound that a letter spells.

A B C books are interesting to young children. Slightly older children take pride in making their own scrapbooks. A B C cards can be made with glue and cornmeal to be traced with the fingers. Large plastic letters can be arranged to spell simple words and to name letters in your child's name.

FIND THE LETTER is played like Bingo. Call the name of a letter, let your child find it and cover it with a bottle cap, bean, or piece of paper. After a row has been covered and your child has "bingoed," have the names of the letters called back to you as the cover is taken off.

Front

FIND THE LETTER

FREE	D d	B b	M m	I i	FREE
P p	H h	V v	E e	C c	S s
Y y	A a	Z z	G g	K k	O o
R r	W w	L l	T t	U u	F f
FREE	J j	Q q	M m	X x	FREE

Back

Figure 10.3
(© 1975 Chattanooga, Tennessee Public Schools)

MATCHING PARTS

Ideas are developed before the math words are taught to go with them. Your children learn about circles and squares, but we do not tell them they are learning geometry.

Learning about symmetrical figures will help them in geometry, too. They will not need to learn this big word now. Instead, talk about the matching parts. Some figures (circles) can be folded several ways and have matching parts. Others (valentines) can be folded only one way to match exactly.

* Fold a paper in half.
* Cut out heart on the FOLDED edge. A heart can be folded only one way to have both sides the same.
* What happens when you fold the tip to the top? Are both parts the same then?
* Cut a circle and show that a circle can be folded several ways and have matching sides.

Front

MATCHING PARTS   You will need: * Newspapers (Sunday comics are grand!)
                                   * Scissors

To make shapes that are the same on both sides:

Fold the newspaper in half. Cut any shape—on the fold. It is most important to understand the "fold" and the open edges. Let your child cut other shapes on the fold.

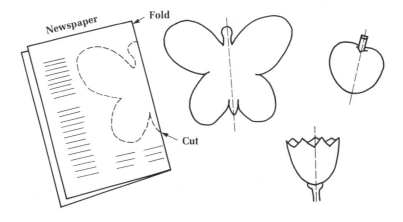

Back

monitoring progress, and recognizing what has been accomplished: how to conduct orientation workshops, get parent reactions to the program throughout the year, keep track of activities that have been sent to each home, and follow children's progress in mastering the emphasized skills.

As a teacher in such a program, you work with the parent advisory committee to introduce parents to the activity card program through letters, explanations, and a workshop. In the workshop, you demonstrate how to prepare materials to use with the cards, and how to use and vary the suggested activities.

Select a few appropriate cards to send home with parents from the workshop, explaining that they are to keep and use them with their children for a few minutes (or more) every day. Additional cards will come home from school every week, selected specifically for each family and child. The information covered in the workshop should be sent to those parents who were unable to attend.

Monitoring of the program begins as soon as cards start going home. The Chattanooga program has a simple, one-page "Activity Card Record Form," consisting of columns of numbers corresponding to the numbers of the activity cards. When a card is sent home with a child, the corresponding number on that child's sheet is circled. When the child moves to the next grade or to another school in the system, the Activity Card Record goes along, and the program continues without interruption. Of course, sending a card home does not mean that the child has mastered that skill, so if additional practice is needed, send parents a reminder to refer back to a previous card.

Keeping track of what parents are actually doing with the cards is more difficult. Give parents a chance to say what they like and do not like about the program at meetings, conferences, and through response sheets sent home and returned by the children. Sheets can be modeled on the one shown in Figure 10.4.

The simplest form of the School Bag System uses library books sent home in drawstring bags. The most elaborate uses activity packets containing everything parents need to play a particular game or activity, including directions and suggestions for extension of the activities. You can also use this system to put school-related materials directly into the hands of parents and children by sending home instructional supplies, toys, books, games, and other materials to be used at home and returned the following week. This approach requires more advance preparation as well as constant maintenance.

Because of the investment of time and money in even the most modest of these programs, parents should be closely involved in every step of the process to make sure the right books and materials—and approaches to the parents—are selected.

As a teacher, you will work closely with the advisory committee and parent coordinator, if there is one, to make sure the books, packets, and toys reflect the interests and needs of the children and classroom. For younger children, you may want to purchase or make sturdy but portable manipulative toys and develop activities around them. Older children can use instructional games made of posterboard, cardboard, and pictures. Suggestions for these are available in almost any book of activities for young children (see Lorton, 1976). However, directions to the parents will have to be prepared by someone,

Figure 10.4
Reaction Sheet: Activity Card Program

My child and I enjoyed doing the activities on the cards.	Yes	No
I learned some things about teaching my child from the cards.	Yes	No
My child learned some things from the activities we did together.	Yes	No
I think the activity card program has helped me to help my child do better in school.	Yes	No

We especially liked these cards and activities:

Please share with us any ideas or feelings you have about the card activity program and its effect on you and your child.

usually the teacher or a group of teachers, Examples of some "To Parents" pages prepared for one school's lending library are given in Figures 10.5 and 10.6. One example uses simple, readily available art material to encourage creative expression, the other describes a more specific teaching activity.

Put these directions and the accompanying materials in a large manila envelope with a sturdy metal or string closer, print the name of the activity and any other identification on the outside with a felt-tip pen, and the packet is ready to go. Prepare in advance at least enough for a month. If the children return the packets on Thursday, other children can take them home on Friday. You will not be able to count on complete exchange, however, because of the wide range of abilities and interests found in any group. Also, time will be needed to make repairs.

A variation on the school bag approach checks out cards and packets to parents rather than to children. Parents meet at the school, in each other's homes, or come to the school individually to pick up the packet and discuss it and their child's needs. In this way, personal contact between parents and the school is maintained.

Use the School Bag System itself to recognize parents' contributions; for example, send home a note of appreciation, select a special card or activity to acknowledge a family's interests, share with other families an idea contributed by a parent, or report something a child said or did that showed the family was

Figure 10.5
*(Adapted from Richland County School District One,
Columbia, South Carolina; used by permission)*

```
To Parents


   Skill area:  Language

   Materials in packet:  Pictures and three cards with labels

   Tasks:  Classifying pictures according to categories and
           explaining how the objects are related

   Activities:

      1.  Name each picture, describe it, and talk about how it is
          used.

      2.  Group the pictures according to classes.  Tell why the
          pictures belong together.

      3.  Mix up the pictures and spread them out.  Take turns
          drawing a picture and describing it.  Let the other
          player draw a picture that belongs to the same group.

   Extended activities:

      1.  Cut from catalogs and magazines pictures that illustrate
          other categories such as buildings, vehicles, and plants.

      2.  Name three things, including two that belong in the same
          group, and let your child tell which does not belong and
          why.

      3.  Name two things that belong in the same group and let
          your child name another that would belong also.

      4.  Name items that go together such as cup and saucer,
          comb and brush, knife and fork, ball and bat, hammer
          and nail.
```

using the suggestions. Keep track of these incidents through the year and share some with parents at a final recognition meeting.

Make and Take Workshops   Make and Take Workshops are parent meetings with a plus. The plus is that parents make and learn how to use toys, games, and activities to promote their children's learning. Schools and other educational institutions have used the workshop way of learning for many years, but only recently has that approach been adapted to parents. We will discuss two examples.

Four Chicago mothers saw the possibilities for parent involvement through this method and formed a group called Parents as Resources (PAR). Through workshops, books, newspaper columns, and television programs, they show

Figure 10.6
(Adapted from Richland County School District One,
Columbia, South Carolina; used by permission)

To Parents

  Skill areas: Art and visual perception

  Materials in packet: Scissors, glue, paper, and crayons

  Objectives: To learn to express ideas, thoughts, and feelings through
               art media and to develop eye-hand coordination

Activities:

  1. Encourage your child to use the crayons and paper to express
     his or her own ideas and feelings through artistic creations.
     Perhaps the child will want you to write a story about his or
     her art work.

  2. Make a collection of items with various textures (yarn, cloth,
     cotton, twigs, pine needles, bark, feathers, seeds, ribbons,
     wood shavings, string, straws, and so on). Discuss the textures
     and describe how they feel. Then your child can arrange the
     materials on a piece of paper and paste them down, using his
     or her imagination.

  3. Use multicolored comic strips. Tear them into different sizes
     and shapes: tiny, large, narrow, wide, round, square, and so
     on. Make a mural of shapes and colors. A grocery bag cut open
     will make a good background on which your child can paste the
     design.

Extended activities:

  Encourage your child to have other art experiences.

  1. Rolling, squeezing, pounding, and bending--these are some of
     the enjoyable activities of working with clay. With clay the
     child can create objects with a three-dimensional effect.
     Play-dough works well as a substitute for clay at home.
         Recipe for easy play-dough: 3 cups flour   1 cup salt
                                      3/4 cup water   food coloring
         Work the mixture together and add more water until the
         dough is workable but not sticky. One tablespoon of alum
         may be added to each two cups of flour as a preservative.

  2. Provide opportunities for your child to paint.
         Homemade paint: 1 cup liquid starch   6 cups water
                          1/2 cup soap powder
         Dissolve soap in water and mix well with starch. Add coloring.

  3. Plan a family trip to the Columbia Art Museum at 1501 Senate
     Street.

parents how to use readily available materials to teach their children. The workshops, in which parents make the items that are being discussed, are central to their whole approach. Another group, the Institute for Family and Child Study of Michigan State University, investigated the effects of workshop activities and procedures (Boger et al., 1971). They called their workshops Parents Are Teachers Too (PATT). We will use the PATT program as an example to help us describe the workshop as a parent involvement strategy.

In parent-teacher workshops, parents construct toys or games to use at home with their children. Active involvement of parents in these workshops is likely to have the following beneficial results:

1. Parents are more interested in coming to the workshops. One parent remarked, "I'd have come in earlier if I'd known you weren't just sitting around talking" (Boger et al., 1971, p. 293).

2. The cooperative production of materials gives parents and teachers a chance to get acquainted, discuss mutual concerns, and learn from each other in a situation where they have like interests.

3. The material that the parent makes for the child is special and is likely to be highly motivating for both parent and child.

4. The workshop itself, with its exchange of ideas, group involvement, interest, and encouragement, is motivating. Parents go home with something they have just made and learned how to use, which is quite different from a prepared packet that they simply open and use.

The content of the workshops will vary to meet the needs and interests of the children, parents, and teachers involved. The PATT program stresses two content areas for children—language development and perceptual-motor skills—but mathematics, reading, health, physical development, and other content areas can be emphasized. Content for the parents can also be varied. For example, some parents may be learning how to encourage children to think for themselves, while others may simply be learning how to keep a child engaged for ten minutes.

Goals are very similar to those of other programs: to increase the amount and quality of adult-child interaction, and to increase participants' knowledge and skill in whatever content is emphasized.

We will now look at what is involved in implementing a series of workshops to establish home-school partnership. As the teacher, you will need to be in the workshop, so it cannot be scheduled during regular school hours. Parents must be able to participate for at least two hours, so child care services must be considered by having evening meetings, child care at the school, or both. Let parents know why this workshop meeting is different from others they may have attended in the past. Include in the invitations examples of the kinds of materials they will be making, reactions of previous participants, and pictures of people involved in workshop activities. Stress that parents will enjoy making the materials and that both parents and children will enjoy playing with them.

Be sure to specify who will be paying for materials and whether parents will be expected to bring household discards.

Locate a comfortable and attractive room for the workshop. Adult-size chairs and tables are essential. Storage for workshop supplies, scissors, glue, contact paper, and other items makes getting ready and cleaning up much easier. Plenty of coffee, tea, or a fruit drink will add to the relaxed atmosphere.

Unless you have time to develop your own workshop ideas, we suggest that you obtain a guide for implementing a series of workshops, such as that developed by the Parents Are Teachers Too program.[2] With a guide that specifies the steps, materials needed, patterns, and background information, a teacher with a supportive parent committee can implement the workshops. Decide well in advance what toys and games will be made. It may take several weeks to collect the necessary discards for a particular project, and many stores do not carry a sufficient stock of craft supplies for workshops. Unless parents have everything they need to finish a project, some of the sense of satisfaction and the impetus to go right home and try it out will be lost. Give specific, step-by-step instructions for construction, demonstrating as necessary. A list of future needs and a place to store household discards and supplies until they are needed will encourage parents to save and bring in needed supplies.

You will need to explain and demonstrate how to help children learn, then provide a time for parents to role-play and practice the necessary skills. Select activities and materials to help children and parents with needed skills. The activities should (1) be economical and easily constructed within the allotted workshop time, (2) be appealing to children, (3) be adaptable to a moderate range in children's attention span and developmental level, and (4) relate to but not duplicate materials and activities being used in the classroom.

Monitor the progress of both workshops and parents so that interest and motivation are kept high. A written evaluation of each workshop is not in keeping with the spirit of sharing and partnership that the workshops are designed to foster. Instead, have a few minutes of sharing just before the workshop ends. What did you enjoy most about this workshop? What could we do better (or differently) next time? In addition, teachers, parent involvement coordinators, and the parent committee should be sensitive to individuals and to the group as they work together. Not every workshop can be a memorable success, but most of them will be if you are attuned to the likes, dislikes, and needs of the parents that are involved.

Attendance is the simplest and most basic way to monitor parent involvement and progress. How many parents are attending? How many make an effort to come and get patterns and materials when they are unable to attend the workshop? But you should also find out what is taking place at home: whether there are changes in parent attitudes and behaviors. In the workshops or on forms sent home, ask parents questions such as:

1. What did you and your child do with this game (activity, toy)?

2. How many times did you and your child work with this activity?

3. Did you and your child enjoy doing this activity together?

4. Would you recommend that we make this material next year in our workshops?

Use these reactions to guide you in selecting or adapting workshop materials.

Recognize parents' contributions and involvement in all the usual ways, such as sincere and warm welcome and mention in newsletters, newspaper stories, and end-of-the-year programs, but take advantage of the workshop approach to use other forms of recognition, too. Post pictures taken at the workshops in the hallway, parent room, and classroom. Compile suggestions of ways that parents have used workshop games and materials to send home to all the parents, with proper credit for each idea. Every parent—even those who are unable to attend the workshops—can collect and share household discards and "recycles" to use in the workshops. This should also be acknowledged. Encourage parents to get involved in planning a workshop using ideas they think others would enjoy. If necessary, help them write up the activity and organize the process, but be sure their names are attached. These recognitions, combined with the enjoyable, satisfying activities of the workshops and playing with the children, will help to keep parents interested and learning.

Traveling Teacher   The Traveling Teacher works part of the day in the classroom and part of the day in the children's homes, linking the two by her presence and by the teaching suggestions she takes to the home. The home visits are carried out as described in Chapter 8, but there is very close coordination and cooperation with the classroom teacher and activities. This coordination is accomplished in several ways: (1) by the presence of the traveling teacher in both the home and school, (2) by the classroom teacher's participation in planning the home visit, and (3) by the home visitor's instruction of small groups and individuals in the classroom.

The classroom teacher has two primary roles: teacher and leader in the classroom, and co-worker with the home visitor in planning the home visits. The first role is no different from working with any paid aide or assistant except that the home visitor brings to the classroom many insights about children's backgrounds and home situations that enable the teaching team to work more effectively. The second role, working with the home visitor to plan the home visit, may be quite unfamiliar to many teachers.

If you are the teacher, your most difficult task may be to find the necessary time to plan with and train the home visitor. The two tasks are accomplished as you and the home visitor do the following activities (Greenwood and Kaplan, 1976):

1. Review and discuss the last home visit and any problems.

2. Select from existing materials or make an activity appropriate for each child and parents.

3. Decide the way to present the home learning activity to the parent and what teaching skills to stress. You may want to demonstrate these to the home visitor.

4. Role-play the demonstration. You take the part of the parent and have the home visitor conduct the demonstration, so you agree on teaching strategies and emphases.

The aim is to select activities and teaching strategies that will help child and parent learn together. As an example, let's look at the Morgan family. Rosella, a child in your first-grade class, knows how to count to twenty, but needs help in counting accurately and in recognizing the numerals. Rosella's family likes to play card games and have enjoyed the educational card games the home visitor has taken. Using cardboard and felt-tip pens, you and the home visitor construct 40 cards, four of each number, zero through nine, with a large numeral in the center of each card and the corresponding number of dots or pictures for Rosella to count. The two of you have worked out a game procedure for Rosella and her mother to play. You have also planned an extension activity for the following week to keep interest high. There are two objectives for Rosella's mother: to play with Rosella ten minutes every day and to concentrate on what Rosella knows by praising her when she tries and when she is correct. You suggest including a counting and number book and a puzzle that shows the sequence of numbers and numerals. The home visitor will also show Mrs. Morgan how to use numerals commonly found around the house for teaching, and will remind the family to watch "Sesame Street" to help both Rosella and the younger children. The home visitor will cover all the cards with clear contact paper to protect them, collect other needed materials, and be ready to go.

You can plan more quickly and effectively if you keep notes during the week about the skills with which children need help, and if the home visitor keeps records about what the families like to do and can do, as well as where they need help. Also, making an occasional home visit yourself will help you know more about the family and whether or not the plans you and the home visitor make are appropriate and will strengthen ties between home and school. You may also help the home visitor decide if a family has needs beyond what the school can meet, and where to refer them for additional assistance.

Monitoring a home visitor program coordinated with a classroom is complicated because there are so many elements involved. Here are some common questions you as a teacher can ask.

1. Am I turning all the planning for home visits over to the home visitor so that my insights as a teacher are being missed?

2. Are we using the same activities over and over again?

3. Is the number of parents actively involved in the program increasing or decreasing?

4. Is there evidence in the children's behavior that their parents are working with them at home?

5. Is the home visitor becoming a more skilled instructional aide?

6. Are home visits conducted regularly and for the full time period?

7. Are careful records of home visits being maintained, including activities and books that are taken?

8. Am I, as the teacher, incorporating into my planning the insights that the home visitor has about the child's home environment?

9. Are parent reactions being solicited and heeded?

If you detect problems, adjust what you and the home visitor are doing before the problems get larger.

Successful home visits with a warm and encouraging home visitor and responsive children are the best rewards for parents. But there are some other things you can do. Distribute the ideas for home learning that have been suggested by a parent; when a parent comes to the classroom to visit or participate, mention a particular home learning activity he or she did well, and perhaps ask the parent to play it with one or two children; give special awards to parents who were home for every visit; ask parents who responded well to the program to explain it to next year's parents; and post in the parents' room at school the names or pictures of all who participated in school activities through the home visitation program.

Review

We have discussed some elements of the review process as we looked at the three major types of home-school partnership. Monitoring and recognizing parents' contributions are closely tied to the type of program that is being carried out. Reviewing, evaluating, and sharing with others what has been accomplished and what modifications need to be made are the same whether you establish a home-school partnership through the School Bag System, Make and Take Workshops, or Traveling Teachers. Summarize and draw some conclusions from the records that have been kept during the year. How many books, games, and instructional supplies went into the homes? How many parents participated in some way? How many home visits were attempted and completed? What did parents and children have to say about the program? This and other pertinent information should be pulled into a brief report and made available to all interested parties, including the advisory committee, principal, superintendent, director, and school board or board of directors. Take slides throughout the year and use them to illustrate a more informal report for the parents at a program meeting. If the program is new or unique in your area, the education editor of the local newspaper may be interested.

As you summarize the records and reflect on the triumphs and failures of the year, recommend changes. Perhaps the cards or packets went home too often or too seldom. Maybe the games were too complicated. Maybe the process for having parent volunteers come to check materials in and out was poorly planned and should be revised. Whatever the suggested modifications, write them down to guide you and the parents in another year's efforts to establish a school-home partnership.

ADDITIONAL SUGGESTIONS

Almost all schools and centers use a combination of approaches to establish links with homes. These tested and proven ways can be used to complement an intensive program such as the School Bag System, Make and Take Workshops, and the Traveling Teacher. They can also be used to establish less intensive home-school links. Most involve take-homes, so remember that parents will be more likely to look at and use any ideas or suggestions if they are sent home one or two at a time. Note the following suggestions:

1. Include activities for parents to do at home in your room or school newsletter. Some day care centers send home such a newsletter on Friday, suggesting things to do over the weekend.

2. Use a distinctive color of paper for notices about parent-child activities, so that parents recognize it. Send home half-sheets reminding parents of special television shows, community events, seasonal ideas, and so forth. Include suggestions for discussion.

3. Set up a telephone hot line, using a telephone answering service machine to transmit a recorded message about what you and the children are doing each week and how parents can help at home. As an alternative, have a specific time each week that a teacher can be reached by telephone.

4. Send home a list of library books for parents to read to children, or children to read to parents. Both general lists and lists related to current classroom interests are appropriate.

5. In November, send home a list of gifts appropriate for the children.

6. Send home recipes for food that the children cooked at school.

7. Post parent-child activity suggestions just outside the classroom door or in the parent room.

Make the time and effort that go into creating instructional materials go further and last longer by using sturdy materials and procedures that help organize and store materials for easy access. We suggest a few ideas.

1. Laminate or cover with clear contact paper everything that you can.

2. Let each parent make an individual chalkboard for the home by painting a 12 by 12 inch square of hardboard with chalkboard paint. Divide

the back side into 4-inch squares for playing Concentration, tic-tac-toe, and other games.

3. Make open-ended game boards for playing games with any skill that needs to be practiced. Draw or glue the game inside a file folder, laminate or cover it with contact paper, write the names of the board on the tab, and it is ready to use. Figure 10.7 shows examples. Make up your own rules—the important thing is to add an element of fun to working together. Parents can keep these boards at home to be used with different skill games, or the boards can be part of an activity packet, with different rules and skills tucked inside as the year progresses.

4. Tape one side of a flat box together to make a hinge. Draw or paste a game board on the inside of the box, add the dice, cubes, spinner, and other things that are needed to play, close the box, label the outside, and you have another game ready to go home.

5. Make spinners out of sturdy posterboard, cardboard, or clear plastic lids. Divide the spinner board into colors, numbers, letters, geometric shapes, and so forth. Use a brad to attach a small key, paper clip, or safety pin for a spinner. Use the margarine or whipped topping container the plastic lid was on to store a couple of small cars, molded plastic animals, or other small toys for "players." Figure 10.7 shows an example.

6. Cover the pages of homemade books with contact paper; or make books by mounting or drawing pictures and words on both sides of construction paper, place in acetate pages, and bind.

SUMMARY

School-home partnerships represent a shared approach to the education of children. The programs aim to develop continuity and cooperation between the home and the individual child's classroom, so that children's learning is enhanced, parents' teaching skills are improved, and parents acquire positive attitudes toward their role as teachers. The teacher's role in this approach is that of parent educator and school partner of the parent. The content of home and school partnership programs is usually related to the school. Parents are taught the behaviors and attitudes that research and accepted practice indicate help children succeed in school. The most widely used method is focused interaction around a joint task, such as books, toys, games, or a structured activity.

The advantages of the home-school partnership are that it gives additional attention to children so that they may learn faster; it communicates trust and confidence in the family's ability to teach children; it is noncontroversial and relatively inexpensive; it establishes a method of regular communication with the home; and it gives a way of varying attendance and staffing patterns for children with special needs. The disadvantages are that parents and children

Figure 10.7
Game Boards

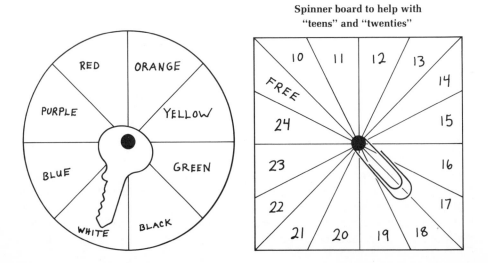

START							CALENDAR
S	M	T	W	T	F	S	
1	2	3	4	5	6	7	
8	9	10	11	12	13	14	
15	16	17	18	19	20	21	
22	23	24	25	26	27	28	
29	30	31					
						FINISH	

Spinners

Spinner board to help with "teens" and "twenties"

RED ORANGE PURPLE YELLOW BLUE GREEN WHITE BLACK

10 11 12 13 14 FREE 15 24 23 16 22 17 21 20 19 18

Figure 10.7
(continued)

Closed for storage

Open

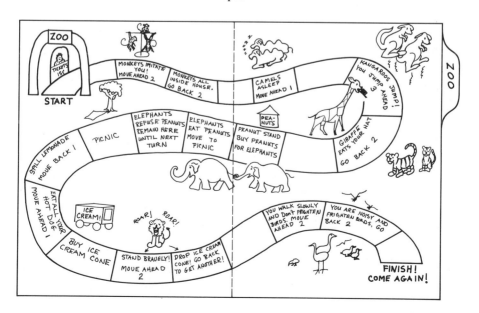

may get too emotionally involved and frustrated with the tasks; the tasks are overly school-oriented; and there is additional work for the teacher.

Although schools, homes, and communities use many approaches to help parents be better teachers of their children, we looked in depth at only three. The first two, the School Bag System and Make and Take Workshops, can be implemented with little cost in almost any community. The third, Traveling Teacher, requires additional staffing and travel money. The School Bag System links the home and school through instructional materials and suggestions that the children carry back and forth. Parents use these ideas and materials to teach their children. Make and Take Workshops bring parents to school to make toys, games, and instructional materials to take home to use with their own children. In the workshops, they learn how to use the materials to help children learn, an essential element in all these approaches. The Traveling Teacher works in the classroom part of the day and in the home part of the day. He or she becomes the link between home and school.

There are other ways to establish this linkage, of course, and we gave some additional suggestions at the end of the chapter.

FOR DISCUSSION AND FURTHER STUDY

1. Send representatives from your class to find out what local schools do to promote home-school partnership.

2. What are some things you could do if you found out that a child felt angry and defeated and the mother felt frustrated because the child was not learning the home tasks as fast as the mother expected?

3. Construct a file folder or box game, as shown in the section on Additional Suggestions. Write out the rules for the game as if you were going to send it home, and then demonstrate how to play it with a fellow student.

4. One of the criticisms of both home-based programs and home-school partnerships is that the learning tasks are too narrowly focused on school activities. In small groups, brainstorm some natural home learning activities. Report the results to the class.

5. Make up a sample school bag packet of home-school learning activities. Use the format in Figures 10.5 and 10.6 to write out directions to parents. You might want to try a packet to promote one of the home learning activities your group generated.

6. Research and write a short paper on one of the many research and demonstration projects of the last few years that used this approach to parent involvement. In addition to *Parents Are Teachers Too*, you might be interested in the *Florida Parent Education Follow-Through Model*, the Appalachia Educational Laboratory's approach, the *Portage Project*, or the *Home-Center Based Parent Training Model* developed at the University of Oregon. (The last two are briefly described in Lillie et al., 1976.)

BIBLIOGRAPHY

Apples Are for Teachers: Desirable Teaching Behaviors for Home Teachers and School Teachers. Chattanooga, Tenn.: Educational Planning and Development Company, n.d.

Bell, Terrell H. *Active Parent Concern: A New Home Guide to Help Your Child in School*. Englewood Cliffs, N.J.: Prentice-Hall, 1976.

————. "A New Role for the Neighborhood Elementary School." Address delivered at the annual convention of the National Convention of the National Association of State Boards of Education. Portland, Oregon, October 10, 1973.

Boger, Robert P., et al. *Parents Are Teachers, Too: A Curriculum Module for Increasing Positive Parent-Child, Parent-Teacher, and Parent-School Interaction*. East Lansing: Institute for Family and Child Study, Michigan State University, September 1971 (Grant No. 9931, Office of Economic Opportunity).

Chattanooga Public Schools. *Home/School Education Learning Products*. Chattanooga, Tenn.: Chattanooga Public Schools, n.d.

Cole, Ann S., Carolyn B. Haas, Elizabeth H. Heller, and Betty K. Weinberger. *Recipes for Run*. Northfield, Ill.: PAR Project, 1972.

————. *Workshop Procedures*. Northfield, Ill.: PAR Project, 1976.

Duncan, Linda J. and Barbara Vonbehren. "Pepper—A Spicy New Program." *The Reading Teacher* 27, no. 3 (November 1974):180–83.

Fredricks, H.D., Victor L. Baldwin, and David Grove. "A Home-Center Based Parent Training Model." In *Teaching Parents to Teach: A Guide for Working with the Special Child*, ed. David L. Lillie et al. New York: Walker and Co., 1976.

Goodson, Barbara D., and Robert D. Hess. *Parents as Teachers of Young Children: An Evaluative Review of Some Contemporary Concepts and Programs*. Stanford, Calif.: Stanford University Press, 1975.

Gordon, Ira J. "Significant Socio-Cultural Factors in Effective Parenting." In *Parent Education: Ecological Perspectives*. Occasional papers available from the School of Education, University of North Carolina, Chapel Hill, November 1977.

Greenwood, Gordon, and L. Kaplan. "The Role of the Teacher." In *Building Effective Home-School Relationships*, ed. Ira J. Gordon and William Breivogel. Boston: Allyn and Bacon, 1976.

Jackson, Nancy E., Halbert B. Robinson, and Philip S. Dale. *Cognitive Development in Young Children*. Monterey, Calif.: Brooks/Cole, 1977.

Lillie, David L. (ed.) et al. *Teaching Parents to Teach: A Guide for Working with the Special Child*. New York: Walker and Co., 1976.

Lorton, Mary. *Work Jobs for Parents*. New York: Addison-Wesley, 1976.

Loveless, P., and K. Kelly. *University of Hawaii Language Curriculum Guide*. Honolulu: University of Hawaii Head Start Evaluation and Research Center, 1968.

Nimnicht, Glen, et al. *The Parent/Child Toy-Lending Library*. Berkeley, Calif.: Far West Laboratory for Educational Research and Development, 1972.

"Parent Activities." Columbia, S.C.: Richland County School District One, n.d.

Powell, Douglas R.   *The Interface between Families and Child Care Programs: A Study of Parent-Caregiver Relationships.* Detroit, Mich.: Merrill-Palmer Institute, 1977.

Updegraff, Ruth, et al.   *Practice in Preschool Education.* New York: McGraw-Hill, 1938.

NOTES

[1]These desirable teaching behaviors—applicable to both teachers and parents— were developed by Ira Gordon and his colleagues at the Institute for the Development of Human Resources in Gainesville, Florida. *Apples Are for Teachers*, an illustrated booklet listing these behaviors and simple explanations and examples for parents, is available from the Educational Planning and Product Development Company, 7416 Twin Brook Circle, Chattanooga, Tennessee 37421.

[2]Information on the Parents Are Teachers Too program is available from the Institute for Family and Child Study, Michigan State University, East Lansing, Michigan 48823.

11 Parent Education

Parent education aims to help parents become better informed about child rearing and about family life as it affects child rearing. This aspect of parent involvement, often called "parenting education," "education for parenthood," or just "parenting," is much broader than parent involvement as teachers, policy makers, or supportive resources for the school. Society expects parents to perform many roles in relation to their children, and it is these parenting roles on which parent education focuses.

Although no one can tell parents exactly what they should do to raise the kind of children they want, parents are eager for information to make parenting easier and more fulfilling. Indications that schools should be involved can be found in the results of Gallup polls of public attitudes. In 1976, three of every four adults in the United States approved of "offering courses to parents as a regular part of the public school educational system" (Gallup, 1977, p. 41). The majority of parents of children currently in the schools indicated a willingness to pay additional taxes to support such programs. These findings are substantiated by the 1976–77 American Family Report, which found that although 90 percent of today's parents would still have children if they had it to do over, they "would welcome help to make the job easier" (Yankelovich, Skelly and White, Inc., 1977, p. 27). Many nursery schools, kindergartens, Head Start centers, and research and demonstration centers have recognized this need and responded to it. Public elementary schools are increasing their services to parents as parents.

In this chapter, we will describe the many types of parent education that are available, and then tell how to set up and lead a parent education group. Because parent education is a controversial subject, particularly in public schools, we discuss at some length the ethical issues, contradictions, and problems involved. To help parent educators move away from one or two overworked approaches, we provide information on the many types of content and the diversity of methods and resources that are available. The chapter ends with a list of information sources about parent education.

PARENT EDUCATION: A DESCRIPTION

A Look at One Program

The door closed behind the last parent and Anita sat down to relax a minute, reflect, and make a few notes about the meeting that had just ended. This was the first of a series of meetings that her school was sponsoring, and she was glad that it had gone well. As a kindergarten teacher, Anita was well aware of the number of parents who wanted someone to talk with about their children. When the school principal asked her if she would be interested in doing some parent education, Anita quickly said yes.

Anita had been involved in parent education groups at the cooperative nursery she had taught at for several years, and she was familiar with the principles and techniques. She, the principal, and a small parent advisory group were able to set up basic guidelines rather quickly. The series of meetings would last for six or eight weeks. The group would meet once a week, on a night to be decided after parents had expressed their preferences. Topics and goals would be set following this also. The list of possible topics would be restricted to those for which Anita thought she could get good materials and resources, and those that would be appropriate for a meeting sponsored by a public institution. For example, she knew that several families were concerned with their children's religious development, but felt they should seek this advice elsewhere. Medical and legal problems would be excluded, too.

The preselection of content and materials would help the group retain its focus and interest but would allow little time for personal parenting concerns to be discussed. Knowing from her work with the parent cooperative how important such discussion is, Anita and the parent advisory group decided to start the ninety-minute meetings early in the evening so that parents could stay later to discuss their personal concerns with Anita or other parents.

A needs assessment survey of parent interest and availability was sent home with all children who had younger brothers and sisters at home, with an extra copy for them to give to a neighbor who had younger children. A tally of the responses showed that parents wanted to know more about guiding and disciplining their children, what children could be expected to know and do at various ages, and what they as parents needed to do to help their children grow and develop normally.

Anita and the advisory committee decided on six topics that would cover portions of the content parents requested. Materials for in-depth study by parents who wanted to explore the ideas further would be placed in the parents room at school to be read there or checked out.

As Anita looked at the topics, she decided to combine the study of children's growth and development with a discussion of the practical implications of what parents should do. Parents would go home with a number of simple things they could immediately put into practice. Each week they would try to make some change in their behavior toward their children; that effort would begin the discussion for the following week.

A flyer giving topics, dates, times, and invitations to all interested parents was sent home with the children and posted in the school and other neighborhood places. Between the date on which the flyer went out and the first meeting, Anita collected materials, obtained additional resources, and got the meetings organized.

Everything was prepared when the first parent walked into the school library—a sign-up sheet, name tags, and the parent advisory group acting as hosts. Coffee, comfortable chairs, and some easy conversation helped everyone feel at home, even Anita.

Anita started the meeting promptly with introductions, an overview of the meetings, and the approach they were going to use. Parents seemed particularly interested in improving the way they actually guided and talked with their children, and they were pleased that they would be trying out some practical ideas. Anita started the film she had selected to be the point of departure for discussion, and the parent education series, "How Do Your Children Grow?" was under way.

Distinguishing Characteristics

Settings   Parent education takes place in public schools; child development, day care, and Head Start centers; mental health and doctors' clinics; privately and publicly sponsored nursery schools and co-ops; homes; hospitals; college classrooms; and churches and synagogues. It is sponsored by a multitude of organizations, public and private, profit and nonprofit, secular and church-related. Our primary concern is parent education associated wih early childhood schools, whether these are public or private, primary or preprimary. However, we cannot ignore the many other ways parent education is delivered, such as television, magazine articles, and family study groups, because schools and centers can use these resources for the benefit of the children and their families.

In the past, kindergartens and cooperative or university-sponsored nursery schools were leaders in parent education. At one time, the PTA sponsored and organized parent education groups in the public schools, but the emphasis of these groups gradually changed from parent education to supporting the schools. However, schools that involve parents in any way—as teachers of their own children, supportive resources, policy makers, aides, or volunteers—soon find that they cannot avoid giving advice, counsel, and support to parents about child rearing. More and more of them are deciding that they might as well do this in a systematic way. Schools have contact with most families, so they may be able to extend parent education to those who want and need it easier than any other delivery system, with the possible exception of commercial television. In the process, they will probably enhance the family's ability to nurture the child.

Goals   Although the aim of parent education is always to produce better parents, interpretations of what is "better" are often vague, if indeed they are stated at all. A recent position paper defined some of the goals of parent education as "developing educational potentials of parents for the social, mental, emotional, and physical growth of children"; improving parent-child communication throughout the life cycle"; and "clarifying parental responsibilities and competencies in developing emotional stability of all family members" (Cromwell and Bartz, 1976, pp. 18–19). We can hardly disagree with those goals, but it is not immediately obvious how to become more specific about them.

Even in the areas of child growth and development where there is fairly general agreement, it is not always clear what parents have to know, do, and believe to meet children's needs. In areas of greater controversy and ambiguity, such as cultural values or moral and spiritual development, the problems are even greater. Brim (1959, p. 94) described the situation this way:

> The establishment of working goals requires a conception of the ethically most desirable parent, as well as certain assumptions about the way in which parents are educated and the effect they have on their children. . . . These matters are far from clear in parent education theory. Many ethical issues are unresolved; and in spite of the vast research on child development, our knowledge of the effects of parents on children's personality is still in a rudimentary stage; and in a like way, our understanding of the limitations imposed by personal and social characteristics of parents upon their ability to learn and change in child rearing is still in a primitive state.

As a result of the expansion of research in child development since that time, more is known, particularly about family patterns that influence children's achievements in school (I. J. Gordon, 1977). However, there are many areas where, as always, the experts disagree or are silent, and parents and parent educators must rely on judgment, common sense, or established practice.

In the past, the ideal of parent education was conceived in several ways, according to the theoretical and philosophical convictions of the people involved. Brim (1959) grouped these into seven types:

1. The *rule follower* has expert knowledge and opinion about child rearing, and is trained to follow it.

2. The *loving and accepting parent* also follows expert advice, particularly in his or her unconditional acceptance of the child.

3. The *parent with knowledge of child development* is able to understand and interpret the child's behavior in a way that leads to better parenting practices.

4. The *parent with understanding of the effect of parental behavior on children* changes his or her behavior to achieve the desired effect.

5. The *problem-solving parent* can analyze a child-rearing problem, obtain necessary information, and then use judgment and creativity in applying the information to solve the problem.

6. The *home manager* has the techniques and skills to set up the home environment to make family living and child rearing as pleasant and problem-free as possible.

7. The *natural, confident parent* is secure, comfortable, and relaxed about his or her own self, and has the ability to sense and do what is best for the child.[1]

Present-day parent education programs contain many elements of these ideals. For example, parent educators who teach behavior management techniques such as positive reinforcement try to get parents to understand the effect of their behavior on children's actions. Child study and discussion groups depend on parents' abilities to define, discuss, and look at several possible solutions to child-rearing problems and then make their own decisions about the best course of action—in other words, to solve their own problems. Some parent education programs simply offer support and encouragement to parents who are learning to trust their natural abilities to do what is right for them and their children. They try to reach parents such as the one who reported: "It is really the mother, with her isolation and sometimes overwhelming feelings of guilt, who needs help the most and receives it the least" (Weisser, 1977, p. 44). Most parent education programs try to help parents learn more about how children grow and develop. As Dr. T. Berry Brazelton, a popular pediatrician, puts it, "Mothers and fathers want to begin to understand their infant as a person, and knowing more about what he or she is capable of helps them do this" (1977, p. 24). Each of these approaches has strengths and weaknesses, and some are more appropriate at different times and with certain groups of people than others. For example, parent discussion groups that regard parents as problem solvers assume a high degree of motivation, access to information, and ability to apply that information to a new situation, which all parents do not have.

Most programs do not restrict themselves to any one "ideal" parent or goal, but attempt to work toward several simultaneously. Unfortunately, sometimes the parent education goals are in conflict. Parents who are relaxed and comfortable with themselves and their children may engage in some practices that are in conflict with goals of good home management and are detrimental to their children. They may, for example, have very casual and haphazard eating patterns that deprive their children of needed nutrients. Knowledge of child growth and development, home management, and behavioral change are needed for the sake of the child. For further discussion and critical review of these goals, see Orville Brim's classic *Education for Child Rearing* (1965).

In spite of possible conflicts and confusions, the complex task of child rearing will continue to require multiple conceptions of good parenting and thus multiple goals of parent education. Emphasis will vary according to the ages of the children, personal convictions, the discipline in which the parent educator is trained (the psychologist in a mental health clinic may see children and parents differently from the home economics teacher), and parent preferences and needs.

Recent large-scale parent education efforts have tried to be more sensitive to parent preferences and needs by using a systematic planning process that begins with a needs assessment. Although such a technique yields information only on parents' *perceptions* of needs, it can be combined with other kinds of information to help parent educators learn more about their parent/students and the kinds of things they want to know and do. Such an approach helps parents and parent educators become a team working toward the same goals, and can avoid some of the problems that result when cultural and ethnic differences in child rearing are ignored. Let's look now at what parents throughout the nation said they wanted to learn.

In 1975, the Appalachia Educational Laboratory (AEL), in preparation for a television series on parenting, conducted a survey of 1,799 parents of elementary school children throughout the United States.[2] The purpose was to find out what parents said they needed or wanted to know or be able to do to be more effective parents. In 1972, the Education Commission of the States interviewed 144 parents in the Rocky Mountain states of Colorado, Utah, New Mexico, Arizona, Nevada, and Idaho as part of a larger survey to determine the educational needs of people caring for young children.[3] The results of the two surveys support each other. (For simplicity, we have combined the priority categories. For exact rankings, see the reports issued by the two agencies.)

Parents in both surveys wanted to know more about the following:

1. Children's growth and development, such as what to expect of children at different ages and how children grow into special, one-of-a-kind people.

2. Treating a child like a person, such as building self-confidence, helping a child accept his or her own feelings, handling anger and problems, and learning how to get along with others.

3. Identifying and caring for health problems in the family and making sure that a child's physical development is progressing satisfactorily.

In addition, respondents to the Rocky Mountain survey identified a need to help the child learn about his own and other cultures and communities, and how to develop language skills.

Parents in the AEL national survey wrote in other items that were important to them, such as developing productive home-school relations; developing parenting strategies that result in increased personal and social competence of children; interpreting and responding to sensitive areas and events, such as sex, divorce, and death; coping with and improving parenthood, marriage, and total family relationships; and helping children with special problems.

The care and management of infants was not a high-priority item for parents who had at least one child above age three.

The goals that would result from developing a parent education program based on what these parents say they need would be very similar to traditional programs that frequently combine general knowledge of child growth and development with specific help on typical problem areas of discipline, home-school relationships, and sensitive areas in family relationships. The question of goals will be discussed again in the section on implementation, along with the content and methods to help parents achieve those goals.

Parent and Teacher Roles In parent education, parents become students, with all the different roles that students assume and the activities that they do, such as discussing, volunteering information, questioning, receiving information, and preparing assignments.

Teachers assume a variety of roles. The most common is that of group discussion leader for a parent group; but they are frequently called upon to be listeners, referral agents to help parents find specialized community services they may need, and resource people for information. Because of the personal and sensitive nature of much parent education, the teacher's role is often quite subtle—sometimes sensing an unstated question, giving a word of reassurance or a nod of understanding, or asking a clarifying question. Teachers are not counselors or therapists, but they do have much knowledge they can share, particularly if they have been trained in parent education.

Content Family life and child-rearing studies involve all the complexities of human development in modern society. They involve dealing with the problems, concerns, and priorities of parents as well as the needs of children. As a result, although child growth and development, child guidance, and discipline appear to dominate content, parents are also taught how to provide for physical growth and health (safety, exercise, rest, immunizations, medicines), manage home and family life (food purchase and preparation, clothing care, organization of time), meet social and emotional needs (show love and affection, and develop security, trust, and healthful relationships between family members), stimulate intellectual growth (talking and reading with children, answering questions, providing things for them to play with), foster moral and cultural development and socialization, as well as know how to use community resources when additional help is needed. Indeed, a comprehensive outline of what is involved in parent education would look like a course in living. With the family and family forms changing, the parent educator cannot assume a stable two-parent household with the child as the focus of both parents. In these changing family forms—single-parent families (both fathers and mothers), divorced and remarried families, communal families, isolated families and families where both parents work outside the home—the needs of the parents as well as the children must be considered.

The developmental stages of the families involved also affect the content of parent education. Parents of infants and preschool children are more likely to seek parent education than are parents of older children. The Children's Bureau has distributed far more copies of its publication *Infant Care* than its publications about the care of older children. Membership in discussion groups, enrollment in correspondence courses, and the content of child care books support the observation that the infant and preschool child is the focus of parents' concern (Brim, 1965). This emphasis may be the result of the assumption that "parental behavior during the period of early childhood is more influential on the child's physical and mental health" (Brim, 1959, p. 118) than during the later years, or it may simply be the result of parent uncertainty and concern for this tiny and vulnerable human being.

However, each age and stage of child growth and development has its own worries and concerns for parents, especially with the oldest child, when the family is experiencing these growing pains for the first time.Also, family life changes of any kind, for either parent or child, may make the need for parent education more acute. When a mother starts to work outside the home and the child goes to a day care center, or when the first child starts to kindergarten, the resulting changes in the family may make parents seek education to meet their special needs. Divorce, death, the birth of another child, or finding that a child is disabled is a family crisis that often makes parents seek support and advice, regardless of the child's age. The content of parent education should be responsive to the changing needs of families as they move through the generational cycle.

Methods   Most school or center parent education programs use group meetings, usually with a presentation by a speaker or a film, followed by discussions or questions and answers. Yet there are many other methods available. We will explore both content and methods in greater depth in the implementation section of this chapter.

Advantages and Disadvantages

As an approach to parent involvement, parent education has several advantages and disadvantages. There are four primary advantages: (1) the comprehensive and in-depth nature of parent education; (2) the systematic way of responding to parent concerns; (3) the assurance and support it gives parents, particularly those with special needs; and (4) the opportunity it affords schools and centers to move out into the community. The disadvantages are: (1) schools often do not see parent education as part of their responsibility, partly because of the ethical issues involved; (2) it requires skilled human relations; (3) parents who most need it often do not participate; (4) it is difficult to evaluate; and (5) people expect it to do more than it can.

Advantages   The comprehensive nature of parent education allows for a more complete view of the child/parent/teacher relationship. Everyone concerned has an opportunity to go beyond the sometimes narrowly conceived school-related concerns of being a volunteer in the classroom or preparing the child for school. A mechanism is available to address parents' and children's critical needs.

Parent education is a way for teachers to respond to parent concerns systematically and efficiently. One kindergarten teacher began a small-scale parent education program because there was not enough time for her to answer all the parents' questions individually, even though they were working as volunteers in the classroom. Efficiency is evident in other ways also. When parental knowledge and competence are increased, all the children in the family are affected and many problems may be prevented. Parents who have knowledge of what their children can be expected to do at given stages of growth and development are less likely to have unrealistic expectations that result in frustration, anger, and possible abuse of the child (McAfee and Nedler, 1976).

Parent education, particularly when strong parent groups are formed, has advantages that go beyond the actual information and skills that are involved. At the present time, this benefit is most frequently voiced by parents of handicapped children.

"From the point of view of the individual parent, [the] greatest value [of parents' groups] is probably the unique kind of understanding and support they can give. . . . It helps to know one is not alone, and to have the advice and encouragement of others who 'have been through it.' Parents strengthen one another, and, by joining hands, are often able to accomplish miraculous changes in their own communities" (National Information Center for the Handicapped, 1974, p. 17).

Finally, parent education can use the many educational institutions and organizations in our society, such as newspapers, magazines, clinics, families, peer groups, and voluntary organizations. This larger concept of education has characterized and been one of the strengths of parent education throughout its history. Schools that embark upon educating for parenthood will be part of this many-faceted enterprise, and will be the richer for it.

Disadvantages One of the problems of parent education is that many schools and centers, both primary and preprimary, do not see it as part of their responsibility. Teachers often are not trained to work with parents, feel unsure of themselves, and do not want the additional responsibility. Administrators often feel the same way, seeing the school's task as educating children, not adults.

The ethical problems in parent education cannot be avoided. Parent education sometimes is perceived as meddling or violating family privacy and responsibility. Whose family will be considered "ideal"? Which childrearing practices are just "different" and which are "detrimental"? Conceptions of the "good" child and parent are influenced by cultural, ethnic, social class, and generation differences, among others. Parent educators must know that these values sometimes conflict with what is accepted. Parent educators must also be aware of their own values and how they enter into any educational program.

Parent educators must be unusually skilled and sensitive to the needs of others. They are dealing with a part of family life that is close to people's hearts. Parents often see any difficulties with their children as a reflection of themselves. Guilt, uncertainty, and self-doubt are close to the surface. Unless it is sensitively carried out, parent education can add to people's problems instead of helping.

Often the parents who appear to need information and guidance the least are the ones who participate. However, it is difficult to judge need. Child abuse and nutritional problems are not confined to any class, educational level, or socioeconomic group of families. Certainly divorce, single-parent families, families in which both parents work, and handicapped children are not.

There are no adequate measures of the change that may result from parent education. You can measure what parents know by tests, and you can solicit their reactions to a given program, but what really matters is what they do at home with their children, and that is difficult to determine, especially on a wide scale.

Perhaps the biggest problem with parent education is that people expect it to accomplish too much. The many social, economic, and personal problems that beset parents cannot be solved by parent education. Parents with the best of intentions, adequate knowledge, love, affection, and all the other attributes we consider desirable can be totally overwhelmed by circumstances in which they find themselves. Parent education will neither cure nor prevent the problems of poverty, discrimination, overwhelming social change, and family disintegration.

PARENT EDUCATION: A GUIDE FOR IMPLEMENTATION

Parent education is not *an* approach to parent involvement but is rather many approaches, depending on what goals, content, and methods are used and who is involved. Because of this complexity and the wealth of resources, this section will concentrate on what a parent educator must do to become familiar with what is available. We will suggest a way of reviewing these many materials in order to decide whether they are appropriate to use in a particular situation. Parent educators have to evaluate resources to see if they are consistent with the purposes of the parent group and the organization that is sponsoring the parent education program.

Most parent education programs involve group meetings of some kind; general guidelines for conducting such meetings are given in Chapter 6 and will not be repeated here. Rather, we will concentrate on implementation strategies that are specific to parent education.

Advance Planning and Preparation

In planning and preparing for parent education, you will need to spend time finding out if parents are interested and what they are interested in, and then surveying and deciding on resources, content, and methods to help achieve the goals of the program. Because there are many topics for parents to study and many resources to help them learn, we will examine in detail the needs assessment, content, methods, and materials to help you be aware of the alternatives available.

Assessing Needs and Interests   You will want to assess not only whether parent education is needed and wanted, but also what parents want to know. They are much more likely to participate and learn from a parent education program if it meets their needs and interests. The easiest way to determine those is through a questionnaire. A sample is shown in Figure 11.1. You will want to vary it to meet your situation; for example, make sure that you can actually develop programs, materials, and approaches on anything you ask about.

Leave some space for parents to write in concerns or topics that you may not have considered. Some needs assessments ask about the types of meetings parents would prefer, such as workshops, speakers, films, or discussion groups. If you are able to make these approaches available, you will find this additional information helpful. Try out the questionnaire on a few parents to make sure the

Figure 11.1

SAMPLE INTEREST AND NEEDS ASSESSMENT

Dear Parents,

Central School is planning a program for parents this year, and we want to make it interesting and helpful to you and your family. Your answers to the questions below will help us. We've left some space for you to write in topics or problems we may not have considered.

Check beside each topic how interested you are in knowing more about it.

How interested are you in learning more about:	Very interested	Somewhat interested	Not at all interested
I. How children grow and learn			
A. What to expect your child to know and do at different ages.			
B. How parents can help children grow and learn.			
C. How to build children's self-confidence.			
D. How to tell if your child has a growth and development problem, and what to do about it.			
II. Health and safety			
A. Planning and preparing healthful food.			
B. How to keep your child from getting hurt and how to take care of a hurt or sick child.			
C. How to keep your child well-- health habits, exercise, shots, sleep, etc.			
D. How to tell when your child needs to see a doctor.			
III. Helping children learn to get along with others			
A. How to know what behavior to expect at different ages.			
B. What to do when children quarrel and fight.			
C. How to teach right from wrong.			

Figure 11.1 (continued)

	Very interested	Somewhat interested	Not at all interested
D. How to guide and discipline children--help them learn how to behave.			
E. How to teach respect for other people.			
F. How to express feelings in an acceptable way.			
IV. Helping children with school readiness			
A. How to select and use activities (books, games, toys, family outings) to help your children learn.			
B. How to teach children to listen and follow directions.			
C. How to help children enjoy learning.			
D. How to help children improve their language.			
E. How to teach children to think and solve problems.			
V. Family living			
A. How to plan your and your family's day so things go smoothly and you have time for important things.			
B. How to locate good child care.			
C. How to make money go further-- buying, repairing, credit, sewing, and so forth.			
D. How to meet your personal needs--for talking with other people, encouraging, discussing problems, etc.			
E. Getting along in the family-- television, bedtime, meals, sharing, and taking turns.			
F. How to show love, affection, and concern in the family.			

Figure 11.1 (continued)

	Very interested	Somewhat interested	Not at all interested
VI. Learning about the world			
A. Telling your child about sex, death, divorce, and other things we find difficult to discuss.			
B. How to teach your children about their own and other cultures and people.			
C. Explaining about the world in a way children can understand-- such as the natural world, things they see on television.			

Some other things I would like to know more about are:

(CIRCLE YOUR CHOICES)

I could attend a meeting on: Monday   Tuesday   Wednesday

      Thursday   Friday   Saturday   Sunday

I would like to meet: Morning   Afternoon   Evening

I would like to meet: Every week   Every two weeks   Once a month

I have _____ children, whose ages are _____

Please return these questions and answers to Central School as soon as possible. We will let you know the results of our survey.

                    Thank you,

                    (Signature)

directions and questions are clear. In small discussion groups that meet frequently, parents and leaders usually discuss and decide what topics and types of meetings will be of specific interest to them rather than using a formal needs assessment.

Meetings should be scheduled to coincide with the times most parents prefer. Making child care available enables more parents to come. Many parent education groups are set up as joint parent education and preschool programs, in which the children have a pleasant and educational group experience during the parent meeting.

An advisory committee composed of parents, the school or center administrators, teachers, and interested community agencies can give guidance on the topics that should be included in the needs assessment, in deciding exactly what to offer after the results of the needs assessment are in, and in developing goals and guidelines for the actual implementation of the program.

Goals   In spite of the complexity of setting clear and achievable goals, some must be set before planning can proceed. If parents indicate that they want to learn more about how their children grow and develop, you can develop several reasonable goals, depending on how many times the group will meet. One goal might be to increase parents' knowledge of children's physical, intellectual, and social-emotional development. However, if parents indicate that they want specific behavioral guides for working with their children, the task is more difficult, not only because the experts disagree, but because you must decide if the goal is going to be just to make them informed about guiding children's behavior or actually to change their behavior, which is a much more difficult task. Changing parents' *attitudes* toward children, child rearing, and parenting is still another type of goal, often expressed as: to help parents develop positive attitudes toward parenting and toward helping children learn. The goals determine much of the content and methods of the parent education program, so work closely with the parent advisory group to make sure the goals are reasonable and appropriate for your community.

Content   Once goals have been determined, you can consider content, which is the knowledge, attitudes, and skills that you want parents to acquire. There are several problems at this stage. First, there is an overwhelming amount of knowledge for parents. You will have difficulty selecting the small amount that can actually be learned. Second, the available content changes as new information and theories emerge. Only a few years ago, the normative work of Gesell and his colleagues and the psychodynamic theories of Freud dominated much of parent education, particularly with middle-class groups. Now, behavior modification, transactional analysis, Piagetian theories, and training in skills such as first aid, positive reinforcement, active listening, and home management compete with more traditional content. The relationship of these varying approaches is unclear, and their implications for parents often conflict, as we pointed out earlier in the chapter. Third, the content seldom takes into account the pressures, complexities, and emotional context of family life. Whenever parents are dealing with their own children, the close emotional ties that hold them together sometimes overwhelm efforts to change. Most of the available materials scarcely touch on this aspect of child rearing.

However, because much of the content is related, you can start at almost any point of interest and concern and still reach a given goal. For example, what if your observation of parents and children indicates a broad need for understanding child growth and development and its implications for working with children, but parents are interested primarily in problem areas such as discipline, children's fighting, and mealtime conflicts? Start with a problems approach, and bring in the necessary knowledge and understanding of children's growth as parents learn a number of specific skills and techniques for dealing directly with the problems.

In selecting content, remember the following points.

1. Change in parents' knowledge and attitude is not always reflected in behavior. If you want to change behavior, select content to help parents change.

2. Different kinds of content may be more appropriate for some groups than for others. Take into account parents' education, income level, cultural background, age, and other differences as you choose content.

3. There is little research on the relative effectiveness of various types of content, and most content is still chosen on the basis of theoretical conviction about its merits.

You and the parents will have to rely on good judgment and a sensitivity to the needs and interests of the group to guide much of your selection of content.

Methods and Materials: General Comments   Methods refer to what is actually done. For example, are parents to watch a television program, read a book, participate in a group discussion, practice a specific behavior under the watchful eye of a tutor, or listen to a lecture? *Materials* refer to the actual books, films, pamphlets, cassette tapes, illustrations, and other materials that are used to help people learn. A parent group that simply wants information on how children grow and learn may well select films and books that present that information in an efficient and straightforward fashion. A parent group that is trying to work out its own feelings about discipline, the role of the young mother in today's family, or being parents of a disabled child will probably choose other methods, such as group discussions or a combination of group discussions with readings.

We have grouped these methods into four basic types: group interaction, mass media, one-to-one education, and combinations. Each has several variations, which will be discussed under the major headings. We will also give the names and addresses of several resource centers and clearinghouses where you can get additional information.

Group Interaction Methods   Parent education through group interaction depends upon the sharing of information, experiences, attitudes, feelings, and skills within the group. Although most such groups have skilled leaders to help them focus, provide necessary expertise, and facilitate the interaction, they assume that members of the group can help each other learn. Discussion groups, study and discussion groups, workshops, role-playing, and informal support groups are in this category.

Most parent discussion groups focus on the interests and concerns of the participants. Parents share their knowledge, experiences, and problems in child rearing. The leader helps the group explore the topic, adds information, and guides the discussion. Each parent is expected to work through his or her resolutions to problems, perhaps going home to try out a new approach or perhaps simply being assured that such feelings or behaviors are normal. Many of the parent education groups sponsored by the Child Study Association and by parent-cooperative nursery schools are of this type. Auerbach's book, *Parents Learn through Discussion* (1968), describes and tells how to conduct such groups.

In study and discussion groups each member studies a given topic before the meeting and comes prepared to discuss it, sometimes reacting to a list of questions. The study material may be a television program, a cassette tape, book, pamphlet, or one's own child. The national PTA has available a series of short brochures designed to be used in such study and discussion groups. The packet, entitled *Today's Family in Focus* (Schlossman, 1977), has separate brochures on the following topics:

- Parent Education: Where It's Been and Where It's Going
- Children's Rights and How Parents Can Protect Them
- Work and the American Family
- The Family in Today's Educational World
- Parents, Children, and Preventive Medicine
- Children and Values: A Guide for Parents and Teachers
- Developing the Mind of the Child
- The ABC's of Children's Social Development

In each brochure, five or six pages of summarized information on the topic are followed by "Questions for Reflection or Discussion," such as "How much exhibition of aggressive behavior do you think is 'healthy' for young school-aged children? How and when should it occur? How can or should it be controlled?" (Clarke-Stewart, 1977, p. 6).

In workshops, the focus is on learning by doing. There is usually a double purpose: the learning that results from the actual making or doing; and certain understandings, skills, and/or appreciation related to what is being done. For example, a workshop on making children's toys teaches parents how to make them and gives them the opportunity to make some, but is also designed to help parents learn that toys need not be expensive, that certain kinds of toys are best for children of different ages, and that making things for children is rewarding. In the process, parents learn to play with their children, what the children learn from play, and that parents have much to contribute to play and learning. If toys from different cultures are included, respect and pride in one's own and other cultures may be learned. Parents in workshops also talk, laugh, make mistakes, help each other, share child-rearing and family experiences, and get to know each other. The action will generate and sustain interest in a way that is difficult to do with other approaches, especially if the participants are tired of too much talk.

Role-playing is often used in group discussions or workshops. It can create a parent-child situation for later discussion, show a discipline technique learned from group study, or demonstrate how to use something made or done in a workshop. Most people have little trouble projecting themselves into these family situations. You can also use games that simulate actual experiences.

Another type of group interaction takes place in informal support groups. These groups help take the place of the extended family and stable neighborhood that reassured and supported young parents in years past. Such groups need little more than a relaxing place to meet, a refreshing drink, and a sympathetic ear. They may form around a sewing group, class for new mothers, parents' council or committee, or a group that congregates informally in the parents' room at school. As parents share frustrations, joys, problems, and hilarious experiences, they help each other gain perspective on rearing children and find confidence in their own abilities and comfort in knowing that they are not alone.

All of these group interaction methods except the informal support group require a skilled leader who knows not only the content being learned but also group dynamics and the leader's role in helping the group achieve its goals.

Mass Media   The term *mass media* refers to methods designed to reach a mass audience, the individual members of which are not known to the people preparing the material. Newspapers, books, booklets, magazines, television, and radio are the most common mass media, which also include films, film strips, audio and video cassettes, slide/tape sets, lectures, speeches, and panel discussions. These materials, of necessity, are general in nature and cannot speak to individual problems and concerns.

Magazines and newspapers present informtion through articles, regular columns, question and answer features, feature stories, and advertising. *Parents' Magazine*, devoted entirely to parents and children, is an American institution. Popular magazines and newspapers reach a vast audience, and the people who speak to parents on their pages, such as Dr. Spock, Dr. Brazelton, Dr. Bettleheim, and Dr. Lee Salk, become friends of the family. Even Dear Abby and Ann Landers dispense advice to parents. Advertising in these commercial enterprises is also a persuasive educational force. The selling of alternatives to breast feeding, various types of special foods, educational toys, and paraphernalia to help care for young children shapes parents' attitudes and behaviors. Such education is not necessarily bad, but it should be regarded cautiously.

Booklets, pamphlets, leaflets, brochures, newsletters, and other types of short, informative, printed materials are available on almost any subject. Baby food and pharmaceutical companies, government agencies, professional organizations, independent organizations such as the Alexander Graham Bell Association for the Deaf and the Child Study Institute, special-interest groups such as the National Education Association, and others distribute these materials at low or no cost. Most of them are on a single topic or group of topics, such as the leaflet "What Books and Records Should I Get for My Preschooler?" published by the International Reading Association. Many booklets are available for families with special interests or needs, such as the set of guides, manuals, and charts included in the packet of materials available to parents of retarded children from the Joseph P. Kennedy Foundation. Some are part of a series, such as the twice-a-month commercial publication, *Parent Talk*, (Abraham) and the noncommercial *Pierre, the Pelican* (Rowland, 1967), which is sent by some state agencies once a month to parents of newborn children. These small publications can be used as the basis of a discussion, to send home to arouse interest, or as handouts to help parents recall what was covered in a meeting, to emphasize an idea, or simply to provide information on a specific question that a parent might have. Their biggest advantages are that they are short, to the point, and inexpensive.

Books for parents have been the basis of many jokes about "raising children by the book," but they have also been sources of information, support, and controversy for hundreds of young parents and their families. Dr. Spock's *Common Sense Book of Baby and Child Care* (1946), which sold over 22 million copies, has been credited with influencing a whole generation of American parents and their children. Other books often reflect popular psychological theories or social trends. The popular *Parent Effectiveness Training* (T. Gordon, 1970) contains elements of transactional analysis, for example. Fraiberg's classic *The Magic Years* (1959) presents a Freudian perspective, and Macht's *Teaching Our Children* (1975) tells parents how to use behavior modification principles to make child rearing easier for both parents and children. These psychological orientations and their assumptions about parents and children are the sources of many of the inconsistencies and conflicting advice of experts. As a parent educator, you will need to become familiar with the more popular books, know their approaches, and be able to discuss them with parents. Almost certainly you will be asked to recommend books that deal with particular topics of interest.

Television and radio broadcasts reach more households than any other media, but their potential for parent education has yet to be realized. Radio has done so little that it has been disregarded as a source of parent education. Television has done much more, but the "Sesame Street" for parents has yet to appear. Televised courses in child development have been offered by many colleges and universities in cooperation with their local educational television stations. Educational television stations in many large cities have produced some outstanding discussions with doctors, psychologists, and parents, as well as demonstrations of child care and teaching. However, these programs reached only a select group of parents and none had national impact. Recently, there have been more systematic efforts to use broadcast television to reach the large number of parents who want and need some help in raising their children.

Several independent groups have produced short series of television pro-grams. Two examples of these are a series based on Thomas Gordon's *Parent Effectiveness Training* (1970) and a series of six films called "Look at Me," based in part on the ideas of the Parents as Resources group that mothers and fathers should spend more time talking, playing and learning with their children. Discussion guides are available with both series, and the "Look At Me" films are available for nonbroadcast use.

The Southwest Educational Development Laboratory developed an experimental series of public-service commercial television "spots" and printed booklets geared to the needs of low-income parents. Spot announcements were used to inform parents about a topic and motivate and direct them to write in for a free booklet giving more information. Field testing of the spot announcements was judged successful. The booklets are also available separately.

Regular broadcast television, particularly commercials, also educates about parenting. Two areas relating to child rearing are especially affected: children's toys and games and nutrition. Many parents do not realize this or know how to combat the messages they and their children receive about the desirability and quality of these products. Excessive sugar and carbohydrates in snack foods, cereals, and beverages are endorsed by advertising. This type of parent education is not always for the good of either parent or child.

Nonbroadcast audiovisual materials, such as films, film strips, audio and video tapes, and slides, are other methods of presenting material to parents. Unlike broadcast materials, they can be used at any time, any place, and on any subject. They can be started when the group is ready, stopped for discussion, and shown more than once. Frequently, films and videotapes that have been prepared for television are available to rent or buy. Many films are available on child growth and development, caring for children, and other aspects of parent education, but they must be carefully evaluated before they are used. If they present out-of-date information, are of poor technical quality, or show dated clothing and techniques, parents will not take them seriously.

Film strips and slide sets often have accompanying records or tapes and discussion guides. Although they do not have the action of movies or video-tapes, they can illustrate and focus attention on the points being made. Parents Magazine Films, Inc., sells film strips and records on guiding the growth of young children. The titles of some of the series, which usually include five sound and color film strip sets, are "Conflicts between Parents and Children," "Bringing Up Children," "Children with Handicaps," and "Developing Crea-tive Thought in Children." Other companies and organizations produce similar materials.

Cassette tapes are more appropriate for individual listening than for groups. You can buy prerecorded tapes relating to parent education or you can prepare your own.

Lectures, speeches, and panel discussions usually present information on a specific topic, followed by a question and answer period, large or small group discussion, or other methods of encouraging parents to reflect on the informa-tion and apply it to their situation. If you select interesting speakers and brief them on their audience and how they fit into the total scheme of the program, they will be able to do a better job.

One-to-One Parent Education   As a teacher, you have many opportunities to talk with parents on a one-to-one basis. Home visits, parent conferences, informal conversations as parents bring children and pick them up, and joint observations of a child or group of children are opportunities for one-to-one parent education. In day care centers, the day-to-day interpersonal exchanges between parents and center caregivers as the children are dropped off and picked up are the primary means of communication, which is usually focused on the child and child rearing (Powell, 1977). Teachers must observe one caution in this type of parent education: they must refer parents who need counseling or therapy to the appropriate person or agency.

Combinations   You can keep parent education interesting and effective by using creative combinations of these methods. Any method, when overused, becomes ineffective. Try combining a demonstration of what children learn from toys and how parents can help in this process with a workshop session where the toys are actually made. Combine a film on the misuses of television with a homework assignment on each individual family's use of television. Follow that with an experiment, designed by parents for their own family, in more creative use of the television in the home. Teach parents how to use positive reinforcement, role-play typical parent-child situations to give practice, and provide parents with a chart to keep track of their progress.

Become familiar with the wealth of resources available to parent educators and learn to use many of them. There is no evidence that any one method is superior to another, so fit the methods to the content and the desired outcomes as well as what parents enjoy and learn from.

Implementation and Review

Many of the steps in implementing and reviewing parent education programs have been covered in Chapters 5 and 6 and will not be repeated here. However, some aspects of recruiting and orientation are specific to parent education.

Recruiting   Recruiting parents for a parent education program will not be difficult if you plan the topics and approaches using the results from an interest and needs assessment and the counsel of the parent advisory committee. Plan your advertising specifically to reach those parents you hope to involve. Publicity suggestions are given in Chapter 5. If you are recruiting from a relatively unknown population, such as a school or neighborhood, give a telephone number or return address and ask parents to let you know if they are planning to attend. This will give you some idea of how many are coming. Workshops, study and discussion groups, role-playing, and some other methods of parent education require that you have a fairly accurate estimate of the number of people who are coming. Even if you have a "captive" audience, such as parents of children in a Head Start center or those in a parent cooperative who are expected to attend parent meetings as part of the program, an active recruiting campaign will result in better attendance.

A catchy name for the program will make advertising and recruiting easier. The South Carolina Department of Education calls its parent education program "The Puzzle of Parenting: How to Fit It Together" (1977). Other names that are being used are "Footsteps" (1977); "Parent to Parent"; and "PATH," which stands for Parents Are Teachers at Home.

If the parent education program is open to all who wish to come, ask other people who work with parents to help with recruiting. Social workers, pediatricians, health department personnel, and religious education directors are good contacts. If only a few parents indicate they are coming, ask the parent advisory committee to help you make personal telephone calls to invite more parents, telling them some of the interesting topics and activities that will be covered, and how they and their children will benefit. However, do not think that every parent—or even a large group of parents—must attend in order for the program to be a success.

Do not stop the publicity and interest-building activities after the first successful program, especially if the families are not used to regular attendance at meetings. To sustain interest and involvement you may want to try phone call reminders, postcards, reminder flyers sent home just before the meetings, invitations written by the children, visits by the teacher or fellow participants, and a "buddy" system that pairs participants who can help each other. You might also arrange to have class credit offered and involve parents in the planning and implementation of coming events.

Orientation   Spend some time at the beginning of the program going over what parents will learn, what will be expected of them, how much time it will take, and what they can expect as a result. Demonstrate any instructional techniques that might be unfamiliar to parents, such as role-playing, observing and charting behavior, and critically reviewing a television show and making notes for future discussion. These previews help parents feel more comfortable with what is planned, and will also help them organize their experiences. If you distribute booklets, tapes, or any other material to be used independently, make sure parents know what they are and how to use them. *Don't* hand out everything at once, but distribute material just before it is needed.

Get to know as many of the parents as possible, and help them get acquainted with each other. Have name tags, personal introductions, and a social hour afterwards to help in this process.

Develop an unobtrusive way of checking attendance and explain it in the first meeting. Parents can sign in or pick up prepared name tags (the ones remaining are the absent ones). This information will be helpful as you review the program.

Getting Started and Reviewing the Program   General guides for getting started and reviewing parent education programs are given in Chapters 4, 5, and 6. You will need to adapt them to the specific content and methods you are using, as well as to the specific group of parents. For example, if parents of handicapped children participate in a group support and discussion meeting once a month, combined with weekly home visits that teach them how to use behavior modification techniques to help their child learn self-help and other skills of daily living, they have much in common and need fewer orientation and get-acquainted activities than would a mixed group of parents from a large elementary school, who are unlikely to know each other.

If more detailed information is needed, refer to Auerbach's *Parents Learn through Discussion* (1968), Pickarts and Fargo's *Parent Education: Toward Parental Competence* (1971), Lane's *Education for Parenting* (1975), and *Parent Involvement: A Workbook of Training Tips for Head Start Staff* (1969).

RESOURCES FOR PARENT EDUCATION

In addition to being alert and writing to all sources that are advertised or listed as having related materials, write to these organizations to find out what information they can make available on resources for parent education.

Parenting Materials Information Center (PMIC)
Southwest Educational Development Laboratory
211 East 7th Street
Austin, Texas 78701
Ask for the "User's Handbook."

Educational Resources Information Center Clearinghouse on Early Childhood Education (ERIC/ECE)
805 West Pennsylvania Avenue
Urbana, Illinois 61801
Ask for information on using the ERIC system, and abstract bibliographies on parent education. You may also ask any large library to conduct a computer search of parent education materials in the ERIC system, which includes all current journals.

The Administration for Children, Youth, and Families
U.S. Department of Health, Education, and Welfare
P.O. Box 1182
Washington, D.C. 20013

U.S. Office of Education
U.S. Department of Health, Education, and Welfare
Washington, D.C. 20201

Center for the Study of Parent Involvement
5240 Boyd Street
Oakland, California 94618
This group publishes a newsletter called "Apple Pie" that contains current information and resources relating to parent education.

The Home and School Institute, Inc.
Box 4847
Washington, D.C. 20008
or

Trinity College
Washington, D.C. 20017

Child Welfare League of America, Inc.
67 Irving Place
New York, New York, 10003
*The Child Welfare League has many useful publications as well as a library/
information service.*

SUMMARY

In parent education, parents learn to be better parents. Most parent education is
for parents of preschool children. Goals are often broadly stated and sometimes
contradictory, but recent large-scale needs assessments have found that parents
want to know more about children's growth and development, discipline, and
family relationships, especially as they involve problem areas such as anger and
expression and acceptance of feelings. Health care and knowing more about
one's culture are also high priorities.

The advantages of parent eduation are its comprehensive and in-depth
nature; the systematic way of responding to parent concerns; the assurance and
support it gives parents, particularly those with special needs; and the opportunity it gives schools and centers to move out into the community. The
disadvantages are that schools often do not see parent education as their
responsibility; there are thorny ethical issues; it requires skilled human relations; parents who need it often do not participate; it is difficult to evaluate; and
it is likely to promise more than it can deliver.

There are a multitude of approaches to parent education and we looked
closely at some of these, dividing methods and materials into group interaction,
mass media, one-to-one parent education, and combinations, giving numerous
examples of each. Content and specific goals can be varied along with the
method. We gave an example of an interest and needs assessment to help
determine what a specific group of parents would like to know. With that
knowledge, parent educators can select from the wealth of resources those that
best meet the needs of a particular group. The chapter closed with a list of the
most comprehensive sources of information about parent education.

FOR DISCUSSION AND FURTHER STUDY

1. What are some of the reasons for so many different ideas about parent
    education?

2. Find out about the parent education programs in your community. Who
    sponsors them? Who attends? What approaches do they use? What are their
    goals?

3. Some people contend that parent education is an invasion of a family's
    privacy, rights, and responsibilities. Discuss that viewpoint with your
    colleagues, listing as many arguments as you can on both sides of the issue.

4. Have you or your parents ever been involved in parent education? What kind was it? Was it helpful?

5. For a class project, list some sources of parent education materials in your community with the names and prices of the material. Try the state Department of Education, mental health clinics, the library, the Federal Extension Service (County Home Demonstration Agent), the Department of Social Services, the Head Start agency, parent cooperatives, and others.

BIBLIOGRAPHY

Abraham, Willard. *Parent Talk.* Scottsdale, Ariz.: Sunshine Press.

Auerbach, Aline B. *Parents Learn through Discussion: Principles and Practices of Parent Group Education.* New York: Wiley, 1968.

Brazelton, T. Berry. "The Infant's World: How Babies Learn about Taste, Touch, and Smell." *Redbook* 150, no. 1 (November 1977): 24–28.

Brim, Orville G. *Education for Child Rearing.* New York: Russell Sage, 1959, 1965.

Cahoon, Owen, and Jean M. Larsen. "The Art of Parent Education: A Selection Approach for Parents." Paper presented at the National Association for Young Children Conference, Dallas, Texas, 1975.

Callahan, Sidney Cornelia. *Parenting: Principles and Politics of Parenthood.* Garden City, N.Y.: Doubleday, 1973.

Clarke-Stewart, K. Alison. "The ABC's of Children's Social Development." In *Today's Family in Focus: A National PTA Program in Parent Education,* coordinated by Steven L. Schlossman. Chicago: National PTA, 1977.

Coan, Donald L. *Parenthood Education Needs: A National Assessment Study.* Charleston, W. Va.: Appalachia Educational Laboratory, 1976.

Cromwell, R., and K. Bartz. *The American Family: Its Impact on the Quality of Life.* Paper presented at Bicentennial Congress on Adult Continuing Education. New York, November 19, 1976.

Dorman, Lynn, and Freda Rebelsky. *Growing Children.* Monterey, Calif.: Brooks/Cole, 1976.

Families Play to Grow. Washington, D.C.: Joseph P. Kennedy, Jr., Foundation, 1977.

"Footsteps." The Parent Education Television Project. Silver Spring, Md.: Applied Management Sciences, 1977.

Fraiberg, Selma. *The Magic Years: How to Understand and Handle the Problems of Childhood from Birth to School Age.* New York: Scribner's, 1959.

Gallup, George A. "Ninth Annual Gallup Poll of the Public's Attitudes toward the Public Schools." *Phi Delta Kappan* 51, no. 1 (September 1977): 33–47.

Goodson, Barbara Dillon, and Robert D. Hess. *Parents as Teachers of Young Children: An Evaluative Review of Some Contemporary Concepts and Programs.* Stanford, Calif.: Stanford University Press, 1975.

Gordon, Ira J. "Parent Education and Parent Involvement: Retrospect and Prospect." *Childhood Education* 54, no. 2 (November/December 1977): 71–79.

Gordon, Thomas. *Parent Effectiveness Training.* New York: Peter H. Wyden, 1970.

Lane, Mary B. *Education for Parenting.* Washington, D.C.: National Association for the Education of Young Children, 1975.

Lauderdale, Michael L., and Martha S. Williams. *The Needs Assessment for Child Development Resources.* Report prepared for the Education Commission of the States, Denver, Colorado, 1973.

Lazar, Joyce B., and Judith E. Chapman. *The Present Status and Future Research Needs of Programs to Develop Parenting Skills.* Washington, D.C.: George Washington University, 1972.

"Look at Me!" A six-part film series for parents, with follow-up activities and discussion guide. Northfield, Ill.: Perennial Education, n.d.

McAfee, Oralie, and Shari Nedler. *Education for Parenthood: A Primary Prevention Strategy for Child Abuse and Neglect.* Report No. 93, ECS Child Abuse Project. Denver: Education Commission of the States, 1976.

Macht, Joel. *Teaching Our Children.* New York: Wiley, 1975.

National Information Center for the Handicapped. *Practical Advice for Parents.* Washington, D.C.: National Information Center for the Handicapped, 1974.

Parent Involvement: A Workbook of Training Tips for Head Start Staff. OEO Pamphlet 6108-12. May 1969.

Pickarts, Evelyn, and Jean Fargo. *Parent Education: Toward Parental Competence.* New York: Appleton-Century-Crofts, 1971.

Powell, Douglas R. *The Interface between Families and Child Care Programs: A Study of Parent-Caregiver Relationships.* Detroit, Mich.: Merrill-Palmer Institute, 1977.

The Puzzle of Parenting: How to Fit It Together. Columbia: South Carolina Department of Education, 1977.

Rowland, Loyd D. *Pierre the Pelican Series.* New Orleans: Family Publications Center, 1967.

Schlossman, Steven L. "Before Home Start: Notes Toward a History of Parent Education in America, 1897–1929." *Harvard Educational Review* 46, no. 3 (August 1976): 436–67.

Schlossman, Steven L., coordinator. *Today's Family in Focus: A National PTA Program in Parent Education,* Chicago: National PTA, 1977.

Spock, Benjamin. *The Common Sense Book of Baby and Child Care.* New York: Duell, Sloan and Pearce, 1946.

Weikart, David P. "Designing Parenting Education Programs." Paper presented at the Working Conference on Parenting Education, Charles Stewart Mott Foundation, Flint, Michigan, September 1977.

Weisser, Susan. "How I Learned to Cope with My Difficult Baby." *Redbook* 150, no. 1 (November 1977): 42–47.

White, Burton L. "Guideline for Parent Education, 1977." Paper presented at Working Conference on Parenting Education, Charles Stewart Mott Foundation, Flint, Michigan, September 1977.

Yankelovich, Skelly and White, Inc. *Raising Children in a Changing Society: The General Mills American Family Report, 1976–1977.* Minneapolis: General Mills, 1977.

NOTES

[1] Adapted from Orville G. Brim, Education for Child Rearing, pp. 95-106. © 1959 Russell Sage Foundation, New York.

[2] The Appalachia Educational Laboratory is an independent research and development laboratory in Charleston, West Virginia.

[3] The Education Commission of the States is a compact of 47 states and territories. Located in Denver, Colorado, the organization conducts research and acts as a clearinghouse for the states on educational matters.

12 Citizen/Parents as Advisors and Policy Makers

OVERVIEW

In the United States public schools are governed and supported by informed citizens and their representatives. Because of size, increasing state and federal regulations, professionalization, and other forces, many schools are perceived by their patrons as being unresponsive to and uninterested in the concerns of citizens. Federal and state laws and regulations as well as citizen advocate groups have tried to increase citizen participation in school policy. This chapter will describe some of these efforts, focusing on the teachers' role in relation to citizen advisory and policy groups. Following a description of some typical citizen/parent groups and their advantages and disadvantages, we will present what teachers need to know about parent councils, and what they may be called upon to do *for* and *with* parent councils.

CITIZEN/PARENTS AS ADVISORS AND POLICY MAKERS: A DESCRIPTION

Introduction: Changing Expectations

Parents relate to schools as concerned citizens as well as parents. In the former capacity they vote on bond issues and taxes, elect and serve on school boards and parent boards, make recommendations about school matters on advisory and policy councils, complain about or support the way schools are run, organize themselves to influence policy, and carry out other rights and responsibilities of participatory democracy. Parents acting as citizen advisors and decision makers can be involved in a center- or home-based program, a combination, a parent education group, or even a program with no form of parent involvement other than advisory or policy boards. Parents learn to exercise their rights as citizens, taxpayers, and community members.

The approaches to parent involvement discussed earlier in this book are concerned with helping parents be better parents and teachers of their own children. To help clarify the distinction between the other types of parent involvement and this one, note that parents who are given the opportunity to participate in a home visiting program can choose whether or not they wish to participate, when the home visitor comes, and the activities they prefer. But parents who are making policy might decide whether there is even going to be a home- or center-based program, help select the home visitors, and advise on curriculum emphases.

Schools in the United States began with lay (nonprofessional) and community control over school policy, but the growth of larger schools and school districts combined with professionalization to make many schools seem remote and unresponsive to the needs of particular community groups (see Chapter 1). In the 1960s several forces worked to counteract this trend. Many poor and minority children did not benefit from the educational programs available to them; perhaps if parents contributed their ideas about school curriculum and organizational change, schools might be better places for their children. Researchers and theorists argued that people who have some sense of control and power over their own and their children's lives are more likely to feel responsible for their children's development and education. Federal legislation and regulations tied money to parent involvement on policy and advisory boards and began to institutionalize "parent power." The Office of Economic Opportunity and Head Start began the process in 1965, and other federal programs and laws followed. Parent involvement in advisory and decision-making capacities was mandated by several Titles of the Elementary and Secondary Education Acts of 1965; by Public Law 94–142, which guarantees education for the handicapped; and by Follow Through regulations as well as the early childhood programs of the Administration for Children, Youth, and Families that complement Head Start.

Some state laws have similar requirements. In California, for example, legislation directs the governing board of the school district to seek community, parent, and teacher involvement in all phases of planning and developing early childhood education master plans. Florida laws direct school boards to establish school advisory committees to include parents, students, and community representatives. Other local areas have policies, regulations, or informal procedures that encourage or require parent advisory or policy committees, in addition to the regularly elected school board or school committee.

As these changes were beginning, citizen groups throughout the country organized to find out what schools were doing, and how parents could help make education more responsive to the needs of children and the desires of parents and communities. The Public Affairs Program of the Ford Foundation encouraged this institutional change by providing financial support and leadership. Sometimes parent organizations represented special interests, as in the case of parents of handicapped children. Sometimes they were simply concerned citizens seeking a way to solve problems such as declining test scores, vandalism, and high dropout rates. Sometimes they worked within established parents' groups such as the PTA, and sometimes they formed their own organizations. Often they used politics and confrontation to make their voices heard, and united with other parents across the country to gain support and leadership experience. The National Committee for Citizens in Education, for example, established "The Parents' Network" to support existing local parent/citizen groups and mobilize them for action to improve schools.[1] The Institute for Responsive Education was formed to conduct action research and publish materials about citizen/community action for better schools.[2]

Most of these issues and events revolved around agencies and institutions that had public funding, such as public schools, Head Start centers, publicly supported day care and parent-child centers, and other special programs, and did not directly affect private nursery schools and day care centers. However, one private delivery system for early childhood education—parent co-operatives—has always been governed by parents. These small, independent groups are usually formed by interested groups of parents with the purpose of starting or maintaining an existing private school—usually a nursery school or kindergarten, but sometimes an alternative elementary or secondary school. Parent cooperatives may well have been the model for the developers of Head Start guidelines. Because the amount of money and numbers of children involved in parent cooperatives are quite small, they have never been as controversial as parent control of public programs.

The relationship of teachers to parent advisory councils, parent policy committees, citizen advisory committees, parent boards, and other governance and advisory groups varies from setting to setting. In a small parent cooperative or Head Start center, the teacher may be the administrative head of the school and work directly with the policy-making group. In a large school district, teachers may never work directly with the advisory group; the director or principal has that responsibility. In some programs, teachers may help parents organize. On the other hand, grass roots citizen councils, which parents themselves organize to solve particular problems, would probably resent such help and probably do not need it.

We will not attempt to give guidelines to cover all these possible variations, but will concentrate on general principles to guide teachers as they work with policy and advisory groups beyond the classroom. Teachers who wish to study citizen/parent groups in depth should refer to the list of materials and organizations at the end of this chapter.

Distinguishing Characteristics

Settings   Strong, active parent *policy* councils, as opposed to *advisory* bodies, are generally found in two settings: parent-cooperative nursery schools and federally funded preprimary programs such as Head Start. Parent councils associated with public schools are likely to be advisory, with restricted decision-making powers because of both the limitations and responsibilities of the elected representatives on the school board and the established ways of operating. Proprietary, or privately owned, centers and schools seldom have parent policy or advisory councils, As a result, parents of preprimary children are more likely to have an active voice in the operation of school or center programs than are parents of school-age children.

Goals   We can group the goals of parent involvement through advising on and participating in school decisions into three areas. First is the political goal of increasing parent power by giving parents greater control over educational decisions that affect them and their children and building political support for schools.

Second is the goal of making schools, including administrators, teachers, and staff, more responsive to the needs of the children and families of the community. When parents advise on and monitor personnel, curriculum, buildings, procedures, and other matters of substance, the schools are more likely to be sensitive to parents' wishes and to recognize that the school is not a separate, independent institution, but a part of the community. It is within the context of this second goal that the phrases "accountability" and "community control" have acquired meaning.

The third goal, increasing the parents' sense of control over their own lives in a way that will influence their behavior with their children, is considered to be a result of achieving the first two goals. Parents who feel that they have some power and influence are more likely to feel responsible for and take an active part in their children's education.

Teacher and Parent Roles   When parents become active advisors and decision makers in the schools, parent and teacher roles are not very clear-cut. Parents who are involved in governing a school are employers in the sense that a school board or school committee is an employer of teachers. They interview and help select faculty and staff, and they set policies such as when school will be in session, tuition and fees (if any), transportation policies, who is eligible to attend, budget, and curriculum emphases. An advisory group has much less power, but may be asked to advise on all those matters, plus others such as traffic safety, lunch room problems, playground equipment, volunteer programs, and school social activities.

Parents may also become advocates for children and the school, lobbying the state or national legislature, or contacting the school board or local taxpayers to gain support for a particular point of view. Many of the recent laws and regulations guaranteeing certain educational rights for handicapped children came about as a result of efforts by concerned groups of parents.

In schools and centers with Title I or Head Start funds, money is budgeted for a parent coordinator who serves as a liaison with parents, organizes workshops, serves as a resource person, and does other things to help the parent program.

Teacher roles vary according to the administrative structure of the school and center. If the center has more than two or three classrooms, the director or principal usually has the most direct contact with the parent group. In some schools and centers, communication between the classroom and the citizen/parent policy group is through the classroom parent advisory committee. These typical lines of communication are shown in Figure 12.1.

Teachers are also employees who are charged with the responsibility for carrying out policies. For example, if the governing mechanism of a parent-cooperative nursery school decides that there will be so many children of a given age in a classroom, the teacher does not have the freedom to make a

Figure 12.1

Lines of Communication between Citizen/Parent Groups and Classroom Teacher

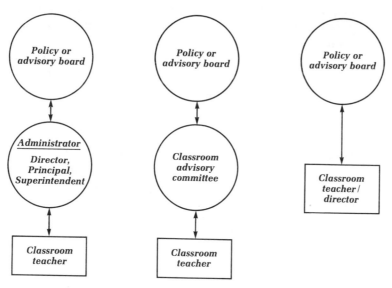

Typical in large schools and centers

Typical in small schools and centers

different decision. A teacher can attempt to influence that policy but cannot disregard it.

But teachers are also professional educators who have had training and experience in teaching young children in groups, and they are frequently called on to supply information, make recommendations, express opinions, and clarify situations. They meet with parents as participants and observers in policy and advisory meetings, so they are seldom passive recipients of rulings that are simply handed down. As one teacher said, "If we want to reduce the pupil-teacher ratio or at least maintain it, the first people we would go to would be the parents because the board listens to them" (Carringer, 1977). In fact, in schools that are unionized, teachers, through their bargaining agents, attempt to negotiate matters that have traditionally been decided by the governing body—classroom size and pupil-teacher ratios, for example.

Both parents and teachers are sometimes confused about their roles, particularly when a school is changing from a "we have all the answers" attitude to actively and systematically inviting parents to take part in all phases of the educational process (Breivogel and Sterling, 1976).

Content Regardless of the specific items that parents are considering in advisory or policy groups, they are learning to identify alternative courses of action, weigh the relative merits of the alternatives, and reach a decision concerning a course of action. In addition to these problem-solving and decision-making strategies, they learn how to deal with professional educators and administrators. They learn how to identify and voice their concerns for children and the schools.

Methods   The methods used to help parents learn to be advisors and policy makers may vary slightly according to the skills and backgrounds of the participants, but the primary method is learning by doing. If an inexperienced group needs to learn to conduct meetings, they may receive some training, but most of their learning takes place on the job. Citizen/parent groups may receive training and support from other citizen groups and national organizations formed for that express purpose, such as the National Committee for Citizens in Education and the Institute for Responsive Education. Both groups publish and distribute guides for parent actions. The booklet, "Parents Organizing to Improve Schools" (National Committee for Citizens in Education, 1976), is an excellent primer for parents. The National School Boards Association and state school board associations provide information, guidance, and service to public school board members, primarily through meetings and written material.

Advantages and Disadvantages

The advantages and disadvantages of active citizen-parent involvement in school policy depend somewhat on your viewpoint—whether you are a parent, teacher, administrator, or nonparent taxpayer. In general, the advantages can be grouped as (1) gaining political power; (2) having joint responsibility and support; and (3) soliciting and respecting perspectives from *all* parents in the community, not just those who have traditionally held leadership roles. The disadvantages relate to (1) the reluctance and hostility of some principals, superintendents, and school boards to invite wider participation; (2) lack of agreement over what are professional and what are lay concerns; and (3) the heavy investment of time and interest that citizen/policy groups must commit.

Advantages   The funding and control of public schools are governed by a political process. Schools must compete with other public and private agencies for funding and support. To do this successfully, they need the support and backing of the taxpayers of the community. The public's disenchantment with education is expressed most strongly when citizens vote against increasing mill levies and passing bond issues. Bringing citizen/parents back into this political process on the side of the schools is one of the biggest advantages to successful parent involvement in policy making. This does not mean that parents will always do what school people want. Rather, it means that solutions will be found that everyone can support—for the good of the children. For example, parents who participate in preparing a school budget appreciate the hard decisions that are made when money is allocated, and they understand the way that allocation is reflected in the educational program. They are often better prepared to defend those decisions to other parents (and voters) than are either school administrators or teachers.

The school and the home share responsibility for educating children.

Schools must have the understanding and support of the communities they serve. Also, parents bring a different perspective that can develop fresh insights and approaches to problems. Almost every organization or group of people benefits from getting another opinion and viewpoint on what they are doing. In a parents council or advisory group, parents, teachers, and administrators can discuss sources of possible misunderstandings, such as discipline, customs, language, and expectations. Changes may result that enable both home and school to work more closely and effectively toward their common goal of caring for and educating children.

Parents of all income levels and backgrounds can be involved in parent and citizen groups to influence what goes on in schools. Low-income parents whose children are in federal programs that require parent policy advisory groups, such as Head Start, Follow Through, and Title I, may find in those groups their first opportunity for such participation. Working together, all parents can acquire skills, such as how to ask for and get information, how to visit the school, how to avoid being "put down," and how to make viewpoints known when decisions are being made. These skills often carry over to other community efforts.

Disadvantages School boards and administrators have certain powers and responsibilities delegated to them; they have acquired other powers and responsibilities through tradition. They are reluctant to relinquish any of these, and many *cannot* be relinquished because of legal requirements. Yet the lack of trust between school boards, administrators, and communities prevents greater parent involvement in many policy areas. State education agencies attribute professional and administrative reluctance to have parents involved to fear that involvement would erode the power and authority of the board of education and the administration, fear of interference in the system, and professional insecurity (Safran, 1974).

People do not agree on which are appropriate concerns for citizen groups. Are school curricula and books appropriate for a lay board to choose, or should these specifics be professional decisions? Parents have recently taken action against specific books they consider unsuitable for children, as well as against an entire social studies curriculum, "Man, A Course of Study" (Carringer, 1977). Even when people agree on the things in which parents should have a voice, such as student discipline, curricula, and general educational policy, they may disagree on how specific and binding those recommendations should be. These gray areas represent persistent problems that exist in all public policy making, however, and are not confined to only schools or parent groups. Although these ambiguous areas are more visible in large public schools, they are present even in small parent cooperatives that draw from a relatively homogeneous population. Some parents want their three- and four-year-olds to be learning letters, numbers, and reading and writing skills, while others think general social, physical, intellectual, and language development is more appropriate. Professional guidance for parent groups is needed, but when and about what are not clear.

Informed participation in parent/citizen councils requires sustained interest and commitment and a lot of time for both parents and administrators. Many parents do not have the time or interest to participate, and some do not see this type of participation as their responsibility. Often parents will rally around a cause, but are unable to sustain participation after the immediate problem is resolved. For teachers and administrators, working with parent groups takes more time and energy than simply making decisions without consulting parents. In addition, if the parents group has little experience in organization work, school personnel may have to help them learn to conduct meetings and make decisions.

Some of these disadvantages may be avoided with skilled leadership, while others are inherent in this approach to parent involvement. Parents, teachers, and administrators are sometimes confused about who has a right to do what, and misunderstandings result. Successful policy and advisory boards operate with a clear sense of their responsibilities and functions, usually spelled out in bylaws.

Other Issues   Active citizen involvement in education raises other issues that are neither advantages nor disadvantages, but cannot be ignored.

Citizen and parent groups work toward the ideal of local control to make education more responsive to children's needs and families' wishes. Yet in today's complex society, more and more decisions are made at the state and national levels through laws, court orders, and regulations tied to funding. The parent involvement movement itself is a good example of the way national policy affects local practice. To get money, programs had to involve parents, so they did. The only local choice was in *how* the involvement was to be done. This trend toward decision making at the state and national levels may severely curtail the real influence of parent groups, just as it has restricted the autonomy of local schools and school boards.

Schools are part of an increasingly complex society that is large, frequently impersonal, and rapidly changing. Keeping institutions in that society responsive to individual needs will be difficult, regardless of individual and group efforts.

Also, the traditional division of responsibility between home, school, church or synagogue, community, and other educating forces is changing, and that change itself creates strain. For example, the emerging body of law concerning children's and parents' rights in relationship to schools requires changes in the way school decisions are made and carried out. Children have a right to "due process"—procedures safeguarding their interests—in discipline and placement in special programs. Parents have a right to participate in these decisions and to know about and see any charges against a child and any records maintained by the school. These civil rights issues change the traditional relationship between teachers and parents (Apple, 1977).

Parents, teachers, and administrators must work together to improve educational practice, yet all too often parent activism results in resistance by teachers. Sometimes classroom teachers and their concerns are completely overlooked, yet it is the classroom that most closely affects children. When teachers' unions and collective bargaining are involved, avoiding confrontation becomes very difficult.

People have differing perceptions of what parents' groups are about, and some of these perceptions may be irreconcilable. For example, school systems may encourage parent participation through policy and advisory councils as long as parents are supportive, but they feel very differently when parents want major modifications in the system itself (Gordon, 1977). Teachers may encourage citizen involvement to remedy overcrowding or high pupil-teacher ratios, but resent parent "interference" in negotiations about teacher salaries or curriculum changes.

Parent involvement in policy and decision making is an evolving concept, changing in response to the people, problems, and places involved. It is not one approach or process, but many. One principal, for example, may develop and sustain an excellent working advisory group that falls apart when she is transferred to another school. Government policies that mandate or permit one type of parent participation may change, leaving those involved feeling betrayed or overwhelmed. As a rapidly emerging force in education, citizen/parent power can be expected to undergo many changes, some of which may be uncomfortable for all concerned. How parent policy and advisory councils "function and what problems emerge will be determined in the future" (Gordon and Breivogel, 1976, p. 18).

CITIZEN/PARENTS AS ADVISORS AND POLICY MAKERS: A GUIDE FOR TEACHERS

Teachers' roles and responsibilities in relation to citizen/parent policy and advisory committees are quite different from their roles in other forms of parent involvement. Because of this, we will not present guides in the same way as in the previous chapters. Instead, we will discuss the things you as a teacher need to know and do *about, for*, and *with* parent councils.[3] Additional information is included in Chapter 4.

About Parent Councils

As a teacher, you need to know as much as possible about the formal and informal structures and procedures of the parent council and your school or center. Formal structures and procedures include administrative relationships and organizations showing who is responsible to whom for what functions; legal requirements, which may include federal, state, and local laws and regulations; funding sources; policies of the agency under whose auspices the school or center operates; and bylaws of the parent council. In school districts, most of this information is readily available in printed form, with the possible exception of laws and regulations. In smaller centers, relationships may be understood rather than written down.

The bylaws of the parent organization are often quite specific about what matters the parent council will address and what the council will actually do. School councils that are not tied to a specific program may perform a variety of functions. The most common are (Davies, 1976, p. 160):

1. Assessing community and student needs; identifying facility needs.

2. Identifying goals and priorities for the school; setting school budget priorities.

3. Improving community support for the school; investigating student or parent complaints and problems; mobilizing school and community response to crises.

4. Selecting (or participating in the selection of) the principal; evaluating the principal.

5. Participating in the selection of teachers and other staff; evaluating or assisting in staff evaluation.

6. Reviewing and approving new school programs, curricula, and student activities.

7. Evaluating extracurricular activities.

8. Coordinating volunteer programs and other programs to provide parent/community assistance to the school.

9. Communicating school problems and needs to area or district councils and/or the school committee.

In the bylaws shown below, the advisory function of a Title I council is made quite clear ("ESEA Title I District Advisory Council Bylaws," n.d.).

The purpose of this council shall be to assist School District 6 to bring about the cooperation of community resources which may be of value to the schools in the operation of the ESEA Title I Program. In achieving this purpose, the council shall provide advice and assistance in:

1. Advising the school district through recommendations on the educational needs of the community.

2. Acting as liaison between the Title I Office and the School Advisory Council of each Title I school.

3. Acting as a disseminator of information for the ESEA Title I Program.

4. Acting as an advisory group in the planning, implementation, and evaluation of the ESEA Title I Program.

This section of the Bylaws shall in no way be construed as giving the ESEA Title I District Advisory Council veto authority over the ESEA Title I Program. The council shall have no powers beyond those expressly set forth herein, or specified in federal, state, or school district rules, regulations, or policies.

Other articles specify membership, election procedures, officers, committees, meeting times, quorum, and decision processes. This information gives a clear idea of the formal structures and procedures.

However, decisions are not always made according to the formal charts and procedures. Often there are informal structures and processes that determine how decisions are actually made and who or what group wields power. Learning about these structures is not so simple. You can listen, watch, ask questions, find out what happens to requests for action, and be sensitive to human relationships in the school, in parent councils, and in other policy and advisory groups. The school politics often shifts with changes in personnel.

For Parent Councils

You may be expected to do things *for* a parent council. For example, teachers with special areas of expertise may be asked to share these with the parent council. If you have experience and training in organizing and conducting meetings, you may be asked to help parents learn parliamentary procedure, how to develop an agenda and follow it, and how to hold discussions on a controversial issue. Not all parents have these skills. Either directly or indirectly (through an administrator), you may be asked to supply information that a parent council needs to make an informed recommendation or decision.

You can also lend support by being informed about and respecting the council's decisions and actions, encouraging parents to participate in all meetings and other functions, and identifying and encouraging potential leaders to get involved.

With Parent Councils

In many schools and centers, you will be expected to be a member or observer of the parent or citizen council, either automatically or as a representative of a group of teachers. As such, you may or may not have a vote, depending on the bylaws of the council, but you will almost always have tremendous influence, which you must use judiciously. Professionally trained people tend to dominate when they are in a group of nonprofessionals. You may have to discipline yourself to refrain from speaking while other members of the group arrive at a solution that seems obvious to you.

Sometimes you may act as advisor or guide, making recommendations on certain courses of action. In these cases, make your recommendations in nontechnical language, backed up by reasons and explanations. For example, if the parents in a small Head Start center solicit your advice on a proposed plan to have a long graduation ceremony for the children that would exhaust both the children and the slender budget, you can recommend alternative ceremonies that will be just as satisfying to the parents and more appropriate to the developmental level of four- or five-year-old children.

Invite parent council members to go to professional meetings, special topic conferences, and events in which they would be interested. Title I and Head Start conferences have special workshops for parents. Local, state, and national meetings and conferences of professional organizations, such as the National

Association for the Education of Young Children, Association for Childhood Education International, Council for Exceptional Children, and the International Reading Association, encourage parents to attend and have interest groups specifically for them. Federally funded parent councils frequently have money for such activities. Local lectures, demonstrations, and workshops may cost little or nothing, yet pay off handsomely in increased understanding, fresh ideas, and a sense of shared experience.

While working with parents in parent groups or councils, you will get to know them in roles other than as parents. The parent who is shy and inarticulate in the classroom may argue long and persuasively for something she strongly believes. The parent who speaks only once all evening may put forth the solution that had eluded other members of the group.

You will also have the sometimes exasperating, sometimes exhilarating experience of seeing participatory democracy in action. It is often inefficient, boring, and cumbersome, but it is probably the best process we have to help schools and communities work together for a common purpose.

Conclusion

Teachers who work with parent councils assume a new and challenging role. These teachers and those who work as home visitors, involve parents as volunteers, conduct parent education programs, supply parents with information so they can become home partners of the school, or set up parent resource centers build relationships and understandings that can have both immediate and long-range benefits. Such efforts will not be easily or quickly implemented.

Good collaboration requires time, energy, effort, and commitment. To ignore these requirements means underestimating both the real costs and the potential benefits for all participants—parents, administrators, teachers, community members—and above all, students (Davies, 1976, p. 158).

SUMMARY

Since the 1960s citizen/parents have become increasingly involved in advising and making school policy. Poor and minority groups wanted a greater voice in how schools were run, federal and state laws mandated parent involvement, and beleaguered schools sought greater support. The types of advisory and policy groups vary from setting to setting. Policy in public schools is usually made by representative school boards, and other parent groups advise; in cooperative nursery schools, parents may make all policy decisions.

The goals of parent involvement through policy making include building political support, making schools more responsive and accountable to the community, and increasing parents' sense of control over their own lives.

The advantages of citizen participation are the possibility for greater political support for the schools, joint responsibility for both popular and unpopular education decisions, and the opportunity to secure the perspectives of *all* parents. Disadvantages are the reluctance and hostility of some school administrators and the existing governance mechanisms to allow wider participation, lack of agreement on what aspects of school policy are appropriate for citizen discussion, and the time and interest that citizen/policy groups must commit. There are many unresolved issues and conflicts in this type of citizen participation.

Teachers are seldom as directly involved in citizen/parent groups as they are in other forms of parent involvement. However, they do need to know *about* the citizen/parent groups, including the school board, in their communities. In addition, teachers are often expected to do things *for* and *with* such groups. Such cooperative efforts may be difficult and time-consuming, but they often have long-lasting benefits for all concerned.

RESOURCES FOR TEACHERS AND PARENTS

Organizations

Institute for Responsive Education
704 Commonwealth Avenue
Boston, Massachusetts 02215

National Committee for Citizens in Education
Suite 410, Wilde Lake Village Green
Columbia, Maryland 21044

National Parent-Teacher Association
700 North Rush Street
Chicago, Illinois 60611

Publications

Bloomenthal, H. *Promoting Your Cause.* New York: Funk and Wagnalls, 1974.

Burges, B. *Facts for a Change: Citizen Action Research for Better Schools.* Boston: Institute for Responsive Education, 1976.

Buskin, M. *Parent Power: A Candid Handbook for Dealing with Your Child's School.* New York: Walker and Co., 1975.

Clasby, M., and J. Lema. *Together: Schools and Communities.* Boston: Institute for Responsive Education, 1975.

Huenefeld, J. *The Community Activists' Handbook: A Guide for Citizen Leaders and Planners.* Boston: Beacon Press, 1970.

Jones, Phillip, and Susan Jones. *Parents Unite: The Complete Guide for Shaking Up Your Children's School.* New York: Wyden Press, 1976.

Linking Schools and the Community. Arlington, Va.: National School Public Relations Association, 1977.

Lurie, E.   *How to Change the Schools: A Parents' Action Handbook on How to Fight the System*. New York: Random House, 1970.

Making School Work: An Education Handbook for Students, Parents and Professionals.   Boston: Massachusetts Advocacy Center, n.d.

Parents Organizing to Improve Schools.   Columbia, Md.: The National Committee for Citizens in Education, 1976.

Parents' Rights Handbook.   Linwood, N.J.: Advocates for Education, n.d.

Prentice, L.   *Words, Pictures, Media: Communication in Educational Politics*. Boston: Institute for Responsive Education, 1976.

Sarason, S. et al.   *The Community at the Bargaining Table*. Boston: Institute for Responsive Education, 1975.

FOR DISCUSSION AND FURTHER STUDY

1. Sometimes parent involvement in policy making is thought of as returning schools to the community control that existed in the early days of our country. What changes have taken place that make this comparison invalid?

2. Interview a school principal or director to determine what kind of parent organization or council exists in that school. Obtain a copy of the bylaws, if possible. Find out what issues or problems the parent group has addressed in the last six months and report this information to your class.

3. Write to one of the organizations listed on page 255 to get information about its purposes and services.

4. Working in small groups, list as many reasons as you can think of that parent policy or advisory groups are often controversial.

5. Exchange lists. For each reason for controversy, think of something parents, teachers, or administrators could do to help avoid it.

6. Is all controversy between citizens and schools bad? When might it be good?

BIBLIOGRAPHY

Almy, Millie.   *The Early Childhood Educator at Work*. New York: McGraw-Hill, 1975.

Apple, Michael W.   "Children's Rights and How Parents Can Protect Them." In *Today's Family in Focus: A National PTA Program in Parent Education*, coordinated by Steven L. Schlossman. Chicago: National PTA, 1977.

Breivogel, William F., and Dorothy Sterling.   "The Role of the Administrator." In *Building Effective Home-School Relationships*, edited by Ira J. Gordon and William F. Breivogel. Boston: Allyn and Bacon, 1976.

Campbell, Roald F., Luvern L. Cunningham, Roderick F. McPhee, and Raphael O. Nystrand. *The Organization and Control of American Schools.* Columbus, Ohio: Merrill, 1970.

Carringer, Helen. "A Growing Voice." *Citizen Action in Education* 4, no. 3 (May 1977): 8.

Davies, Don, ed. *Schools Where Parents Make a Difference.* Boston: Institute for Responsive Education, 1977.

"ESEA Title I District Advisory Council Bylaws." Greeley, Colo.: Weld County School District Six, n.d.

Goodson, Barbara, and Robert D. Hess. *Parents as Teachers of Young Children: An Evaluative Review of Some Contemporary Concepts and Programs.* Stanford, Calif.: Stanford University Press, 1975.

Gordon, Ira J. "Parent Education and Parent Involvement: Retrospect and Prospect." *Childhood Education* 54, no. 2 (November/December 1977): 71–79.

Gordon, Ira J., and William F. Breivogel. *Building Effective Home-School Relationships.* Boston: Allyn and Bacon, 1976.

Hess, Robert D., Leonard Beckum, Ruby Knowles, and Ruth Miller. "Parent-Training Programs and Community Involvement in Day Care." In *Day Care: Resources for Decisions,* ed. Edith Grotberg. Washington, D.C.: OEO Pamphlet 6106–1, 1971.

Hess, Robert, Marianne Block, Joan Castello, Ruby Knowles, and Dorothy Largay. "Parent Involvement in Early Education." In *Day Care: Resources for Decisions,* ed. Edith Grotberg. Washington, D.C.: OEO Pamphlet 6106–1, 1971.

Institute for Responsive Education. *Citizen Action in Education* 4, no. 3 (May 1977).

Kirschner Associates, Inc. *A National Survey of the Impacts of Head Start Centers on Community Institutions: Summary Report.* Report No. 889–4638. Washington, D.C.: U.S. Government Printing Office, 1970.

Knitzer, Jane. "Parental Involvement: The Elixir of Change." In *Early Childhood Development Programs and Services: Planning for Action,* ed. Dennis McFadden. Washington, D.C.: National Association for the Education of Young Children, 1972.

Lane, Bess B. *Your Part in Your Child's Education: An Activity Program for Parents.* New York: Dutton, 1948.

National Committee for Citizens in Education. *Parents Organizing to Improve Schools.* Columbia, Md.: NCCE, 1976.

National Institute of Education. *Compensatory Education Services: A Report from the National Institute of Education.* Washington, D.C.: National Institute of Education, 1977. (Available from U.S. Government Printing Office, 1977, 0–729–413/1397.)

National School Public Relations Association. *Citizen Advisory Committees.* Arlington, Va.: National School Public Relations Association, 1973.

Parent Involvement: A Workbook of Training Tips for Head Start Staff. Washington, D.C.: Project Head Start, OEO, 1969.

Safran, Daniel. *State Education Agencies and Parent Involvement: A National Survey of State Legislation and the Policies and Perspectives of State Departments of Education.* Berkeley, Calif.: Humanics Press, 1974.

Smith, Carol E. *Better Meetings: A Handbook for Trainers of Policy Councils and Other Decision-Making Groups.* Atlanta: Humanics Press, 1975.

Taylor, Katherine W. *Parent Cooperative Nursery Schools.* New York: Teachers College, Columbia University, 1954.

Zeigler, L. Harmon, Harvey J. Tucker, and L. A. Wilson. "How School Control Was Wrested from the People." *Phi Delta Kappan* 59, no. 7 (March 1977): 534–39.

NOTES

[1] The National Committee for Citizens in Education is a nonprofit, tax-exempt organization designed to increase citizen involvement in the nation's public schools. It is the successor to the National Committee for Support of the Public Schools, which was founded in 1962 (NCCE, 1976).

[2] The Institute for Responsive Education, 704 Commonwealth Avenue, Boston, Massachusetts 02215, publishes a newsletter, "Citizen Action in Education," and other documents and conducts research (Davies, 1977).

[3] Teachers who move into positions as directors, principals, or parent coordinators assume additional responsibilities for organizing the council, developing bylaws, setting goals, budgeting, complying with guidelines and regulations, organizing committees, holding meetings, and implementing decisions. These are beyond the scope of this book. Interested readers can refer to Gordon and Breivogel (1976) and Taylor (1954).

Index